Pedagogies of Taking Care

Also available from Bloomsbury

Social Theory and the Politics of Higher Education, edited by Mark Murphy, Ciaran Burke, Cristina Costa and Rille Raaper
Wim Wender's Road Movie Philosophy, René V. Arcilla
Critical Pedagogy for Healing, edited by Tricia M. Kress, Christopher Emdin and Robert Lake
Wonder, Vlad P. Glaveanu
Rethinking Philosophy for Children, Tyson E. Lewis and Igor Jasinski
A New Perspective on Education in the Digital Age, Jesper Tække and Michael Paulsen
Hopeful Pedagogies in Higher Education, edited by Mike Seal
Wonder and Education, Anders Schinkel
Postdevelopmental Approaches to Childhood Art, edited by Mona Sakr and Jayne Osgood

Pedagogies of Taking Care

Art, Pedagogy and the Gift of Otherness

Dennis Atkinson

BLOOMSBURY ACADEMIC
LONDON • NEW YORK • OXFORD • NEW DELHI • SYDNEY

BLOOMSBURY ACADEMIC
Bloomsbury Publishing Plc
50 Bedford Square, London, WC1B 3DP, UK
1385 Broadway, New York, NY 10018, USA
29 Earlsfort Terrace, Dublin 2, Ireland

BLOOMSBURY, BLOOMSBURY ACADEMIC and the Diana logo are
trademarks of Bloomsbury Publishing Plc

First published in Great Britain 2022
Paperback edition published 2024

Copyright © Dennis Atkinson, 2022

Dennis Atkinson has asserted his right under the Copyright, Designs and
Patents Act, 1988, to be identified as Author of this work.

For legal purposes the Acknowledgements on p. viii constitute an
extension of this copyright page.

Cover design: Charlotte James
Cover image © Dennis Atkinson, '*Icarus*', acrylic paint, 70x70cm

All rights reserved. No part of this publication may be reproduced or transmitted in
any form or by any means, electronic or mechanical, including photocopying,
recording, or any information storage or retrieval system, without prior
permission in writing from the publishers.

Bloomsbury Publishing Plc does not have any control over, or responsibility for, any
third-party websites referred to or in this book. All internet addresses given in this
book were correct at the time of going to press. The author and publisher regret any
inconvenience caused if addresses have changed or sites have ceased to exist, but
can accept no responsibility for any such changes.

A catalogue record for this book is available from the British Library.

A catalog record for this book is available from the Library of Congress.

ISBN: HB: 978-1-3502-8832-4
PB: 978-1-3502-8836-2
ePDF: 978-1-3502-8833-1
eBook: 978-1-3502-8834-8

Typeset by Newgen KnowledgeWorks Pvt. Ltd., Chennai, India

To find out more about our authors and books visit www.bloomsbury.com
and sign up for our newsletters.

For Karen

Contents

Acknowledgements		viii
	Introduction	1
1	Education, Politics and Subjectivity: An Ethico-Aesthetic Project for a Pedagogy of Taking Care	13
2	*Parrhesia* and *Epimeleia* and the Scandal of the Truth: Changing the Value of the Currency in Pedagogic Work	51
3	Pedagogy, Conditions and Value	71
4	Gilbert Simondon: Transduction and Pedagogic Practice	97
5	On the Idea of Speculative Pedagogies	125
6	The Scandal of the Truth of Art and Its Implications for Art in Education	145
7	The Gift of Otherness: Ontological Adventures in Pedagogic Work	171
8	Thinking par le milieu: Pedagogic Work and Art Practice	193
9	Pedagogy of the Interstices: Trust and Uncertainty	213
References		237
Index		247

Acknowledgements

I want to thank a number of friends and colleagues who have read and commented upon draft chapters for the production of this book. They are John Baldacchino, Paul Dash, jan jagodinski, Rosalyn George, Tony Brown and Jusso Tervo. I also want to thank all those who have participated in presentations I have given in various locations and for the debates from which I learned a great deal. These include David Rousell, Raphael Vella, Carl-Peter Buschkuhle, Catarina Martins, Catarina Almeida, Miranda Matthews, Kevin Tavin and Fernando Hernandez. Thanks also to the artist-teacher discussions with the Freelands Foundation that have continued online throughout the pandemic organized by Kate Thackara and Andy Ash. Thanks to the reviewers for their detailed and helpful comments and to Bloomsbury for taking on this project.

Introduction

This book continues the explorations of pedagogy in art education and pedagogy more generally, as well as practices of art, that were developed in my previous book *Art, Disobedience and Ethics: The Adventures of Pedagogy*. It does so by advocating pedagogies of 'taking care' and advancing the idea of otherness as a gift that may lead to a modification or even a decolonization of thought and practice and subsequent transformations in practice. Both pedagogy and art practice are explored through a range of themes including truth, contingency, individuation, ecologies of practices, cultures of interstices, ethico-aesthetics, *parrhesia*, *epimeleia*, conviviality, speculation, ecosophy, divergence and mesopolitics.

Recent studies in anthropology that deal with those disruptive experiences and which challenge the anthropologist's frameworks of understanding, a common phenomenon of anthropological practice, argue that anthropological insights do not emerge only from discursive reasoning but also from what Willerslev and Suhr (2018), recalling Kierkegaard, call 'leaps of faith' through which new understanding may transpire. Such leaps, let us say leaps of speculation or imagination, involve leaping out of the certainties that hold us and which provide the ground for our leap. The task and trust, as Alfred North Whitehead describes (1978: 5), is to make a leap, a speculation, in the knowledge that we will return and that the ground to which we return will vindicate our leap. If the leap is successful, then new understandings of the world, of the practice, from which we leapt, will be formed. Such leaps therefore involve a trust and a risk that the ground to which we return will meet us. This is not as straightforward as it might appear because the ground which receives our leap will not be the same as that which we leapt from. This is the entire purpose of a leap of speculation in that it is not to confirm what we know, the ground from which we leap, but to create new modes of thought or practice that will meet the challenge of those encounters that necessitate a leap, encounters that cannot be met by established thought or practice. Such leaps indicate that the world is not to be conceived as a static entity but, as William James put it, an ongoing pluralistic universe, a world in the making, and the leaps that we take are very much part of this making.

This book draws parallels between such studies and the domains of pedagogic practice in that by advocating a pedagogy of 'taking care'; pedagogic work sometimes requires similar leaps of faith or trust when obligated to respond empathetically to the difference and divergence of children's and student's pathways of learning that may not be commensurate with a teacher's established frameworks of practice. A pedagogy of taking care is thus concerned with the becoming-making of worlds and the leaps of faith and trust that are often required by teachers to respond to the ways in which learning encounters are conceived and constructed by children and students. This approach to pedagogic work is contrasted to that which has dominated educational policy and practice in recent decades, one that is composed of controlled curriculums, teaching methodologies, assessment programmes and inspection regimes according to which pedagogical identities are preordained to meet the requirements of economic ambition and competition. A pedagogy of taking care does not function in accordance with prescribed pedagogical subjectivities but is conceived as an adventure through which subjectivities emerge in their difference and divergence. A process that involves not only drawing upon established forms of knowledge, values and practice but also engaging with uncertainty and the not-known as it encounters the diversity of ways of learning and their respective potentials. Meeting and acknowledging such diversity may require speculative leaps that result in modified or new understandings of practice. Such moments are not uncommon in pedagogic work when there is an openness to the diversity and difference in how children or students respond to their learning encounters. These pedagogical encounters may require a modification or even a decolonization of pedagogical practice that arises from speculative leaps whilst engaging with learners' practices and whose success results in a broadened understanding of practice.

If education in schools prioritizes certain curriculum subjects and reduces access to others, if it is driven by prescribed models of competences or standards and if teacher education is subject, as in England, to prescribed methodologies that are constantly subject to a rigid regime of inspection, then the effect of such patterning or norming could obscure 'other' modes of practice (in both learning and teaching) that don't fit but which may extend the variety of individual and collective flourishing. In contrast, pedagogy might adopt the notion of the gift of otherness as both a generative opportunity to examine established values and modes of practice and in doing so expand how practice is conceived. This would place otherness, along with uncertainty and not-knowing as part of practice, a 'calling' for new ways of understanding; a summons to artefactualize ways of responding and learning with otherness. Pedagogy thus requires a practice of trust in such speculation and enterprise, a trust that motivates, amplifies and proliferates thought and practice. We might say that pedagogic work functions according to the actions that are taken arising from established modes of practice, but it also requires a facility to receive the gift of otherness, a facility concurrent with existential uncertainty. This denotes a tension between what is known and that which challenges understanding.

Since the late 1980s, educational policy in schools in the UK and elsewhere, driven by economic ambition, has prioritized those subjects such as science, technology, engineering and mathematics (STEM) and reduced the time allocated to the arts and other subject domains. The impact of this policy is that children and students have been denied or given restricted access to the arts and their specific modes of experiencing and learning. If we accept that education is a process whose task is to facilitate each learner's capacities for a flourishing life and in doing so extend collective capacities for convivial relations in order to meet the many and increasing challenges facing co-existence, then the current and continuing emphasis upon STEM subjects, driven by economic imperatives, is, I would argue, limiting such flourishing and its convivial potentials. The aim of this book is to provide an advocacy for what I call a pedagogy of taking care that embraces two practices of becoming-making – that which concerns the potentials, aptitudes, interests and capabilities of each child or student to advance individual and collective pursuits and that which evolves and expands each teacher's understanding of pedagogical practice.

In passing, many working in the university sector are dismayed by the effects of economic imperatives upon university life and do not recognize these establishments to those in which they began their academic work when they were driven by intellectual curiosity, the desire to discuss, debate and share knowledge and practice, to engage in critical thinking with students and colleagues in the pursuit of research and teaching.

The chapters in this book provide explorations of this process of becoming-making in pedagogical practice more generally and also with a specific focus upon art education. Such practices are conceived in relation, but not exclusive, to Felix Guattari's notions of ethico-aesthetic adventures and ecosophy, Michel

Foucault's lectures on truth, Gilbert Simondon's work on individuation, and Isabelle Stengers's ideas of an ecology of practices and cultures of interstices.

Chapter 1 develops a position statement to advocate a pedagogy of taking care. It articulates a critique of current educational policy for schools motivated by economic ambition and the subsequent valuing of STEM subjects and their respective pedagogized subjectivities. The background circumstances to this policy are not to be viewed totally in terms of the effect of neoliberal economic policy; this would be too reductionist but involves a more complex assemblage of different vectoral forces, some of which I will discuss in Part One. This will include considering not only the effects of neoliberal rationality on education but also what we might call a failure of a social and liberal mentality to grasp and develop what John Dewey called a 'cooperative experimental intelligence', which, I argue, was integral to the social and educational concerns of a line of thinkers that has a long history but, in more recent times, can be found in the UK in the work of Richard Hoggart, Stuart Hall and Raymond Williams. Part One provides a brief discussion of their approach to education. Such work seems to have lost momentum in educational policy and its application today. The failure to advocate and fight for the need to develop this social, cooperative and convivial intelligence could be levelled against the centre left that, in coming to power in the late 1990s, chose not to reverse the individualist, competitive and market principles of Thatcherism that circulated through institutions such as schools, universities and hospitals. By then government itself had been realigned to serve markets. Educational institutions and organizations, such as universities, that had power to resist the forces of economization gradually became complicit. Part One continues to consider the effects of economism and marketization upon the school curriculum and upon teacher education in England with particular reference to the School Direct Research Project (Brown, Rowley and Smith 2015) that examined the introduction and impact of school-led teacher-training upon university teacher education.

Part Two is informed by the work of Felix Guattari, Maurizio Lazzarato and Mikhail Bakhtin. It presents an argument for an alternative educational project, a pedagogy of 'taking care', that is grounded in valuing the autonomy of difference and potential in relation to collective and mutual responsibility. As discussed in Part One, education policy driven by economic ambition prioritizes those subject disciplines on which such ambition depends (STEM subjects) and marginalizes others (e.g. the arts). By implication it prioritizes the production of subjectivities that are required to realize such ambition. A pedagogy of taking care begins with a *concern* for each child or student's learning pathway, its modes of experiencing, its concerns and sensibilities, working with and expanding these capacities across a range of subject domains. Taking care also involves a critical obligation towards what we might call the dispositifs of pedagogic practice, the conceptual and practical frameworks that inform pedagogic work, to ascertain their relevance for each student's learning pathway. Taking care thus involves an ethico-political challenge, to value difference and divergence whilst simultaneously aiming to promote and construct collective participation. It is grounded in the notion of 'common sense' as proposed by Alfred North Whitehead, which does not refer to the idea of common knowledge but to an interest in and obligation towards the way others (in this case, students and children) make their world matter and the possibilities and potentials that may stem from such mattering.

To deepen the pedagogical concern for ways of making sense, Part Two explores the process of subjectivation as developed in the work of Felix Guattari. In this work subjectivity is not viewed in substantialist terms of a constituted individual but as a local assemblage (*agencement*) of evolving vectors of subjectivation composed of material practices, semiotic orders, virtual realities and intensities and existential affects. The point here is to provide a theoretical discussion that places emphasis upon viewing subjectivation as a series of actual and virtual vectors whose potentials are always informed by their environmental milieus. If the milieu is rigidly pre-established, then subjectivation is regulated strictly according to its practices and values. We might argue that this form of subjectivation is pervasive in current educational policies in the UK and elsewhere. If the milieu facilitates open and equal access to wider domains of study and a corresponding sensitivity to each student's learning pathway and modes of learning, this would enable what we might call more democratic routes for learning *agencements* and in doing so may extend the parameters of pedagogic practice.

Chapter 2 deals with the notions of *parrhesia* and care (*epimeleia*) as explored in depth by Michel Foucault in his final lectures given at the College de France in 1983–4, titled *The Courage of the Truth*. Practices of *parrhesia* and care are explored in relation to pedagogic work. Foucault's discussion becomes pertinent for such work when he describes how the complicated relation of *parrhesia* to politics and democracy in early Greek society moves to *parrhesia* being linked to an ethics concerned with care (*epimeleia*) of the self, or put differently, to the truth of and responsibility for the self, which also implies care for others and the world. Here it is important not to think of the self as a self-contained entity but as an assemblage (*agencement*), an ecology of practices, discourses, relations, values – an assemblage of existential struggle and propagation (with others). This process is explored through the Cynic notion of an ethico-aesthetics of existence and what Foucault terms 'the scandal of the truth', a process through which the truth of 'another life' exposes constraints, discriminations and biases of established habits, values and traditions. An illustration of this scandal is explored in the work of contemporary art practices.

The chapter then turns to the philosophical explorations of the Czech philosopher Jan Patočka, giving particular focus to his work on the notion of 'care of the soul' that involves a concern for otherness, equality, detachment and the idea of the 'post-idea'. The aim is to draw upon Patočka's writings on philosophy and politics in order to unpack their relevance for my concerns with education and a pedagogy of taking care. In the last section, I draw together the discussion and, briefly, contrast the stupidity of current educational policies grounded in *homo economicus* with an advocacy for a pedagogy of taking care.

Chapter 3 offers some thoughts towards a re-evaluation of education and pedagogic work in order to exit the practice of education that functions almost exclusively as the production of human capital for economic ambition and competition. After a brief introduction highlighting some of the issues raised by questions pertaining to conditions and values, the chapter considers the work of Ivan Illich, particularly his books *Deschooling Society* and *Tools for Conviviality*. The chapter draws upon John Baldacchino's book, *Educing Ivan Illich*, in which he provides a scholarly and discerning deliberation of the notions disestablishment, contingency and reform, through which he interrogates Illich's opus covering the domains of education, healthcare, religion, technology, the environment and more. The intention is to show how the writings of Illich aided by Baldacchino's text still have relevance for education and pedagogical work and continue to offer radical alternatives to our current systems of education that are largely grounded in the values of economization. Though there are those who regard Illich's proposals for education and other services as being too radical, utopian or impractical, I suggest that the writings I discuss still contain profound lessons for developing what I have called a pedagogy of taking care, although, perhaps, it is not a term that Illich would employ. The discussion of Illich's work and its relevance for a pedagogy of taking care that seems inherent to his notion of a convivial society is followed by a brief engagement with Isabelle Stengers's ideas on idiotic events, the cosmopolitical proposal and her work on an ecology of practices (revisited in later chapters), which I believe resonates with the idea of conviviality proposed by Illich.

Chapter 4 provides an account of Gilbert Simondon's work on the process of individuation all the while trying to view it in relation to pedagogic practice and processes of learning. The task is to introduce some of Simondon's key concepts in order to elaborate his notions of individuation and ontogenesis; these include modulation, preindividual, transduction, disparation and transindividual and then apply these to pedagogic practice and practices of learning. Emphasis is placed not upon pre-constituted individuated subjects but upon ongoing encounters (events) of individuation, or perhaps more precisely, *events of individuating*, that lead to the ongoing production of a subject as a metastable state. Put another way, a body or individual is not conceived as already constituted but rather as a process of individuating and forming assemblages (affective, cognitive, practical, embodied) with other bodies, objects, technologies, environments or milieus. The pedagogical task of a pedagogy of taking care has, therefore, to try to engage with each learner's modes of individuation that produce local assemblages of learning, with a focus upon the dynamic processes of becoming and open potential in contrast to the preforming forces of hylomorphism. Finally, a very brief account of some contemporary art practices is provided, viewing these in turn through the lens of Simondon's theory of disparation and transduction.

Chapter 5 builds upon the critical engagement with current educational practices driven by economic ambition set out in Chapter 1. The focus of this chapter, however, concerns established curriculum practices and planned routes of teaching and learning that involve pedagogical methodologies, regulatory assessment, competences and standards that anticipate preordained pedagogized subjects, such as those produced in different curriculum subjects and their respective modes of assessment.

In sharp contrast to this prescriptive approach to education and pedagogic work, the chapter explores the process and practice of speculative inquiry as conceived by Alfred North Whitehead, Isabelle Stengers, and similarly by Maurice Merleau-Ponty and Hannah Arendt. The chapter proposes the idea of speculative pedagogies, which advocate a more uncertain pedagogical adventure characterized by novel modes of subjective engagement that emphasize a subject-yet-to-come and where the notion of the not-known is immanent to such adventures.

Though it is important for pedagogical practices to introduce learners to the inheritance of tradition and established forms of knowledge and practice that constitute the known world, it is also crucial to view teachers and learners as innovators enabling potentials for a world to come, a world that is not yet known and which cannot, in the didactic sense of prescription, be controlled or predicted nor accommodated by established orders. In a trite sense, we can say that if inquiry or learning that occurs on the cusp of a 'developing present' is not speculative, then it is not learning, but the obviousness of this remark does seem to have been obscured within those instrumentalist approaches to educational practice that dominate many countries. Speculative pedagogies emerge from the ground of inheritance but try to remain open to the potential for invention that may arise in learning encounters experienced by children or students and their diverse forms of expression.

The chapter explores the notion of speculation in the philosophical work of Whitehead paying particular attention to his notion of 'proposition' as a 'lure for feeling', as that which causes thought to think, a situation, for example, such as a learning encounter, that forces thought and practice. It argues that in responding to a learning encounter, we must be careful not to impose established modes of practice to guide pedagogic work but to remain open to the possibilities and potentials of a student's learning pathway. In such a speculative key pedagogic work becomes an adventure in constructing a future, a constructing that often requires receiving the gift of otherness, which lies beyond established orders of practice. Other important concepts developed by Whitehead are considered to develop the advocacy for speculation; these include *importance, relevance, care* and *mattering*. Speculation is then considered in relation to an ethics and politics of speculation and in particular in relation to Isabelle Stengers's work on the cosmopolitical proposal and its concern for what I call the gift of otherness.

Speculation is then briefly considered in relation to art practice and the notion of artfulness proposed by Erin Manning. Artfulness is considered as a wager on an unfinished present and its potential of cultivating experience that may lead to new or modified ecologies of practice. It involves an otherness that lurks at the edge of experiencing and which may open new possibilities for practice. This links with Whitehead's claim that 'life lurks in the interstices', which we can transpose to art practice as lurking in the interstices, a practice in which there are no 'objects' or 'subjects' as such but an ongoing assemblage of intensities and relations.

Chapter 6 builds upon the scandal of the truth discussed in Chapter 2 in relation to Cynic practices. Part One proceeds to explore the scandal of the truth of art as a practice that breaks new ontological and aesthetic grounds and in doing so brings to light new possibilities for expression and modes of existence. As a site of irruption, art practice can be viewed as a courageous site of refusal of established orders, a challenge to existing traditions and values. The chapter explores these ideas through a range of art practices connected to the scandal of the 'readymade' that first appeared in the work of Marcel Duchamp and which he saw as a conceptual event but which in this chapter is conceived as an intensive affective force that constitutes its crucial and scandalous aspect of practice. In disrupting established representational orders and values, the readymade, which I extend to the notion of readymade-making, may open new possibilities and sensibilities for practice. The otherness of art then, as formulated through readymade-making, can create explosions that fracture or disrupt established orders of perception and understanding. This can be viewed in terms of a politics of practice through which established orders and values are confronted with alternative modes of practice and existence. The chapter proceeds to explore different manifestations of readymade-making in the works of several contemporary artists including Adrian Piper, Tehching Hseih, Ingrid Pollard and Zarina Bhimji.

Building on the discussion of the readymade and the notion of speculative practices that lure thinking and making to unforeseen possibilities, the chapter proceeds to consider Francois Laruelle's challenge to the 'sufficiency' (its authority) of philosophy through his notion of *non-philosophy*. This has some similarity to the challenge and scandal of contemporary art to the sufficiency of established practices. Laruelle's non-philosophy is discussed in relation to Whitehead's notion of creativity and 'novel creatures'. Laruelle's challenge is concerned with expanding the field of philosophic practice through his notion of the 'non' as it applies in non-Euclidean geometry to an expansion of this domain of study. The 'non' is an operator for an expanded field. In relation to this, Laruelle offers what might be viewed as a decolonization of thought which has equivalence to those art practices already discussed. The chapter applies Laruelle's notion of the 'non' to develop the idea of 'non-pedagogy' in terms of an expanding pedagogic field.

Part Two turns to practices of art in education and contrasts current emphases upon competences and standards of practice as illustrated in the European context by the European Network for Visual Literacy (ENVIL), and the search for more efficient assessment criteria, with an emphasis upon ecologies of affect as generated through art encounters. Such emphasis is elaborated through the notion of an ecosophic pedagogy of taking care. The idea of ecosophy and its concern with affect is taken from the work of Felix Guattari. Part Two explores Guattari's idea of an ethico-aesthetic paradigm and the importance of affect in generating new sensibilities and applies this concern for affect to pedagogic work. This includes a consideration of the import of Guattari's three ecologies (subjectivity, social structures, environment) for pedagogic/educational practices and policies. The idea of ecosophy brings these three ecologies together and relates to the struggle for what Illich calls a convivial collective. An ecosophic art education is proposed in which the focus is placed upon the intensity of affect generated through art practice and its potential for generating new sensibilities, for transforming modes of practice, where art and life are constantly making and unmaking each other. The gift of art practice, its otherness, enables a metastable production of becoming.

Chapter 7 builds upon Laruelle's notion of the 'non' as an operator for an expanded field of practice. It works with the notion of the gift of otherness. In doing so, it turns to anthropological studies that are concerned with encounters with otherness; these include the works of Roy Wagner, Marylin Strathern, Eduardo Viveiros de Castro, Martin Holbraad and Morten Axel Pedersen. The task is to learn from these studies to advance an advocacy for an ecosophic pedagogy. The anthropological question, 'how does an anthropologist enable her ethnographic material to reveal itself by allowing it to dictate its own terms of engagement so as to compel her to see things she had not expected or imagined to be there?' is transposed to the pedagogical context in which a teacher may often confront practices that lie beyond their pedagogical frameworks. How does this otherness reveal itself in pedagogic work? The ontological question is therefore concerned not with seeing things differently but with seeing different things. In a pedagogical context, instead of trying to grasp a child or student's point of view of the 'same' object or encounter, can we put established epistemological frameworks aside in order to allow that which is 'other' to grasp us and, in such grasping, change or even transform the ground of our pedagogical practice? The chapter proceeds to outline some key concepts from the studies of Wagner (challenging convention, culture as invention), Strathern (relation, comparison, post-plural) and Vivieros de Castro (perspectivism, multinaturalism, careful equivocation), all of which are elaborated in relation to a pedagogy of taking care. Following on from these anthropological enquiries, the chapter returns briefly to the notion of speculative ontologies and the process philosophy of Whitehead; it introduces the notion of instauration from Etienne Souriau that is central to his writing on art practices. Instauration concerns the complex relational processes of becoming-making, a reciprocal composing and collaboration involving body, mind, materials and affects. These ideas are applied to pedagogic work as children's and students' practices are considered in terms of local instaurations that constitute local ethologies and ecologies of learning.

Chapter 8 deals with politics, pedagogic work and art practices. It begins with a discussion of macropolitics and micropolitics as discussed by Deleuze and Guattari, giving illustrations of their interrelations – for example, the macropolitics of neoliberal economics and the micropolitical diffusion of its values and desires and the macropolitics of educational policies and the diffusion of their values in domains of teaching and learning. The work of Suley Rolnik provides an illustration of the capture of individuals and collectives through what she calls a *colonial-capitalistic unconscious*. Micropolitics is also considered in terms of resistance and change, drawing on Deleuze's and Guattari's ideas on minoritarian practices. Rolnik argues for a concern for those affects and forces that are not captured by our subjection to capitalist forces and which lie 'outside-the-subject' as constituted by capitalism, which traverse bodies and relations and may offer potential for transformation. The notion of 'outside-the-subject' is explored through the idea of empathy towards otherness that may generate embryos of other worlds, of a people yet to come. This empathic collaboration is applied to pedagogical work constituting a micropolitics of empathy.

The chapter then turns to the idea of mesopolitics as developed by Isabelle Stengers. The meso is concerned with sites and processes of invention rather than with established micro- or macro-positions or orders. It pertains to a pragmatics of invention, with what rises up in practice, with the malleability of materials, with affects generated, with resistance or accommodation – in short, the events and affects of becoming-making. Here materials refer not just to things in art practice such as paint, brushes, clay, wood, computers, video equipment and so forth but also to concepts, bodies and affects. Mesopolitics deals with the relational materialities and affects of events of becoming-making that may lead to new or modified modes of existence, individual and collective. The chapter provides more detail of Stengers's mesopolitics all the while relating to pedagogical work; it also includes reference to Whitehead's notion of 'common sense', a concern for the way others make their world matter. It considers the notion of thinking and acting *par le milieu* from Deleuze and Guattari, in relation to meso thinking and to the gift of otherness that a situation may present and that may provide possibilities for a mesopolitics which leads to challenging existing orders and values of practice. The chapter proceeds to argue that the practice of mediation in a pedagogy of taking care functions at the meso level, operating *par le milieu* within a feeling that something may grow here and with a concern not to impose prior aims or prejudices.

Chapter 9 tackles the notion of a pedagogy of the interstices that involves speculation, uncertainty and contingency. In proposing a pedagogy of the interstices, cultures and discourses of identity are held in abeyance, whilst emphasis is placed upon those pedagogic encounters that precipitate interstices that open new or modified modes of practice and ways of conceiving practice. Whitehead's ideas on abstractions, societies, prehension and concrescence are considered to support and develop a concern for the interstices of practice along with Isabelle Stengers's notion of a culture of interstices. The idea of a pedagogy of interstices is further elaborated through an engagement with the local domains of artist–teacher assemblages and artist–teacher conversations that address the situatedness of pedagogic work to advocate a pluralism of pedagogies, each developing through their local ecologies of practice.

In this discussion and elaboration of artist–teacher conversations, importance is placed upon the active part of the practitioner to problematize, speculate or artefactualize pedagogical and practical issues or encounters. A pedagogy of taking care does not provide 'models' for practice but advocates a demanding and rigorous pragmatism that acknowledges established conceptions and modes of practice both in pedagogy and in art practice but does not get stuck in their groove when encountering that which challenges them. For example, new forms of art practice in the domains of contemporary art or that which emerges in a child's or student's practice challenge or disturb how art or pedagogy is conceived in art education. A pedagogy of taking care makes speculative leaps from the ground of practice and returns to a world-in-the-making where the teacher's leap can only be evaluated by the effects they produce as part of the becoming-making of pedagogic practice in a particular situation. The advocacy for a pedagogy of taking care in contrast to current emphasis upon the imposition of prescribed curricula and controlled methods of teaching involves a risk in that advocates of the latter persuasion are likely to dismiss it with disdain. There is also the risk of accepting such an approach to pedagogy too lightly and thereby diluting the importance of a demanding and attentive disposition towards the difference and divergence of practice. Pedagogies of taking care therefore place importance upon the creative initiatives of teachers to formulate and develop their pedagogical practice within their specific milieus of practice. They maintain the tension between established knowledge, values and practice and the potentialities for future modes of practice as we encounter the contingencies, surprises or divergences of practice, producing what Cecile Malaspina calls a 'reservoir of potentials and virtualities that we may activate collectively in order to invent solutions to the situations, problems and encounters we face'.

1

Education, Politics and Subjectivity: An Ethico-Aesthetic Project for a Pedagogy of Taking Care

Introduction

The task of this chapter is to develop a position statement that advocates a particular approach to the purpose of education and the practices of teaching and learning that is grounded in a pedagogy of taking care. Part One articulates a critique of current educational policy for schools motivated by economic ambition, consumption and competition coupled with the emphasis upon particular curriculum subjects and the production of their subjectivities in the contexts of the school curriculum and teacher education. However, the background circumstances to this policy are not to be viewed totally in terms of the effect of neoliberal economic policy; this would be too reductionist but involves a more complex assemblage of different vectoral forces, some of which I will discuss in Part One. This will include considering not only the effects of neoliberal rationality on education but also what we might call a failure of a social and liberal mentality to grasp and develop what Dewey (2000: 53) called a 'cooperative experimental intelligence', which, I argue, was integral to the social and educational concerns of a line of thinkers that has a long history but, in more recent times, can be found in the UK in the works of Richard Hoggart, Stuart Hall and Raymond Williams. Such works seem to have lost momentum in educational policy and its application today. The failure to advocate and fight for the need to develop this social, cooperative and convivial intelligence could be levelled against the centre left that, in coming to power in the late 1990s, chose not to reverse the individualist, competitive and market principles of Thatcherism that circulated through institutions such as schools, universities and hospitals. By then government itself had been realigned to serve markets.

Educational institutions and organizations that had the means to resist the forces of economization gradually became complicit, universities caved in and unions were weakened.

Part Two presents an argument for an alternative educational project, which I call a pedagogy of 'taking care', that is grounded in the valuing of the autonomy of difference and potential in relation to collective and mutual responsibility. Whereas the former project is informed by an established teleology towards generating and expanding particular skills and knowledge that sustain, develop and transform particular (capitalist) modes of existence, the latter advocates a more open-ended project, and whilst recognizing those skills, practices and forms of knowledge that are required for life beyond school and economic prosperity, the chapter argues that other modes of existence, than those perpetuated by capitalist economics, may be possible and even more desirable. Put in other terms appropriate to this chapter, whilst the former project functions towards the production of prescribed and regulated pedagogical subjectivations, the latter advocates an open, more unpredictable process that, rather than beginning from a dictated ground of method and practice, begins with supporting the existential heterogeneity of experiencing and how this might 'inform' learning encounters and the diverse subjectivations that follow. Subjectivation here is perhaps a more precarious adventure. Such an approach is articulated not by authorized models of educational identities but, in this chapter, by a schizoanalytic metamodelizing of difference as developed by Felix Guattari.

Educational policy in the West is motivated largely by economic ambition and competition; it has emerged from a history of capitalist exploitation that has produced environmental devastation, global warming and increases in poverty and other social inequities. The emphasis upon core curriculum subjects such as science, technology and mathematics has led to a reduction in the value of other subjects such as the arts, a reduction that prioritizes some pedagogical subjectivities over others. A pedagogy of care begins with a metamodelizing according to each learner's modes of experiencing, sensibilities, aptitudes and interests, working with and expanding these capacities across a range of what we call subject domains rather than limiting opportunities according to those domains deemed desirable for prescribed agendas.

To clarify my concerns, education in this book refers mainly to institutional practices in schools and other sites but also to theoretical framings and underpinnings of educational practices, their values and purpose. Politics, in the second part of the chapter, refers to practices in which politics and ethics are indissoluble. What I infer or argue by this articulation is that social relations and their evolution are dependent upon valuing difference whilst at the same time trying to forge collective values and practices; the ethico-political and aesthetic challenge therefore is to value ethical differentiation whilst also constructing collective participation. Subjectivity denotes *processes of subjectivation* and not essentialist notions of a constituted individual. It refers to assemblages of evolving/mutating vectors and processes that emerge across a range of practices and relations, constituting what we might call vectors of subjectivation. The 'subject' therefore is an always emerging, incomplete and perhaps even disobedient process in that disobedience refers to the opening of new values and potentials that break out from established grounds as they arise in processes of experiencing. This raises a complex issue of how potentialities become actualized and break through the boundaries of established existential territories. By referencing Felix Guattari's four ontological domains, the chapter conceives this complex process of subjectivity in terms of an assemblage of actual and virtual vectors and interfaces. These include actual material relations that modulate experience, as well as domains of logic and established practices and fields of inquiry – virtual existential territories and incorporeal universes of affect and intensities that unsettle them and which facilitate novel modes of becoming. Put another way, can pedagogic work in the spirit of a pedagogy of taking care that aims to support and respond effectively to the haecceities (thisness) and heterogeneity of modes of learning and expression open up and extend new sensibilities and modes of practice which in turn, by implication, may disrupt or even challenge the parameters of pedagogic practice? By adopting this processual notion of subjectivity, it opens up questions concerning the 'objectivity' of a curriculum, its methods, its assessment or even the school as institution. I will return briefly to such questions in the conclusion.

My task then is first to develop an account of current educational practices and the kind of subjectivations that are prioritized and then to problematize this mode of production in order to provide an alternative that assumes contrasting ethico-political relations and subjectivations. Whereas the former educational project can be described as prescriptive and driven by economic ambition and competition and the production of human capital (vertical and hierarchical), the alternative is grounded in an open and unpredictable valuing of difference and potential (horizontal and divergent) in relation to collective values and responsibilities.

Part One

Neoliberalism and Education

My discussion of neoliberal politics/economics is not extensive but limited to the basic features of neoliberalism that characterize this economic project and its impact upon educational policy and practice. I draw upon Wendy Brown's persuasive critique of neoliberal rationality that she develops in *Undoing the Demos* (2015) regarding its impact upon higher education in the United States and her later text, *In the Ruins of Neoliberalism* (2019), where she extends the former text's focus upon economics and neoliberal rationality by addressing neoliberalism's moral conditioning, tracing this back to Friedrich Hayek's advocacy for 'markets and tradition'. I follow Brown's critique by considering the neoliberal *condition* (a term given to me by John Baldacchino) as it has affected educational policy and practice in England: first, by engaging briefly with the work of Richard Hoggart, Raymond Williams and Stuart Hall that has been marginalized by neoliberal marketization policies but whose sociopolitical and ethical agendas are important for a pedagogy of taking care; and second, by addressing the impact of neoliberal forces and values on the school curriculum and teacher education.

But is everything that has happened in the past few decades in social, economic, political, educational and ethical domains all down to neoliberal principles and values? This is too reductionist and requires greater in-depth elaboration beyond the focus of this chapter. One might think of the rise of consumer culture and its pervasive and invasive affects; the increasing infiltration of surveillance and administrative apparatuses and practices; the effects of televisual and digital cultures; the rhythms of conformity; the inducement, manipulation and satisfaction of needs generating the desire for more; the rise of nationalisms and protectionism; and the upsurge of fundamentalisms and racism. All such phenomena cannot be attributed to neoliberal economics. But the complexity I infer here will be partly examined in Part Two when I address the complex ontological production of subjectivity as developed by Felix Guattari.

As a form of economic rationality, neoliberalism conceives most human activity as subject to market reason, 'economized in value and conduct' (Brown 2017, *Eurozine*: 5). It is a term that is difficult to pin down, but generally it signifies a preference for markets over government; it prioritizes economic initiatives over social and civic concerns, and it promotes entrepreneurial practices over collective or community values. In short, both politics and the idea of society are dethroned by markets. Brown (2015: 177) argues that there are four aspects of neoliberal rationality that have a direct impact upon education in the liberal arts and, I would argue, that affect other areas of education and its practices in the United States, England and elsewhere. In the second part of this section, I provide a particular illustration by turning to the impact of neoliberal rationality upon teacher education in England and refer to a research project (Brown, Rowley and Smith 2015) that began in 2013 to consider the effects of the changing nature of teacher education in England for university teacher education programmes as it became more regulated and controlled by government interventions steered not only by the values of neoliberal economics and the production of human capital but also by an aspect of a historical undercurrent that abhors progressive educational initiatives.

Brown (2015: 176) states that neoliberal rationality 'formulates everything, everywhere, in terms of capital investment and appreciation, including and especially humans themselves'. The four aspects that she maintains effect education are first, the issue of public goods and services: should they be an entitlement, or should they be paid for? This question implies that in adopting neoliberal economic policies, government moves from a position of civic responsibility to provide public welfare systems to exposing such provision to market forces whereby citizens become consumers. In the UK we have witnessed the opening up of health and education systems to forces of privatization. Second, when neoliberal values, such as economic ambition and competition, saturate nearly every aspect of social existence, democracy becomes transformed 'so that political meanings of equality, autonomy and freedom (however problematic these terms may be) give way to economic valences of these terms' (my bracket). The consequence of this shift is that the market becomes the sole arbiter of value and replaces other humanitarian, justice, moral or ethical considerations. Brown (2015: 177) writes, 'Democracies are conceived as requiring technically skilled human capital, not educated participants in public life and common rule.' Third, the impact of these two aspects of neoliberal rationality upon subjectivity is that subjects become 'conceived in terms of self-investing human capital that are controlled primarily according to market logics and governance' (177). Fourth, a factor deeply affecting educational policy and practice; knowledge, thought and training are valued in terms of their contribution to and development of capitalist economies, and this emphasis marginalizes the focus upon developing civic values and practices as well as cultural practices such as the arts and humanities within educational contexts. Brown (178–9) argues that the effects of these four aspects of neoliberal rationality upon education and society more generally are that they hollow out democracy defined in terms of an engagement with and development of civic good, with debates about how we should live in order not only to develop this good to foster convivial relations but also to generate critical appraisals that might lead to further social and civic transformations.

Brown focuses upon the effects of neoliberal rationality upon the status of teaching and learning in the liberal arts in American universities. Although such effects are of great concern, what cause her even more disquiet are the effects of neoliberal politics upon democratic citizenship, when the functions and purpose of higher education become economized. Though she writes about the American context, there are direct parallels with higher education in many European contexts.

> After more than half a century of public higher education construed and funded as a medium for egalitarianism and social mobility and as a means of achieving a broadly educated democracy as well as for providing depth and enrichment to individuality, public higher education, like much else in neoliberal orders, is increasingly structured to entrench, rather than redress class trajectories. As it devotes itself to enhancing the value of human capital, it now abjures the project of producing a public readied for participation in popular sovereignty. (2015: 184)

Brown argues that the introduction of a liberal arts education in American universities in the 1940s should be viewed as 'a radical democratic event', in that studies aimed at world cultures, literacies, arts, politics, ethics and other fields were made available to a wider public, though there were still problems of access.

> For the first time in human history, higher educational policy and practice were oriented toward the many, tacitly destining them for intelligent engagement with the world rather than economic servitude or mere survival. (185)

This meant that beyond class mobility and the laudable but highly suspect or even mythic idea of 'equality of opportunity', the ideal of democracy was realized in a new way in that higher education was available to the general public to pursue both individual knowledge pursuits and for civic engagement and participation. Such education followed the philosophical and social enquiries of Adam Smith, John Dewey, Alexis de Tocqueville and others that conceived the sole pursuit of economic interests and values as being much too narrow for developing individual lives or the practice of democracy. However, universities and schools today are more generally aligned to and driven by the notion of the market value of knowledge and the production of human capital, the 'income-enhancing prospects for individuals and industry alike' (2015: 187) and not capacities or qualities for developing civic values and democratic citizenship. Brown argues that greater public access to a liberal arts education coincided with the rise of critical democratic movements such as the civil rights movement, feminism and numerous challenges to social inequalities.

Post-war Initiatives in Education in the UK and Later Educational Change

In the UK, probably from the 1960s, as well as some of the aforementioned sociopolitical movements, the introduction of comprehensive secondary education, the rapid increase in higher education numbers, the birth of the Open University and, in wider Europe in 1968, the worker/student protests against capitalism, consumerism and American imperialism reinforced a call for more egalitarian democratic politics and civic organizations. During this epoch a number of educators, writers and academics developed inclusive and socially transformative approaches to education that are worthy of mention, in that such work in recent decades seems to have been sidelined in educational policy and practice.

Richard Hoggart came from a working-class environment in Hunslet, a district of Leeds. His formative years in this social and cultural environment, where community spirit, family and collective support were crucial, were influential upon his later work in the fields of cultural studies and education. This inheritance influenced his approach towards the importance of social responsibility and the ongoing task of developing a shared sense of moral, affective and collective values. Education for Hoggart was a process through which someone could extend their capacities not simply for oneself but also for collective purposes and action. His first venture into adult education where he saw the social and moral possibilities of education was towards the end of the First World War, in the Army Education Corps and the Army Bureau of Current Affairs. There he witnessed how education had a liberating effect upon the adults attending. He proceeded to publish articles on the aims, principles and methods of teaching. But it was the publication of *The Uses of Literacy* in 1957 that sparked debate and new modes of study and research into social and cultural practices, enquiry into how people make sense of their lives in their respective material sociocultural situations that are not static but open to forces of change. Hoggart drew attention to the new proliferation and expansion of mass cultural forms that occurred in the UK after the Second World War and in the 1950s – television, pop music, magazines, advertisements, youth culture, movies and so forth – and he sought to understand the effects of this 'Americanization' by seeking answers to how these commercially driven forms of mass communication were impacting older working-class values. As Stuart Hall, a later colleague of Hoggart, writes, 'What, in short were the "uses" to which this new kind of "literacy" was being put?' Hoggart's view of culture was not hierarchical or elitist, whereby working-class culture was seen as 'limited' but that working classes had cultures, values and traditions of their own. Culture concerns local practices of making sense, shared values and attitudes, and such ways of life need to be studied to understand the effects of cultural change.

Hoggart's interrogation of 'literacies' evolved into new programmes of social and cultural enquiry at the University of Birmingham in 1964 where he established the Centre for Contemporary Cultural Studies; there he was joined amongst others by Stuart Hall. New interdisciplinary methods of study and forms of research were developed, and later, under Hall, this included an intense engagement with semiotics, post-structuralism and theories of discourse. Thus, we might say that Hoggart's work led to the development of new modes of enquiry, teaching and learning that encouraged students to develop an informed understanding of evolving cultural, social and political practices. Hall (2007b: 39) writes:

> It is widely recognised that, without Richard Hoggart, there would have been no Centre for Contemporary Cultural Studies. It isn't always so widely acknowledged that, without *The Uses of Literacy*, there would have been no Cultural Studies.

A year after the publication of *The Uses of Literacy*, Raymond Williams published his seminal book, *Culture and Society* (1958). He was a major figure in the study of culture and cultural materialism, committed to the view that culture concerns the fabric of daily lived experience and not the domain of an elite cultivated people. He came from a working-class background in Wales where education was valued and where he was encouraged and supported. In his work as an adult educator at Oxford, he insisted that 'education was ordinary' and that education should function as a 'public pedagogy' that sprang not exclusively from schools or other educational institutions but from a wide range of social contexts such as the family, libraries, churches, museums, galleries, media outlets (TV, internet sites, movies), pubs and so forth. He recognized that in his work in adult education, people could develop their capacities for learning together by mixing with those from very different backgrounds and places of work, and this togetherness was a crucible for a future expansion of the democratic process (see Williams 1993: 221). This implied that all involved in the educational process, including teachers, would be able to expand their capacities to benefit themselves and the collective. This also assumed a point I have mentioned and to which I will return that at times, a teacher's pedagogical framework may not be able to respond to a learner's form of practice or expression that does not fit, and this then requires an innovation and expansion on the part of the teacher. Williams writes that the teacher or educator 'may not know the gaps between academic teaching and actual experience among many people; he may not know when, in the pressure of experience, a new discipline has to be created' (1993: 225; see also Cole (2008)). He was aware that new and emerging technologies of mass communication often ran counter to the promotion of civic values, social justice and a critically informed public, as such technologies were driven by the interests of capitalist expansion. But he did believe that there are always elements within dominant social orders or cultures that may rise and act as an immanent critique and that educators can play such a role. From *Culture and Society*, the following quotation burns with relevance for me in my concern for the unpredictable valuing of potential in pedagogical practice. We might replace the terms 'culture' and 'community', respectively, with the terms 'pedagogy' and 'classroom'.

> A culture, while it is being lived, is always in part unknown, in part unrealized. The making of a community is always an exploration, for consciousness cannot precede creation, and there is no formula for unknown experience. A good community, a living culture, will, because of this, not only make room for but actively encourage all and any who can contribute to the advance in consciousness which is the common need. Wherever we have started from, we need to listen to others who have started from a different position. We need to consider every attachment, every value, with our whole attention; for we do not know the future, we can never be certain of what may enrich it; we can only, now, listen to and consider whatever may be offered and take up what we can. (Williams 1958: 340)

In pedagogic practice working with what and how something presents to us was a feature of the pedagogic practice of Stuart Hall, who, many would argue, was the most prominent, leading figure in the development and pedagogy of cultural studies in post-war Britain. He was a central figure of the New Left along with Williams. His work in social and cultural practices, theory and politics has had enormous influence. Like Hoggart and Williams, although not the same, Hall insisted that culture consists of a field of evolving, mutating practices – processes of constructing relations between people, their worlds and their futures. This process of production involved languages, customs, beliefs, habits and dispositions through which people made sense of their world and their potentials. Hall knew that the complexification of cultural diversification in Britain required modes of teaching, research and study that recognized the importance of cultural politics, issues of identity and the politics of race.

Hall joined Hoggart at the Centre for Contemporary Cultural Studies and later became its director, developing innovative research practices and the injection of ideas and theory from European sociology, semiotics, structuralism and post-structuralism and the theory of ideology into the study of culture. Asked what makes up the core of cultural studies Hall (1997: 86) replied, "It's quite difficult to define. You could say something very general – that culture is the dimension of meaning and the symbolic – but cultural studies has always looked at this in the context of the social relations in which it occurs, and asked questions about the organisation of power." The articulations of power within social and cultural formations are a key focus of his work. However it was the collegial, intimate and generous force of his practice of teaching, of which many speak, his concerned pedagogic work, that interests me here and in particular his pedagogical practice of *articulation* (Hall 1985, Clarke 2015), which links to the work of Felix Guattari that I discuss in Part Two. This is how Hall (1985: 113–14) describes the term 'articulation':

> By the term 'articulation', I mean a connection or link which is not necessarily given in all cases, as a law or a fact of life, but which requires particular conditions of existence to appear at all, which has to be positively sustained by specific processes, which is not 'eternal' but has to be constantly renewed, which can under some circumstances disappear or be overthrown, leading to the old linkages being dissolved and new connections – re- articulations – being forged. It is also important that an articulation between different practices does not mean that they become identical or that one is dissolved into the other. Each retains its distinct determinations and conditions of existence. However, once an articulation is made, the two practices can function together, not as an 'immediate identity' (in the language of Marx's '1857 Introduction') but as distinctions within a 'unity'.

This idea of articulation seems close to the notion of an assemblage or *agencements* as formulated by Deleuze and Guattari in *A Thousand Plateaus* as a territorialization that orders and stratifies bodies, human and non-human, as well as forms of expression. The relations that constitute an assemblage are not static but can be displaced so that new relations form and dissolve. The parts of an assemblage can be recombined, subtracted or modified; each new mixture can produce a new kind of assemblage. An assemblage can thus be conceived as a fluid multiplicity and what is important for its functioning are not constituting elements but the in-between relations. In order to analyse an assemblage, we have to abandon logics of identity or essence and take up a logic of relations and multiplicities. An assemblage has no fixed identity or essence but is open to the contingencies of social and historical events and processes that continue to effect its becoming. It is not simply a mixture of heterogeneous elements 'but entails a constructive process (an abstract machine) that lays out a specific kind of arrangement' (my bracket), which will be subject to events of disruption, displacement and redistribution.

The resemblance between assemblage and articulation seems close, where analysis has to pay due attention to particular internal and external relations of an articulation. For Hall, the English word 'articulation' can be used to denote an articulated expression and also the idea of connection bringing together heterogeneous elements. Articulation as a pedagogic practice involves trying to draw alongside, to articulate a link with each student, to engage with their differences and their sensibilities in order to create new possibilities, to actualize their potentials.

Angela McRobbie (2000: 212) comments on the effect of Hall's work as a teacher engaging people from a range of backgrounds at the Open University, where pedagogic work became a collective pursuit:

> Stuart Hall has operated throughout his career as a teacher, and indeed as a certain kind of teacher. As he himself said in interview, 'Open university courses are open to those who don't have any academic background. If you are going to make cultural studies ideas live with them, you have to translate the ideas, be willing to write at that more popular and accessible level. I wanted cultural studies to be open to that sort of challenge. I didn't see why it wouldn't "live" as a more popular pedagogy'.

This gives a sense of the pedagogical challenge, of paying close attention and finding a way to develop articulations that are appropriate and commensurate for each student, their different manners and ways of thinking when engaged in a learning encounter, in order to extend their capacities and potentials.

My discussion of the work of these three key academics, teachers and writers is far too brief, and much has been omitted; its purpose is to indicate in historical terms a rich vein of thought and educational practice that in many ways underpins my advocacy for a pedagogy of individual and collective taking care. Their work along with educators in the United States (John Dewey, Maxine Greene, bel hooks, as well as others such as John Holt, Paul Goodman and Ivan Illich) insisted upon the value of education not simply for economic advantage or benefit but also for developing and expanding individual and collective values, for civic responsibility and well-being, what Aristotle termed *eudamonia*, a Greek term referring to happiness comprising fulfilment through the elaboration of human possibility. The creation of the Open University in 1969 in the UK was an important manifestation of such civic pursuits in the domain of education. Emerging from the groundbreaking work of these educators throughout the 1960s and 1970s came a range of social, political and cultural enquiries: the rise of women's studies, ethnic studies, post-colonial studies, multicultural and intercultural studies and radical pedagogies, each of which extended democratic concerns and practices. In current educational policy, the emphasis placed upon economic ambition and prosperity has promoted a de-democratizing effect, in that civic values and collective pursuits for social well-being are pushed to the margins, as neoliberal economics and competition, the pursuit of individual advancement, underfunding of welfare and healthcare and the marketization and economization of education have advanced.

One example of marketization can be witnessed in the domain of academic research in the form of the Research Assessment Exercise in English universities whereby research is assessed according to its uptake in non-academic domains such as commerce, state agencies and NGOs. Lecturers and professors within the university are therefore conceived by the university in terms of academic capital, acquiring research 'points' that translate into the amount of research funding awarded. Research becomes governed by market values. One lamentable consequence of this situation is that the high value placed upon research has led to a reduction in the status of undergraduate teaching. I turn now to other examples of economization and marketization in the school curriculum and teacher education.

School Curricula

In England and elsewhere, neoliberal rationality has affected the school curriculum in that more emphasis is placed upon provision for the STEM subjects that are necessary for economic progress, and this has meant that the arts in many schools have been reduced. (The current planned English Baccalaureate has no provision for art.) This can be viewed as a direct consequence of the effects of economization on the school curriculum. Consequently, the emphasis placed upon STEM subjects is that, by implication, those with interests, aptitudes and proclivities for STEM subjects are prioritized. This produces an educational system that places importance upon particular forms of knowledge, teaching and learning whilst marginalizing others, and this puts those students with interests in the latter domains at a disadvantage. Educational subjectivities are thus produced according to specific socio-economic interests and requirements.

Such emphasis follows the centralization of school education in England and elsewhere and enables government to control the content and purpose of education, which, as already stated, is essential to prepare pupils for the world of work, though some recognition of what used to be called a pastoral curriculum is acknowledged, promoting social values such as responsibility, respect, empathy, cooperation, patience and perseverance. The current coronavirus pandemic has highlighted the necessity for such pastoral provision, particularly because of the effects of the pandemic upon children's and students' mental health. In many ways, a belief in human potential, in the child and their interests, capacities and potentials, has now been replaced by what we might call a prioritization of *homo economicus*, of the production of human capital for the world of economic competition and ambition. This economization of the purpose of school education tends to move away from older community or civic values, which was never perfect, to be replaced by an individualist competitive scenario in which pupils need to work hard and compete for success, not working with and for the community but competing with others for the benefits to oneself. A particular disastrous effect of economization on educational provision is the serious underfunding of resources for special needs education that many would argue has become a national disgrace.

But if the production of human capital for the economic world of competition and progress as defined above is indeed unsustainable and ultimately destructive, as some would argue, then should we begin to reflect upon the consequences for future generations and thus, by implication, the ethos informing the kind of schools children and students deserve? Is it possible to construct an education system that is not totalized by the drive for the production of human capital to service the world of economic competition and ambition, where the ethos of competition and self-interest is morphed more generally throughout social relations? Can we conceive and develop systems of education and schools that are 'community centric, ecologically balanced and culturally sensitive' (Balch 2013)? Can we reimagine schools as places of human flourishing with others beyond the particular vision of economic progress described above; can we reimagine education from the damage (for human and non-human) of this vision? This is not to argue that economic life and prosperity are unimportant; they are, but can we reimagine an economics and prosperity of taking care rather than competition and self-interest? Can we design schools whose central purpose is not the production of human capital but as centres and communities that promote and advance the arts of living and flourishing with others alongside or beyond the forces of economization? This would entail reimagining processes of teaching and learning that are not motivated or controlled by the forces of audit for particular specified outcomes as determined by others but which are informed by an open deliberation of their individual and civic value and purpose and for generating practices and knowledge for the aptitudes, interests and potentials of each student. The deeply embedded nature of audit that pervades the evaluation of curriculum content and practice, as well as the quality of teaching, makes it difficult to foresee other forms of teaching and learning beyond such apparatuses of surveillance and control. I will respond to the questions raised above in the second part of this chapter when I advocate an alternative approach to educational practices in schools. But before that, I want to consider the effects of neoliberal rationality upon the provision of teacher education in England.

Teacher Education in England

I turn now to recent changes to the organization and programme content of teacher education in England. Historically, since the closure of colleges of teacher education in the late 1980s and early 1990s, teacher education was organized, supervised and accredited by universities. It took the form of partnerships between universities and schools. Since the mid-1990s, government made a series of interventions into the content and practice of university-based teacher education driven by economic concerns as well as international comparisons of educational performance of school pupils in which English schools were viewed to be underperforming in comparison with many countries. Teacher education was viewed by government as a key instrument to raise both teacher and pupil achievement. Initially, the concern was to assert some control by establishing a series of 'competences' for university-based programmes (PGCE) that functioned as criteria according to which student-teachers' performance and knowledge should be assessed as they trained to be teachers as well as the quality of their training. These competences later became 'standards' (Teacher Development Agency (TDA) 2008) for the achievement of qualified teacher status (QTS), and these were enforced when the government inspection service OfSTED (Office for Standards in Teacher Education) was extended from school inspection to university teacher education programmes (PGCE). If such programmes failed to meet the Standards, they could be closed.

Teacher 'training' and not teacher 'education' became the preferred term, and this discursive change signalled a conspicuous emphasis upon the practical aspects of teaching whilst marginalizing discussion and debate about pedagogy. Teaching was viewed by government in practical terms, and apprenticeship into the profession was best achieved in schools on the assumption that by spending more time in schools and less within university seminars, this would produce more effective teachers (see McNamara and Murray 2013).

From the late 1990s, in order to reduce the control of teacher education by universities, government introduced different routes into teacher training that were essentially school based, and government funds were largely diverted from universities to schools. Alongside reduced university PGCE provision, Graduate Teacher Programmes and School-Centred Initial Teacher Training (SCITT) programmes were introduced (see Furlong 2001). In 2012, the government introduced the School Direct programme of training, and in this section, I concentrate on this particular model of school-based training and the School Direct Research Project (SDRP) (Brown, Rowley and Smith 2015) and its final report, *The Beginnings of School Led Teacher Training: New Challenges for University Teacher Education*. My intention is to highlight the effect of neoliberal marketization and rationality upon recent government initiatives in teacher education that have impacted upon its previous organization, control and pedagogy by university departments of education.

The School Direct Research Project aimed to understand the implications for university teacher education of this particular school-led initiative in teacher training in which student-teachers would receive the bulk of their training in schools under their control and supervision with a much decreased input from universities. The report draws attention to the changing nature of teacher training that has affected the roles and responsibilities of teacher educators in universities and those teachers training student-teachers in schools. It also refers to how school-based teacher training has reshaped student experience:

> The push to a greater emphasis upon school-based practice and knowledge is also reconfiguring how trainee teachers experience and understand practice-based pedagogical knowledge, or put more simply the relationship between theory and practice. Increasingly, teaching is conceived in craft-based, technicist terms strengthened by increasing prescription and performative measures,

> which require teachers to present and shape knowledge in particular ways. ... Furthermore, many re-conceptualisations of teacher education have privileged practical components to the detriment of theory and analysis. (SDRP: 7)

And later:

> However, within a school-based model progression to pedagogical knowledge is increasingly shaped by demands of the regulative policies and highly structured frameworks as enacted within schools where trainees spend the majority of their time. In this scenario, teachers craft their understandings according to the legislative framework (Standards) in which their practices have become ever more strictly articulated, rather than being educated so much in universities to engage critically with evolving demands. (my bracket) (9)

These quotes point to how student-teacher subjectivations have been radically remodelled in the light of government initiatives to transform teacher education by situating it in schools. It also suggests that school-based models of training have changed conceptions of what it is to teach and how to do this. We can view government initiatives to promote and encourage different routes into teaching and to control the flow of routes as a market-led approach although one with a particular bias towards school-based programmes. By this I suggest, as discussed above, that neoliberal economics have pervaded government policies for education in the sense that great emphasis is placed upon subjects that will meet the requirements of economic ambition and competition, whilst other subjects, not conceived important to such ends, become marginalized. Teacher education, now teacher training, has also given priority to students wishing to train to be teachers in STEM. The emphasis in teacher training is placed upon craft-based, instrumental principles so that little, if any, time is given to discussion and debate about pedagogy and the purpose of education. The implications are that government prefers to minimize university-led inputs to teacher education because such inputs, which historically encouraged exploration, discussion and debate about pedagogy as well as exploring different conceptions of teaching and learning in accordance with helping to promote civic values and social and moral responsibility, do not fit with the much narrower educational function of producing human capital equipped for the world of work. The report writes:

> With respect to subject knowledge, university-based teacher educators also face longer-term changes as academic priorities in schools change the curriculum structure and the relative inclusions of different subject areas. For example, tighter specification of core subjects such as mathematics, English and science

has led to a compression of staff specialising in music, drama and art as student recruitment in those areas has been reduced. (9)

With reference to research into teaching and learning and to discussion and debate over their purpose, conception and suitability for current and changing sociocultural contexts, the report highlights the narrowing approach to conceptions and practices of teaching and learning now imposed by government.

> Attitudes towards research are also changing whilst the function of research is also being crafted as 'evidence' that can be used in a straightforward manner to improve narrowly defined educational outcomes, rather than progressing critical or analytical ideas of what it means to educate. Such conceptions are concurrent with the increase in external specification and surveillance, which conceives teaching in particular ways and, in turn, has an impact upon how teacher professionalism and agency is understood and enacted. (9)

In summary, the report indicates that government has enforced stricter control and prescribed content of teacher training in England in order to meet the requirements of school education, which, in essential terms, is to produce human capital for the evolving demands of economic prosperity. Teaching in schools has been transformed first through increased prescription, compliance and inspection in order to control and shape curriculum knowledge content and assessment and second through constant inspection of the quality of teaching.

Equally, the government has taken control of the discourses and practices that constitute teacher training and its assessment and thereby reconstructed this practice. Emphasis is now placed upon the practical aspects of 'training' in compliance with Standards for QTS rather than an education in pedagogy and associated disciplines alongside more practical aspects of teaching. This can be viewed as symptomatic of the impact of neoliberal forces affecting teacher training in that government prescription marginalizes any debate about pedagogic values, the purpose of education and the quality and relevance of education. This returns us to Brown's comments on aspects of neoliberal rationality affecting democracy and education. To repeat (2015: 177), "Democracies are conceived as requiring technically skilled human capital, not educated participants in public life and common rule." Trainee-teachers are trained to acquire the practical skills of teaching alongside the prescribed knowledge and skills to be taught. They are not viewed as participants who are educated, called upon to think, debate or develop the content or assessment of learning, nor to consider or explore alternative modes of teaching that do not prioritize economic concerns but focus more upon civic values and the ability to develop critical, caring and reflective minds.

This chapter maintains that whilst it is important that education facilitates skills and knowledge required for economic existence, it is also vital that it enables opportunities for children and older students to develop and expand their particular proclivities and potentials, which might include aesthetic, affective, ethical, spiritual, physical or political interests and practices. To restrict education mainly to the skills and knowledge required for economic life could be viewed, as Brown suggests, as a hollowing out of democracy, that is, if we accept the notion of democracy advocated by John Dewey and others, as an incomplete project that values difference to sustain its vitality and relevance for evolving collective participation and civic practices.

I want to turn quickly to Maurizio Lazzarato's work on social subjection and machinic enslavement in order to consider further the effects of neoliberal rationality upon teacher education. Such effects relate not only to new forms of subjection in terms of changes to roles and responsibilities but also, more insidiously, to pathic effects, demeanours and modes of comportment. They also challenge professional ethics and integrity, particularly amongst established university-based teacher educators rooted in modes of pedagogy and practice that were developed for many years before the imposition of government control and regulation of initial teacher education.

In his book *Signs and Machines* (2014), Maurizio Lazzarato draws attention to two interconnected forces that constitute the capitalist production of subjectivity, social subjection and machinic enslavement. The first refers to forms of identity, such as gender, profession, nationality and so forth, that are determined by social divisions of labour, social values and inheritance and produces 'individuated subjects, their consciousness, representations and behaviour' (12). The second is more surreptitious in that it 'proceeds through de-subjectification' and 'dismantles the individual subject, consciousness and representations' (12). In machinic enslavement there are no individuals but 'dividuals' (see also Raunig 2016) acting as cogs in different social assemblages and their respective forms of control, regulation and normalization. We might understand social subjection functioning in school education in terms of specific pedagogized identities that are produced within curriculum subject domains and their processes of assessment. Here both teacher and student identities are constructed according to the specific practices and discourses that constitute particular domains of learning and teaching. We might also view teacher training as discussed above as a process of social subjection to specified and highly regulated discourses and modes of practice. The notion of governmentality developed by Michel Foucault points to such social situations of power whereby practice is constituted and regulated as practice according to prescribed modes, structures and subjectivities.

Machinic enslavement is more insidious in that it refers not to individual identities but to different qualities, desires, attitudes, demeanours, comportments and so forth, demanded by an assemblage, so that in an education assemblage, teachers and learners are not viewed as individual subjects but as components requiring particular capacities for interacting within the assemblage, like cogs in a machine.

> In machinic enslavement the individual is no longer instituted as an 'individual subject', 'economic subject' (human capital, entrepreneur of the self), or 'citizen'. He is instead considered a gear, a cog, a component part in the 'business' and 'financial system' assemblages, in the media assemblage, and the 'welfare-state' assemblage and its collective institutions (schools, hospitals, museums, theatres, television, Internet, etc.). Enslavement is a concept Deleuze and Guattari borrowed explicitly from cybernetics and the science of automation. (Lazzarato 2014: 25)

Andrew Goffey (2019: 43) points to a crucial dimension of this machinic process that Lazzarato discusses in his book *Governing by Debt* (188):

> Lazzarato further points out that under conditions of 'enslavement' human agents not only form part of a broader machinic assemblage, in which the usual oppositions between human and machine break down, but further that 'the component parts of subjectivity (intelligence, affects, sensations, cognition, memory, physical force) are no longer unified in an "I", they no longer have an individuated subject as referent. Intelligence, affects, sensations, cognition, memory, and physical force are now components whose synthesis no longer lies in the person but in the assemblage'.

In an assemblage therefore, as developed by Deleuze and Guattari, we are not concerned with individual subjects but, as mentioned, with a particular machinic relation, the generation and synthesis of particular affects, desires, demeanours, responsibilities, comportments, values and so on, in the micro-production of subjective states. I will discuss this process in relation to the idea of mesopolitics in Chapter 8. The machine of educational assemblages not only interpellates subjects according to specified identities (e.g. as particular kinds of teachers or learners) but also, more stealthily, generates a series of capacities, comportments and attitudes – an infrastructure of affects that the assemblage requires.

In the educational assemblage, social subjection operates through the specification of particular pedagogized identities as constituted through discourses pertaining to standards, assessment criteria, inspection regimes and improvement targets. Such interpellative forces also 'machine' particular desires, affects, attitudes and demeanours, a plural a-signifying semiotics that lubricates the assemblage, thus producing and valorizing a particular kind of pedagogized/ professionalized and politicized subjectivity. So whilst social subjection operates through discursive interpellations as they function, for example, within institutions, crucially, machinic enslavement functions on an existential and collective pathic level (Goffey: 44–5), generating particular habits, drives, propensities and demeanours.

The importance of pathic experience in the production of subjectivity is therefore a pivotal aspect of the force of machinic enslavement entwined with the governmental power of social subjection. We might detect this combination in the analysis of findings in the School Direct Research Project mentioned earlier. This presents a series of comments by university teacher educators trying to manage or come to terms with government changes to the new assemblages of teacher training that have considerable professional and pathic impacts upon their work, in comparison with previous assemblages of teacher education that were organized by universities.

If we look again at the SDRP report discussed above, the effects of government changes to teacher training upon many established university-based tutors have been quite demanding, even demeaning, as they have to comply with new regulations causing radical changes to their work, responsibilities and status, now that teacher training has become largely school based. We might consider the effects of such changes upon these tutors as generating a complex of pathic intensities (affects) on an existential level. Thus, the more overt effects of subjectivation, of changing roles and status, are coupled with subliminal affects ('a-signifying affects', in Deleuze and Guattari's terminology) that may impact more potently professional integrity and ethics. These effects and affects, overt and subliminal, manifest, for example, a mixture of professional resentment, grudging acceptance, willing participation, a new entrepreneurialism or passive resignation. It is clear from the report's analysis of findings (17–25) that in school-based teacher training, university tutors' roles have been diminished. Where prior to government changes, they were responsible for the organization, structure and content of teacher education programmes, but always in close partnerships with schools, the roles of university tutors now involve a real admixture. Now that teacher training has become marketized in the sense that in school-based Initial Teacher Training, the schools hold funding and can 'shop around' for their preferred university package; university tutors become sales representatives as their Initial Teacher Training package becomes a product to be negotiated and sold to schools. Schools often go for the cheapest offer (SDRP: 18), becoming consumers of university Initial Teacher Training packages, whilst, as one tutor stated, universities 'act like gas providers' (18). University tutors' expertise and experience, particularly in academic areas of pedagogic research, are often denied or even denigrated as school-based provision focuses mainly upon the practical aspects of teaching, and when interviewing prospective student teachers, university tutors' views are frequently disregarded (19). Equally, university tutors are sometimes expected to relax their standards or expectations by their own management personnel in order to retain business from schools. On the other hand, some university tutors, often those newly appointed from schools as 'expert' teachers, see school-based Initial Teacher Training as an entrepreneurial opportunity to develop new approaches to school and university partnerships, particularly to develop new masters and postgraduate programmes for teachers.

The report also draws attention (22) to conflicts between long-held pedagogical understandings of established university tutors and the new specified models for teaching established by government.

> For example, one teacher educator described how due to the way that pedagogy of her subject has changed as a consequence to increased specification, her subject and how it is taught was now very different from her own pedagogical conceptions which had been acquired within the academy. As she further explained in relation to recent observations of trainees in schools: Nothing they seem to be doing bears any relation to any kind of research or ideas about learning or how kids learn ... I think it's really sad. (22)

Of course, it may be countered, people have to adopt to new ideas, new ways of working and new roles and responsibilities, but this begs the further question, what kind of pedagogical outcomes do such new ideas and practice produce and who benefits from them? Newly appointed university tutors as expert teachers from schools were far more comfortable with the new school-based arrangements, but they felt undervalued by the university as they were perceived to 'lack capital' in terms of a research profile (22).

Following on from the previous quotation, the report draws attention to a depreciation of theory and critical reflection on school-based Initial Teacher Training programmes and a strong emphasis upon practical matters of training. Equally, the introduction of prescribed subject knowledge in the school curriculum has impacted teacher training subject knowledge content so that whereas previously trainees were encouraged to critically engage with subject knowledge and its relevance and format for learning practices in relation to ways in which children learn, now they are required to follow and deliver a prescribed content and agenda. Equally, lesson structure has become more regimented.

The impact of school-based Initial Teacher Training upon established university tutors, and the new managerialism of government to procure such programmes, has produced new 'controlled' subjectivations relating to roles, responsibilities and new forms of comportment, whilst the existential machinic affects of such subjectivations have precipitated intensities manifesting anxieties, uncertainties, resentments and de-professionalization that unmoor professional integrity and ethics as existed in the previous assemblage of university teacher education.

The marketization of teacher training as within school-based programmes, whereby universities produce training packages and compete to sell these to schools to meet with government prescriptions of curriculum content, has transformed university Initial Teacher Education. Previously, this was viewed as a civic endeavour to produce effective and educated teachers who developed pedagogical understandings to enable children to develop their different proclivities and potentials and not mainly those related to the production of a particular mode of human capital. This seems to me to involve a de-democratization of education, the nihilism of market values applied to the civic enterprise of teaching and learning.

Part Two

Towards an Ethico-Aesthetic Paradigm of Education

In the second part of this chapter, I engage with the writings of Felix Guattari, Maurizio Lazzarato and Mikhail Bakhtin, in order to consider an alternative to educational practice not driven by neoliberal reason but by an ethico-aesthetic paradigm and a politics of potential and taking care. In contrast to grounding educational practices mainly upon the task of preparing students for the world of work, economic competition and ambition, this part advocates an education concerned with nurturing and supporting the diversity and variety of what Guattari terms 'existential territories' and their expanding relations. This does not lower the importance of skills and knowledge for economic livelihood, but rather than knowledge being viewed mainly towards the achievement of such ends, the production of human capital for the world of work, it can also be viewed as instrumental to the creation and valuing of existential affirmation and potential in the proclivities and potentials mentioned above within a shared collective world. Whilst the first pedagogical programme is driven by prescribed and controlled teaching methodologies, content, routes and outcomes for learning, the second, whilst not only supporting the skills and knowledge of this first programme but also valuing other forms of knowledge and practice that it marginalizes, advocates a more open and exploratory approach to pedagogic work that views pedagogy not only in terms of established practices/methodologies but also as an always-evolving 'incomplete' (perhaps even disobedient) adventure of practice – an adventure in which, for example, teachers may expand their pedagogical understanding as they confront the diverse and divergent ways in which children and students learn. In such circumstances children or students become teachers by proxy. The crucial point here is to view the subject as an always-evolving, eventful, sometimes disobedient, adventure, not as a preconceived entity.

Lazzarato on Bakhtin's Speech Genres

I begin by turning again to Lazzarato with particular reference to his comments on Mikhail Bakhtin's notion of speech acts and speech genres. Bakhtin made a distinction between language and enunciation, between linguistic meaning and the sense of enunciation, between words or propositions of language and existential utterances. A speech act consists therefore of an existential function (Guattari) that is sequestered from linguistic categorisation – 'forces that are external to language but internal to enunciation' (Lazzarato 2014: 179). Although language is a crucial constituent of speech acts and the formation of meaning, such acts involve more than language. This draws attention to what we might call the pathic existential dimension of speech acts. Lazzarato, following Bakhtin, makes a series of claims about speech acts as political and ethical events: 'every speech act is an ethico-political act, a question asked of others, oneself, the world', where 'the world (is) viewed as a problem, an event, something that remains to be accomplished' (181). He makes the point that speech acts precipitate or facilitate possibilities for action within a singular, existential relation in an immediate present, opening possibilities for new universes of value and sensibility, subjective mutations through its event. 'Every enunciation is an historic event even if it is infinitely small' (181). He continues, stating that the speech act constitutes a 'micro-politics' of relations between speakers (181) and furthermore, that the other is an active participant in a speech act; it is not a matter of simple reception on the other's behalf but of a co-production of 'linguistic virtualities, worlds of values, and the existential territories in which they occur' (181). The importance of all these statements about the ethico-political aspects of speech acts for pedagogical relations relates to the ability for educators to develop a care and concern for the existential grounding of each child's possibilities and potentials for practices of learning that can facilitate the emergence of new worlds. The crucial point here is that such taking care is prior to the content of learning in that it attempts to comprehend how such content matters for a particular learner and then address this mattering in such a way as to expand each learner's capacity to learn. A persistent difficulty surrounding such a pedagogy of taking care is the subjection to what we might call the molar discourses and practices of guidelines, competences, standards, methodologies or assessment criteria that 'pedagogize' both teachers and students. That is to say, such discourses and practices for the teacher tend to invoke or anticipate specific forms of practice that constitute the understanding of practice. In other terms, such forms precede pedagogic practice in determining practices of teaching and learning. In contrast, by emphasizing the importance of the existential dimension of enunciation in a speech act, or for our purposes, a learning event, that is to say, a specific teaching-learning situation, it is important not to allow the abstraction of established forms and practice (rules, methods, criteria, techniques) to occlude the existential specificities of enunciative events that impact the expression of each learner's practice. Although established and valued forms of knowledge, practice and discourse constitute a vital heritage, it is important to acknowledge that in the situated specificity of each learner's practice, in whatever subject area (mathematics, science, art, etc.), such learning constitutes a novel creation or iteration in its existential mattering. Bakhtin (1986: 120) writes:

> An utterance is never just a reflection or an expression of something already existing outside it that is given and final. It always creates something that never existed before, something absolutely new and unrepeatable, and, moreover it always has some relation to value (the true, the good, the beautiful, and so forth). But something created is always created out of something given (language, an

observed phenomenon of reality, an experienced feeling, the speaking subject himself, something finalized in his world view, and so forth). What is given is completely transformed in what is created.

These ideas on the importance of the existential aspects of enunciation have significant implications for thinking about the production of subjectivity in pedagogic work. If emphasis is placed upon the production of specific preordained, pedagogized subjects to service the needs of economic competition, a production secured by controlled curriculums, assessment and inspection programmes, following prescribed routes determining educational success or failure, then affirmation of diverse and divergent practices and their existential mattering is likely to be occluded. By acknowledging the vital importance of enunciation pertaining to existential difference, whether it occurs within prioritized subjects or those marginalized, a more uncertain pedagogical adventure emerges that attempts to comprehend how a learning encounter matters, how it might be existentially affirmed by a learner. In this more uncertain pedagogical process, subjectivation emerges, is yet to be realized, is constructed, in the enunciative event of learning (the relationalities of the event). Yet things are even more complex because the idea (and fact) of difference is actually what nourishes the neoliberal condition and which it can exploit for market advancement. What really matters here in relation to a pedagogy of taking care is an articulation with the alterity of difference in relation to both existential and collective civic pursuits.

In an earlier passage, Medvedev and Bakhtin (1978: 152) emphasize the novel aspect of communication that is directly relevant to pedagogical work involving relations between teacher and student and the emergent nature of subjectivation:

> The relationship between A and R is constantly changing and generating, and itself changes in the communicative process. And there is no ready-made communication X. It is generated in the process of intercourse between A and R. Furthermore, X is not transmitted from one to another, but is constructed between them, as a kind of ideological bridge, is built in the process of their interaction.

In his work on speech acts, Bakhtin argues that what precedes the subject is not language as such but what he calls 'speech genres' and that learning to speak, that is, to become a subject, is achieved through immersion in such genres. Speech genres 'function as an assemblage composed of a multiplicity of ways of speaking, responding, disagreeing, and cooperating' (Lazzarato 2014: 193). Chains of utterances that constitute speech genres are fluid and constantly changing in their respective contexts and relations (such as in education); they evolve as speakers try to express intentions and meanings both in stereotypical and in more creative or original forms. If we think of speech genres functioning in an educational context governed by standards or competences, prescribed content and routes for learning, they will maintain a high degree of constraint and a politics of standardization and reproduction. Those speech genres that facilitate a more adventurous, less prescribed approach to teaching and learning as they try to draw alongside and value local events of enunciation, as discussed briefly above, would demand a more innovative, sensitive and intimate approach, involving a politics and an ethics of relevance and taking care. The distinction made here between prescribed and reproducible standardization and singular enunciations of practice raises what we might call a contrast between the macropolitics and micropolitics of expression and brings into focus the ethico-political aspect of pedagogic work. The implication is to be able to adopt an articulation, in Hall's sense, between a macropolitics and micropolitics of expression, between practices and expressions of inheritance and conformity and singular creative practices that may disrupt the former but in doing so expand the efficacy of pedagogic work. In trying to meet this challenge, Bakhtin (1986: 120) is again helpful as he calls for a 'science of singularity':

> It is much easier to study the given in what is created (for example, language, ready-made and general elements of world view, reflected phenomena of reality, and so forth) than to study [how and] what is created. Frequently the whole of scientific analysis amounts to a disclosure of everything that has been given, already at hand and ready-made before the work has existed (that which is found by the artist and not created by him). (my additional bracket)

If, in pedagogic work, exclusive emphasis is placed upon prescribed routes for and outcomes of practice, reinforcing prescribed methodologies of teaching, standards and competences for learning and, by implication, particular subjectivations, other modes of practice, forms of expression and subjectivities that do not subscribe to these values are likely to be marginalized or subordinated. By implication, such subordination narrows the heterogeneity of expression emerging from a multiplicity of existential enunciations, their relations and modes of practice. Yet we might argue that real learning is always grounded and affirmed existentially, in its different ways and forms of mattering, and through such grounding and effective support, local forms of expression are made possible and are given coherence, stability and recognition. One consequence of this support for existential affirmation in learning encounters is that it may effect not just a redistribution of the sensible of pedagogic work in Rancierian terms but a puncturing and transformation of the epistemological and ontological grounds of such work.

Felix Guattari: Metamodelization and an Ethico-Aesthetic Paradigm

A concern for the singular runs through the work of Felix Guattari, and I want to turn to his notions of metamodelization and an ethico-aesthetic paradigm in order to build upon those ideas of Bakhtin that I have discussed. Again, this is to inform my advocacy for a pedagogy of taking care that prioritizes the existential cartographies and sensitivities of learners rather than predefined or preconceived subjectivations according to established educational infrastructures and discourses. Guattari is not using the term 'aesthetic' to discuss works of art, though the rupturing forces, the 'mutant coordinates' of art, are of interest to him but to refer to the aesthetics and ethics of life as a lived creative force. He argues that subjectivation should not be viewed only as determined by economic, linguistic or social infrastructures, that is, as determined by external referents, but stresses the importance of autopoietic existential processes that might, in various degrees, reposition or reconfigure social orders. He is concerned then with the processual immanence of local cartographies of existence and their creative potential in contrast to established transcendent or authoritative discourses and orders.

Guattari's idea of metamodelization requires some discussion because it ties in with the points already raised about current subjectivation to neoliberal economic forces, the social models that mould human existence according to their values, 'whose purpose is to regulate our most intimate temporalisations, and to model our relationships to the landscape and to the living world' (Guattari 2011: 111). The notion of model in French can mean 'pattern' in the sense of a learned pattern of behaviour that emerges, for example, from family relations, institutional procedures as in education, the law or healthcare, which establish norms of functioning. Model can also refer to mapping processes and configurations or to established structures (Watson 2008). Schizoanalytic metamodeling is 'a discipline of reading other systems of modelling, not as a general model, but as an instrument for deciphering modelling systems in various domains' (Guattari 2013: 27). Guattari is therefore concerned with the diversity and divergence of modelling systems or modelling functions, and he is against any universalizing pretensions of specific models. Such modelling systems apply to the process of subjectivity, which, though it is likely to be subjugated to particular socio-political modelling, also has the capacity to produce its own 'existential territory' from its surrounding milieu of semiotic materials, physical, technical and social relations. Guattari states that 'subjectivity is always more or less a metamodeling activity' or 'a process of self-organisation or singularisation' (2013: 17)

We might consider the practice of a pedagogy of taking care in terms of a metamodeling practice in its concern not only to respond empathetically to the learning pathways (incipient metamodelings) of each child or student but also, in a critical orientation, to the established pedagogical frameworks (modelings) that guide pedagogical work. The following quote from Janell Watson (2008) has some relevance for pedagogical practice.

> Guattari's metamodeling promotes a radical, liberatory politics. It creates a singularizing map of the psyche. It allows one to construct one's own metamodels. It recognizes, and even borrows from, existing models. It can transform an existence by showing paths out of models in which one may have inadvertently become stuck. Rather than looking to the past, it looks to future possibilities. 'What distinguishes metamodeling from modeling is the way it uses terms to develop possible openings onto the virtual and onto creative processuality' (Guattari 1995: 31). Metamodeling produces, creates, finds new paths.

The process of metamodeling in relation to subjectivity therefore is to open up possibilities for creative expansion. The important point in relation to the creative processuality of subjectivity is that such creation is not confined to established orders of practice or discourses, what we might call established semiotic orders, but is also composed of a-signifying practices. The metamodeling process of subjectivity for Guattari is composed of four ontological functions or functional domains. They concern both the actual real and the virtual real. The actual real consists of material fluxes that involve semiotic, emotional, economic, physical and other material orders, what Guattari calls abstract machines: rules, regulations, plans or guidelines, which form social or political models that establish social norms. The virtual real consists of existential territories of subjectivity that are composed of non-discursive virtual 'graspings' or 'testings' and incorporeal universes that compose the realm of potentiality for new modes of becoming – crystals of singularization or intensification, intensities of affect and virtual possibilities.

The metamodeling of subjectivity is therefore composed by the interaction of these actual and virtual ontological functions. We might think of the experiencing of an encounter or disturbance, for example, in a teaching situation, that does not fit with established frameworks of practice and how the initial affect of encounter, the encounter with otherness, moves from a potential/virtual universe into trying to grasp meaning through signifying processes that employ linguistic or other forms of signification. Initially, the affect disrupts the teacher's existential territory without direct signification, but it requires the support or the articulation of signifying machines which are themselves reconfigured to actualize the material/emotional flows that enable change in the teacher's existential territory. Guattari's four functional domains of the assemblage of subjectivity are interdependent; they form a processual spatio-temporal, signifying and affective-incorporeal (a-signifying) conjunction.

If an existential territory is to continue to expand, to be open to new modes of becoming, it has to be receptive to deterritorialization. As Roberts (2019: 52) insists, the distinction between the *actuality* of material flows and signifying machines and the *virtuality* of existential territories, a-signifying and incorporeal universes that traverse and unsettle them is important. This is because the actuality of material flows and formalized logics can be expressed discursively according to finite coordinates, whilst existential territories and incorporeal universes that traverse and unsettle them (a-signifying domains of intensities and affects as in art practice) cannot be known in the same way. In the struggle to grasp and formulate a world, existential territories are therefore placed between the actuality (discursive semiotics) of material flows and coordinates and the intensities, affects (a-signifying semiotics) and haecceities of incorporeal universes. Subjectivity is conceived as an actual/virtual assemblage involving all four domains. It is vital that virtual aspects of the assemblage are not overpowered by actual aspects. We might say that the assemblage of subjectivity, or more generally processes of *experiencing*, are composed of a series of interfaces between affects, intensities and haecceities (virtual) and the stratifications of different signifying registers that constitute different social settings.

As an evolving assemblage, subjectivity always requires a territory, but the process of territorializing is never complete, and it can also stagnate if its modelling remains, for example, in established material coordinates. The cartography of this assemblage has to remain open to mutations effected by all the domains. Guattari seems then to be offering both a cartographical and an ecological assemblage of subjectivity.

Whitehead's process philosophy and his immanent principle of creativity seem to have some resonance with the articulation or the subject assemblage (*agencements*) of Guattari's four ontological functions. Whitehead (1978: 21) writes:

> Creativity is the universal of universals characterizing ultimate matter of fact. It is that ultimate principle by which the many, which are the universe disjunctively, become the one actual occasion, which is the universe conjunctively. It lies in the nature of things that the many enter into complex unity.

Or put simply: 'The many become one and are increased by one', a disjunctive heterogeneous diversity, conjoined in human experience (but also in non-human experience). Human experiencing articulates a series of differing ontological functions, centres of experiencing, that produce a conjunction from their initial heterogeneity. Subjectivity is made up of different centres of experiencing (across the four domains of Guattari); they are immanent to and conjoined in subjectivity. Creativity is to be viewed as an ongoing diverging process that may effect what Guattari calls 'mutant coordinates' and a change in the cartography and ecology of the assemblage of subjectivity. It is not to be confused with the way it is often used, for example, in art education to denote a substantive internal force (the creative individual) because it does not concern an individual but rather a flow of heterogeneous (unpredictable) relational vectors that constitute a 'creative instance' in Guattari's terminology. This will be mentioned shortly.

My aim is to try to show the relevance of Guattari's concern with existential cartographies for advocating a pedagogy of taking care. A pedagogy that attempts to draw alongside, facilitate and expand each learner's creative capacities (and equally those of teachers) in actual instances of practice as well as their virtual potential that may open up locally what Guattari, in a wider sense, calls new universes of reference and new universes of value. Another way of putting this concern for the actual and the virtual (potential) within pedagogic work is to think of its relation in terms of an interface between the finite and the infinite (see O'Sullivan 2010). So, learning events can be viewed as processes in which the finitude of practice as it occurs in the relationalities of each existential cartography (Guattari's material and discursive domains) holds an infinitude of potential respective to it (Guattari's affective intensities and territories).

When we considered the complex assemblage of capitalist relations discussed earlier, we found that subjectivation in its neoliberal form was reduced to the production of human capital. The transcendent apparatus of capital standardizes the production of human capital, its controlled comportments, demeanours and values, for its specific requirements. One aspect of such standardization can be viewed in the educational assemblage through the valorization of specific prescribed, pedagogized subjects. In sharp contrast, the ethico-aesthetic paradigm envisioned by Guattari affirms the creativity of difference, divergence and singularity, both in its actuality and in its virtuality. He states, 'The decisive threshold constituting this new aesthetic paradigm lies in the aptitude of these processes of creation to auto-affirm themselves as existential nuclei, autopoietic machines' (1995: 106). We can relate the notion of existential nuclei to emerging existential germs or graspings leading to local crystallizations or individuations of experience within particular settings that continually and machinically expand the subject assemblage.

Following this he makes a crucial point: 'The new aesthetic paradigm has ethico-political implications because to speak of creation is to speak of the responsibility of the creative instance with regard to the thing created' (107). This does not refer to the responsibility of an 'individual who creates' but to the assemblage of the *creative instance* or event that can open up new vectors of possibility for new modes of becoming, new or modified political and ethical relations – new vectors that bring about a reconfiguration of established orders and relations from the immanence of the creative instance. In pedagogical work it concerns the opening up of new modes of becoming, new cartographies and ecologies of experiencing. We might say that the creative instance involves a necessary friction between actual and virtual components that opens up new capacities for practice.

Pedagogy becomes more experimental in responding empathically to the heteroglossia of local vectors of learning encounters. This heterogeneity involves divergent existential cartographies and temporalities so that a classroom can be viewed as a heterogenous and heteroglossic composition of different rhythms of becoming, actual and virtual, different foldings or crystallizations producing local ecologies and cartographies of experiencing. The ethico-aesthetic paradigm is thus centred upon the potentials (incorporeal universes) that generate the production of new modes of being, new subjectivations in the form of existential cartographies or, as put by Guattari (1995: 117), 'of new infinities from a submersion in sensible finitude, infinities not only charged with virtuality but with potentialities actualisable in given situations'. By focusing upon the singularities, the situated specificities of existential processes, Guattari's new ethico-aesthetic paradigm configures an ethico-politics by affirming and supporting a 'heterogenesis of systems of valorisation' (117) that may precipitate new modes of social practices and relations. Emphasis is placed upon a self-responsibility for developing subjectivity in relation to others and our world. This would be an important target for a pedagogy of taking care, to be able to respond to, nurture and extend each learner's proclivities, their different pathways and cartographies of learning whilst at the same time trying to encourage a self-responsibility for learning. In a difficult passage from *Chaosmosis* (60–1), we get a sense of Guattari's concern for the singular, for ontological heterogeneity and therefore the need to adopt what he calls a 'schizoanalytic modelisation':

> Schizoanalysis does not ... choose one modelisation to the exclusion of another*(e.g., competences, standards or education modelled upon economic imperatives)*. Within the diverse cartographies in action in a given situation *(a classroom)*, it tries to make nuclei of virtual autopoiesis discernible, *(germs of creative expression)* in order to actualise them, by transversalising them, in conferring on them a diagrammatism (for example, by a change in the material of Expression), in making them themselves operative within modified assemblages, more open, more deterritorialised. Schizoanalysis, rather than moving in the direction of reductionist modelisations which simplify the complex, will work towards its complexification, its processual enrichment, towards the consistency of its virtual line of bifurcation and differentiation, in short towards its ontological heterogeneity. (my additions in italicized parentheses)

This points to remarkable resonances with advocating a pedagogy of taking care and the importance of discerning and developing modes of access to the glimmerings of local germs of expression around which a subjectivity might cohere (nuclei of virtual autopoiesis) as learners engage with learning encounters. This suggests a requirement not to reduce diverse existential groundings of encounter to a particular 'model' composed, for example, of a set of competences or standards but to work with the richness of divergence and diversity, with each learner's mode of comprehension, mattering and practice (a local diagram), thus acknowledging the 'ontological heterogeneity' of pedagogical work. This approach does not reject established models or discourses but through a concern for the diversity and heteroglossia of singular practice attempts to complexify such models, to generate a metamodelization, to make them more apposite whilst simultaneously accepting that they will always be incomplete and imperfect. I will return to the notion of metamodelizing shortly.

Trying to engage with the glimmerings of local germs of expression is initially to engage with affective flows and then with their actualization into modes of coherence (linguistic, visual, etc.), into crystallizations that function pragmatically and strategically for a particular subjective purpose, a kind of existential probing and testing that extends the assemblage of the subject. It is by paying due attention (Stengers) to these affective flows and their actualized probings that we might expand our modelizings, our narratives of pedagogic work. Simon O'Sullivan (2010: 273) sees this process of expanded narrativization as a 'performative fictioning' in that by paying due attention to the intensity and 'singular constellation' of local processes of learning, we might build upon or reconfigure established pedagogical narratives in relation to experiencing the task of expanding local assemblages of coherence and potential. As indicated earlier, it is not a matter of abandoning established narratives or guidelines, but that in paying due attention to local existential practices of learning, we might develop an expanded field of pedagogic work.

'Schizoanalyis', or 'schizoanalytic modelizing', is the term Guattari (and his collaborator Gilles Deleuze) used to denote an approach to psychoanalysis that moved away from its dominant models and concepts, such as the oedipal complex, in order to explore and expand upon other ways of conceiving psychic processes and modelling assemblages of subjectivity. In simple terms and applied more generally, it rejects the controlling and reductive effects of authoritative models (concepts, ideologies) through which particular conditions or subjectivities are understood – to open up enquiry to other ways of understanding that produce different subjectivations (as formulated in the discussion of metamodelizing and the four ontological functions discussed above), thus bringing to light other modes of expression, values and potentials, revealing new rhythms or refrains of subjectivity, a technique that denotes an incessant production and continuous variation of the assemblage of the subject. By pushing through the limitations of authoritative discourses (e.g. in capitalism or education) and their specific subjectivations, we might open new possibilities (a process of metamodelizing) for understanding subjectivity that involve both signifying and a-signifying processes. In the first part of the chapter, I discussed neoliberal economic rationality and its modelling of educational practices to produce a particular mode of subjectivation, a particular mode of pedagogization and standardization.

Returning to the notion of existential territories and emergent germs of expression, Joe Gerlach and Thomas Jellis (2015: 135), following Guattari, state that a subject discipline is composed 'around a set of existential refrains – or what Guattari also terms "graspings" – rather than a set of definitions or procedures'. They take the notion of grasping to refer to 'a tentative establishment of some coherence in chaos'. This notion of grasping (that Guattari takes from Whitehead), in the forming of existential territories, is important for my purpose here in developing a pedagogy of taking care in that it offers a way to think about school subject disciplines or university and other programmes of education and their pedagogies and structures, not only from the perspective of established methods, guidelines, standards or competences but also as a 'heterogeneous assemblage of a plurality of existential territories' (135). These territories, constructed by both learners and teachers, are composed of an 'array of tentative graspings', but there is no stress placed upon the boundary of a discipline or established coordinates so that what constitutes a discipline remains open to creative expansion or, on the contrary, closed to stifling stratifications. We might view pedagogic work as an ongoing complex composition of different vectorial relations and components such as concepts, affects, techniques, materials, discussions, questions, answers, feelings and so on that come together to form existential refrains and territories. It is important to note that existential territories as conceived by Guattari are virtual real and never complete and require the actual real of signifying machines, such as language, which themselves need to be open to change. Perhaps it is better to understand this term in a verbal sense of *territorializing* – a territorializing in which the focus is upon becoming through transversal relations that open possibilities for practice and thinking. The emphasis here is not upon the 'subject' but upon an assemblage of vectors of becoming (*agencements*). Territorializing thus involves not only spatio-temporal coordinates but also incorporeal coordinates or universes.

It is this ongoing complex composition of practice, in our case pedagogic practice, that brings into play the need for what Guattari calls schizoanalytic metamodelization, as in the case of the assemblage of subjectivity already described as an assemblage (*agencement*) that is composed of the evolving relations between the four ontological functions. In pedagogic work the task concerns inventing novel modelizations of practice when pedagogical events challenge existing patterns and techniques, such as when a learner's practice does not fit within a teacher's pedagogical understanding. We might be tempted to ignore such disturbances, or we can face the disturbance and try to develop techniques and sensibilities for addressing the situated specificities of a learner's practice, a process that simultaneously alters pedagogic practice. The development of new techniques, new sensibilities in response to actual episodes of practice, illustrates the immanence of metamodelization. As mentioned earlier, it is important to acknowledge that the process of metamodelizing works within and amongst other models, drawing on, modifying, expanding or discarding previous models as a situation arises. The prefix 'meta' does not denote a 'model of all models', according to Brian Massumi (2011: 103), who writes, ' "Meta" is to be understood here in its etymological sense of "among". It refers not to the on-high of the ideal, but on the contrary to the spontaneous remingling of acquired regularities of practice,' as new events in the flows, spontaneities and indeterminacies of practice emerge. From such intermingling new techniques and sensitivities can emerge that extend pedagogic practice and its potential. We might see that this metamodelizing involves a process of unsettling established modes of practice and understanding and thereby bringing about new ways of conceiving practice, a new ethos of practice that involves a constant 'metamodelizing among'. We might then see that taking on board a process of metamodelizing in pedagogic practice involves an ethico-aesthetics in relation to events of practice and not simply a reliance upon established prescriptive or authoritative practices.

In *Chaosmosis*, Guattari (106) refers to art practice as one that constructs new modes and qualities of being; 'art does not have a monopoly on creation, but it takes its capacity to invent mutant coordinates to extremes: it engenders unprecedented, unforeseen and unthinkable qualities of being'. Guattari's notion of aesthetics widens this creative process so that it is not only confined to art but also relates to other modes of existence and also to what Foucault called a care of the self, which will be discussed in the next chapter. As the complex vectors and the relationalities that compose assemblages of existence modify and evolve, this care becomes an ongoing ethico-aesthetic project for processual development.

The process of metamodelization is important not only for the local processes of pedagogic practice but also, crucially, for the construction of educational policy in a world that has become increasingly complex – a complexity that involves technological innovations, shifting demographic constellations and political affiliations, social and cultural problematics and more. If we regard education not mainly as preparation for the world of work and the economy, though this form of modelization is important, but more widely in terms of processes that encourage and support learners to acquire skills, knowledge and sensitivities across a range of pursuits, then this growing complexity requires not just a single model but an ongoing metamodelizing of educational policy and practice that is commensurate to the immanence of specific demands.

A metamodelizing that considers this production of subjectivity requires a cartographic approach that considers existential cartographies as well as structural cartographies. Guattari (1995: 11) writes, 'In a more general way, one has to admit that every individual and social group conveys its own system of modelising subjectivity; that is, a certain cartography.' Pedagogic work concerns a multiplicity of not only local cartographies of learners and those of teachers but also structural cartographies imposed by government, policy and inspection regimes. What Guattari is arguing for with his notion of schizoanalytic cartography (Guattari 2012) is a concern for local vectors of becoming along cognitive, affective, actual and virtual lines, a more speculative venture than one constrained or regulated by established orders and prescribed subjectivities, though we cannot avoid these. And one outcome of such speculation may be to unsettle the latter and transform the wider structural and existential fields of practice. This would seem to advocate schizoanalytic cartography as always concerned with a processual production of new or modified vectors; cognitive, affective, physical, actual and virtual, new or modified existential refrains; and becomings; trying, Guattari (13) states, to grasp subjectivity, 'in the dimension of its processual creativity'.

The challenge for an education system that advocates a pedagogy of taking care is to encourage metamodelizing as a necessary function of pedagogic practice in order to facilitate, support and be commensurable to the multiplicity of existential territorializings and modes of expression, assemblages and diagrams of enunciation that the divergent learning pathways of children and students may present. The challenge also extends to a metamodelizing of structures that operates a constant vigilance to allow structural mutations to facilitate the ongoing complexities of pedagogic practice. These two modelizings are interconnected; they involve a transversality rather than a hierarchy.

There is a likely conflict here between the position of a teacher wanting to adopt a pedagogy of taking care and the demands of the state machine for a prescriptive pedagogy. We might describe it as a conflict between the molar order of discourses that define and regulate pedagogy and the diverse and divergent molecular orders of local pedagogic experiences, their actual/virtual and cognitive/pathic dimensions, where the former authoritarian orders are unsettled. Structural metamodelizing would constitute a rhizomic assemblage rather than a hierarchical assemblage, able to respond to the diversity of modes of expression and practice, their different cartographies of becoming – a response that deterritorializes established dispositifs into new or modified coordinates.

A pedagogy of taking care, informed by Guattari's metamodelizing of subjective assemblages according to his four domains, would not stress a responsibility for the maintenance of a territory, a form of being, but would emphasize the incorporeal vectors, the affects, intensities and haecceities that animate and inflect it, that is to say, the forces of becoming. It is important to establish a territory, a mode of being, a mode of practice but not so that it rigidifies. The security of being and established structures might relieve us of evolving a *response-ability* when this may be necessary to respond effectively to events of experience that disturb, events of difference and divergence. The stultification of being, in contrast to processes of creative becoming, can be considered as a kind of internal micro-fascism that prevents a freeing up of experiencing to creative potentials. Guattari's ethico-aesthetics refuses to be grounded in the vectors of actualized form but requires a constant reworking in the light of the vectors of virtual potential of events of experiencing.

Conclusion

The world is currently experiencing a global pandemic from COVID-19, a coronavirus that has killed hundreds of thousands, if not millions, and for which, as yet, there is no cure. Economies have been wrecked, millions will be left unemployed and destitute and the impact of the pandemic on mental health and social well-being is incalculable. Will this terrible event make governments reassess priorities and values? This may be too optimistic. But in the UK, neoliberal economics, long years of austerity with many communities suffering from years of neglect, the serious underfunding of social, medical and welfare services, has contributed to an unpreparedness that has exposed the people to dire and tragic consequences.

The social and civic commitments and concerns of Richard Hoggart, Raymond Williams and Stuart Hall discussed briefly in Part One are articulated with Guattari's concern with existential singularities and potentials in order to advocate a pedagogy of taking care. Underpinning this advocacy therefore is the challenge of viewing education not solely in terms of the production of human capital, commodification and individualism but also in valuing the diversity and divergence of human potential, self-affirmation and of collective responsibility and well-being.

Taking care does not refer only to the act of caring, of 'having a care', but also to the idea of concern, not just about 'being concerned' about something but, in its Quaker sense, as a call to action in the absence of desires for individual prestige or power. Upholding this sense of care/concern can often mean doing so even though, as is frequent in pedagogical work, and its implicit relations of power, those we are asked to support act in ways that seem awkward, mysterious or 'incorrect'. Such concern functions upon not only a basis of respect but also the task of generating self-responsibility which implies a responsibility towards others and an evolving conviviality. But taking care must also equally involve having a care for the impact and effects upon practice of the very frameworks through which practice is conceived. Such frameworks may inadvertently marginalize or even dismiss practices that do not conform to their values.

Ivan Illich, whose work I will discuss in Chapter 3, draws our attention to the way we have been schooled into thinking and acting in certain ways, and he argues persuasively and with conviction for the need to be able to step outside such parameters in order to develop visions of alternative modes of thinking and acting practices and forms of social and collective organization that are not controlled by the forces of capitalism but work for the advancement of collective and civic values.

Some open questions with which to end. What kind of school structures and curricula do we require for this purpose, and what values should underpin them? Is the notion of a curriculum in its current form suitable? What would a schizoanalytical modelling of curricula look like in contrast to the subject discipline structure that has been in place, in one form or another, for generations? Do we need examination systems in their current form? Is it possible to devise other structures and programmes that facilitate learning and social values that are not competitive? Adopting a processual notion of subjectivity opens up questions concerning the 'objectivity' of a curriculum, its methods, its assessment or even the school as institution. What would a processual notion of curriculum look like?

2

Parrhesia and *Epimeleia* and the Scandal of the Truth: Changing the Value of the Currency in Pedagogic Work

Introduction

In the previous chapter, I made reference to the groundbreaking work of Richard Hoggart, Raymond Williams and Stuart Hall and its implications for pedagogic practice, particularly for what I am calling a pedagogy of taking care. All of these teachers, writers and academics placed great emphasis, in their respective fashion, upon the importance of education for developing personal and collective values and to unearth hidden potentials, for the affirmation of civic life and respect for divergence and difference. All were totally opposed to the academic virus of conceit and its diverse manifestations. John Clarke (2015: 281) comments that for Stuart Hall, teaching involved trying to forge the 'right modes of address and engagement' for each student, developing modes of articulation with each student that would 'lead towards a new set of configurations and possibilities'. In this mode of articulation, pedagogy becomes a 'process of collective discovery, rather than an act of masterly revelation' (281). For Hall, pedagogical work was not about revealing truths to students, a process of demystification or a deconstruction of 'common sense' to be set right by the introduction of more legitimate knowledge. It was a process through which students are encouraged to construct their truths and values within a spirit of conviviality, in the sense of this term given by Ivan Illich, whose work, *Tools for Conviviality*, will be discussed later. Hall was not turning away from speaking truth to his students, as the following extract illustrates:

> I do think it is a requirement of intellectuals to speak a kind of truth. Maybe not truth with a capital T, but anyway, some kind of truth, the best truth that they know or can discover – to speak that truth to power. To take responsibility – which

can be unpleasant and is no recipe for success – for having spoken it. To take responsibility for speaking it to wider groups of people than are simply involved in the professional life of ideas. To speak it beyond the confines of the academy. To speak it, however, in its full complexity. Never to speak it in too simple a way, because 'the folks won't understand'. Because then they will understand, but they will get it wrong, which is much worse! So, to speak it in its full complexity, but to try to speak it in terms in which other people who, after all, can think and do have ideas in their heads, though they are not paid or paid-up intellectuals, need it. (Hall 2007a: 289–90)

This passage brings into play the Greek notion of *parrhesia*, the notion of truthful speech, and its relation to pedagogic practice, a practice in which students are engaged in learning, each from their respective existential coordinates. Developing articulations with each student's practice is to engage with its 'truth' and its potentialities for each individual student, and this in turn may require, on the part of the teacher, to rethink their practice, to rethink its truth.

In this chapter I will focus upon the notions of *parrhesia* and care (*epimeleia*) as explored in depth by Michel Foucault (2011) in his final lectures given at the College de France in 1983–4, titled *The Courage of the Truth: The Government of Self and Others II* (CT)). I will then try to comment upon practices of *parrhesia* and care in pedagogic work. Foucault's discussion becomes pertinent for such work when he describes how the complicated relation of *parrhesia* to politics and democracy in early Greek society (fifth and fourth centuries AD) moves to *parrhesia* being linked to an ethics concerned with care (*epimeleia*) of the self, or put differently, to the truth of and responsibility for the self, which also implies care for others and the world. Here it is important, in view of recent discussions of subjectivity as processual, not to think of the self as a self-contained entity but as an assemblage (an ecology) of practices, discourses, relations and values – an assemblage of existential struggle and propagation (with others).

Then I will turn to the philosophical explorations of the Czech philosopher Jan Patočka, giving particular focus to his work on the notion of care of the soul that involves a concern for otherness, equality, detachment and the idea of the 'post-idea'. My aim is to draw upon Patočka's writings on philosophy and politics in order to unpack their relevance for my concerns with education and a pedagogy of taking care. In the last section, I draw together the discussion and, briefly, contrast the stupidity of current educational policies grounded in *homo economicus* with an advocacy for a pedagogy of taking care.

Foucault's Archaeologies of *Parrhesia* and *Epimeleia*

In a postscript, reviewing the content of Foucault's 1983–4 lectures on truth, Frederic Gros (2011: 356) quotes the last words from Foucault's manuscript, which he omitted from the end of his final lecture:

> *What I would like to stress in conclusion is this: there is no establishment of the truth without an essential position of otherness; the truth is never the same; there can be truth only in the form of the other world and the other life (l'autre monde et de la vie autre).* (italics in original)

The notion of otherness, of an other life and an other world, is central to Foucault's elaborations of the notion of *parrhesia* and its importance for the care of the self and others as he explores Cynic practices that I will come to shortly. Initially he recalls his work on *parrhesia* from the previous year's lectures when he narrated the different and changing meanings of *parrhesia* in ancient Greek life. *Parrhesia* is the practice of telling all; it can be employed pejoratively in the sense of saying anything that comes to mind, anything that serves the interests of someone. More positively it concerns telling the truth without concealment, being frank and steadfast, even though this may involve personal risk by offending others who may be violent in response. Thus, *parrhesia* requires the courage to speak the truth. Foucault (CT 2011: 13) tells us:

> So, in two words, *parrhesia* is the courage of the truth in the person who speaks and who, regardless of everything, takes the risk of telling the whole truth that he thinks, but it is also the interlocutor's courage in agreeing to accept the hurtful truth that he hears.

In the text *Fearless Speech*, Foucault (2001: 19) summarizes *parrhesia*:

> *Parrhesia* is a kind of verbal activity where the speaker has a specific relation to truth through frankness, a certain relationship to his own life through danger, a certain type of relation to himself or other people through criticism (self-criticism or criticising of other people), and a specific relation to moral law through freedom and duty. More precisely, *parrhesia* is a verbal activity in which a speaker expresses [his] personal relationship to truth, and risks his life because he recognises truth telling as a duty to improve or help other people (as well as himself). In *parrhesia*, the speaker uses [his] freedom and chooses frankness instead of persuasion, truth instead of falsehood or silence, the risk of death instead of life and security, criticism instead of flattery, the moral duty instead of self-interest and moral apathy.

Parrhesia defines a mode of being of courage and truth-telling and also having the courage to bear the speaker's truth. Foucault describes four modes of veridiction or truth-telling that are not isolated practices but often combined. First, that of prophecy, whereby the prophet speaks not in his name but acts as an intermediary for 'a voice which speaks from elsewhere' (15). Second, the truth-telling of wisdom, whereby the sage speaks his own wisdom about being but is not forced to speak, share or teach it. Third, the truth-telling of the professor, technician or teacher who possesses 'know-how' (*tekhne*) and whose obligation is to pass this knowledge on to others, so forming a bond of shared knowledge, heritage and tradition with those being taught. The fourth mode of veridiction is demonstrated by the parrhesiast who is not a prophet, sage or teacher; the parrhesiast does not speak of fate as prophesied, of being and wisdom or of knowledge and tradition. The parrhesiast's mode of veridiction lies in the 'truth of what is in the singular form of individuals and situations' (CT: 25). The parrhesiast articulates the 'true discourse of what the Greeks called *ethos*' (CT: 25). We might view *parrhesia* as a mode of 'disobedience' in the sense that in practising *parrhesia*, the parrhesiast often invokes disobedience towards customs, traditions and norms of habits, to rupture them in order to open up new modes of thought or action. It is an obedience of the speaker to her truth but simultaneously a disobedience to those established orders she speaks against.

Socrates combines these modes of veridiction (see CT: 26–7); he does not give speeches or tells what he knows but remains reserved, confining himself to modes of questioning that challenge and provoke and also 'teach' by encouraging people to interrogate their modes of living and relations with others in order to improve their lives. Thus, in Greek culture at the end of the fifth and beginning of the fourth century BC, Foucault's research illustrates the four modes of veridiction: 'distributed in a kind of rectangle: that of prophecy and fate, that of wisdom and being, that of teaching and *tekhne*, and that of *parrhesia* and *ethos*' (CT: 28).

In Euripides the term *parrhesia* was employed in political practice as referring to the right to speak publicly, to have one's say in public debate about matters concerning the city, a right that applied only to citizens by birth (CT: 34). In later philosophical and political texts, at the beginning of the fourth century, *parrhesia* is transmuted from a public right to speak into a more dangerous enterprise, to be practised with caution. What Foucault (CT: 35) calls a 'crisis of *parrhesia*' is characterized by two phenomena. The first is the criticism of democratic *parrhesia* and the questioning of democratic institutions as places for truth-telling. This is because such institutions lack what Foucault terms 'ethical differentiation'. The claim that democracy was the privileged site for truth-telling, the right to give one's views is challenged so that the right to express ones views, to have the courage to oppose the views of others and traditions, becomes difficult or even dangerous for a couple of reasons. First, because it is dangerous for the city if everyone can express their views in line with their interests, this would constitute a *parrhesia* of 'anything goes' without any sense of civic duty or critical self-judgement, thus suggesting as many governments as there are individuals. Second, the issue of safety for the parrhesiast who opposes the will of others by having the courage to speak against them. In speaking out and opposing others, the parrhesiast disrupts established (democratic) values and consensus and in so doing becomes a danger to democracy itself. This reveals a paradox in that the disobedience, the combat and conflict of *parrhesia* rupture the egalitarian framework of democratic government and equality, and yet it depends upon such a framework for it to occur. By rupturing the equality of democracy and introducing difference, the right of anyone to speak regardless of status, Foucault describes a double danger. First, 'there can only be true discourse through democracy, but true discourse introduces something completely different from and irreducible to the egalitarian structure of democracy' (Foucault 2010: 184), which is 'ethical differentiation' (CT: 35), not ethical and political discrimination (better/worse, good/bad). Second, the danger to the individual who speaks *parrhesia*, Foucault (CT: 38) summarizes this double danger:

> So you see the notion of *parrhesia* splitting. On one side it appears as the dangerous latitude given to everyone and anyone to say everything and anything. And then there is the good, courageous *parrhesia* of someone who nobly tells the truth, even when the truth is disagreeable, and this *parrhesia* is dangerous for the individual who employs it and there is no place for it in democracy. Either democracy makes room for *parrhesia*, in which case it can only be a freedom which is dangerous for the city, or *parrhesia* is a courageous attitude which consists in undertaking to tell the truth, in which case it has no place in democracy.

Commenting upon current Western democracies, Maurizio Lazzarato (2014: 232) argues that 'there is no longer any space left for *parrhesia*. Democratic consensus neutralizes *parrhesia*, cancels the risk of truth-telling and of the subjectivation and action that follow from it.' In drawing our attention to the problem and danger of *parrhesia* in relation to democracy in ancient Greek culture, Foucault concludes that democracy is not 'the privileged site of *parrhesia*, but the place in which *parrhesia* is most difficult to practice' (CT: 57).

He then turns his attention to *parrhesia* as a mode of truth-telling not in relation to the government of the city (*politeia*) but in relation to the field of ethics, to the production of *ethos*, the soul (*psukhe*), the care and government of self, individual relationships and an aesthetics of existence. But this shift in *parrhesia* towards the soul and an aesthetics of life cannot be detached from the conditions for the forms of truth-telling, the organization of relations of power and the modes of formation of the *ethos* in which an individual constitutes themselves as a moral subject of conduct (CT: 66). Here the practice of *parrhesia* considers the question of *ethos*, ethical differentiation, in relation to sociopolitical structures that must try to accommodate the truth of the latter and its differences. In narrating the shift from political *parrhesia* to ethical *parrhesia*, Foucault (CT: 86) describes Socrates' mission to watch over others, to encourage people to take care of themselves, not in terms of material goods but to take care of their reason (*phronesis*), that is to say, reason in practice, enabling good decisions to be made and false opinions rejected, thus caring for their souls and their conduct.

The practice of care that the Greeks called *epimeleia* is central to ethical *parrhesia*, whereby the *parrhesiast* advises others upon their actions and helps them to develop critical and judicious faculties with fervour in the care of themselves and others. In Plato's *Alcibiades* when discussing the education of young people, the focus of the notion of care was the soul, the contemplation of the soul and its divine nature. In the *Laches*, again thinking about the education of the young, Plato develops a different pathway where the focus is not the soul and its immortality but 'life' (*bios*), ways of living or practices of existence (CT: 127). Here, Foucault argues, this difference between the metaphysical reflection on the soul (ontologically distinct from the body) or reflecting upon modes of existence (ways of being and doing, how one lives) comes to define two major and interlinked philosophical practices in the West.

> On the one hand, a philosophy whose dominant theme is knowledge of the soul and which from this knowledge produces an ontology of the self. And then, on the other hand, a philosophy as a test of life, of *bios*, which is the ethical material and object of an art of oneself. (CT: 127)

Therefore, *bios* as the object of care becomes the key focus, particularly when considering the education of the young, and this in turn raises the question of the virtue of care, of the quality of teaching (*tekhne*) or education – teaching not through the lens of competence or of passing on knowledge, but in terms of the form one gives to life (CT: 143–4) throughout life. What we might call an ethico-aesthetics of existence goes to the heart of a pedagogy of taking care in that the emphasis is placed not upon *tekhne*, though this is important, but upon the truth of how something, a learning encounter, matters for a learner and how the truth of this mattering can be supported in its particular *bios*. Here *tekhne* and *ethos* are conjoined but in the space of existential practice and affirmation of *bios*.

Recognition of and support for this imperative on the part of the teacher may require a kind of courage to examine and question, to interrogate the quality and commensurability of their practice and to take care of their practice. This courage extends also to the possible conflict between the *ethos*, the ethico-aesthetics of a teacher's practice and the political organization of teaching, something that will be discussed later. It also extends to the problem of schooling and its subjections, the 'schooled society' as problematized by Ivan Illich (1973), in contrast to the development of pedagogic work that tries to engage with the truth of individual interests, dispositions and potentials, the *bios* of each individual student or child. We might conclude from this that the ethics of pedagogical *parrhesia* is thus concerned with a practice of care for the singular aesthetics of the student's *bios*.

Foucault takes these ideas of care for the self and others, *parrhesia* and aesthetics of existence, and locates them in the practice of ancient Cynicism. In order to practice ethical *parrhesia*, Cynic practice involved being free of all attachments and material goods that would distract from this purpose. The Cynic mode of life stripped away all pointless conventions and material possessions in order to reveal the truth value of those things that are indispensable for human life. It emphasized the importance of modes of existence as acts of truth (*bios* as alethurgy; CT: 180). In doing so such acts provoke what Foucault called 'the scandal of the truth' by revealing or exposing the truth of 'another life' against the background of established conventions, habits, values and traditions. Foucault suggests that traces of this Cynic attitude can be found not only in Christian asceticism but also in various forms of 'militantism' (CT: 183–4) such as revolutionary movements in the nineteenth century and beyond that advocate the possibility of an *other life*.

The Cynic principle of the 'mode of life as scandal of the truth' (CT: 186) can also, according to Foucault, be found in practices of art. This is an important point to which I will return in other chapters. In practices of modern art, the Cynic mode of being can be ascertained in the artistic life as a kind of scandalous break from existing traditions and values, where the artwork or practice reveals the existence of a new reality or, put in another way, brings to expression that which had no form or possibility of expression and which produces an *other world*, that which is not yet known.

> Art … is constituted as the site of the irruption of what is underneath, below, of what in a culture has no right, or at least no possibility of expression. (CT: 188)

Later chapters will discuss the practices of artists including Fred Smith, Regina Jose Galindo, Techsing Hsieh, Ingrid Pollard, Adrian Piper and Zarina Bhimji.

This idea of art is therefore one in which art practice is viewed as that which breaks through established practices, traditions and values. It is an idea in modern or contemporary art in which, Foucault maintains, 'there is a sort of permanent Cynicism towards all established art' (CT: 188). It is an art that is essentially 'anti-cultural' in that its courage is to oppose consensus by opening up the possibility of an 'other' world through its radical forms of expression.

> Modern art is Cynicism in culture; the cynicism of culture turned against itself. And if this is not just in art, in the modern world, in our world, it is especially in art that the most intense forms of a truth-telling with the courage to take the risk of offending are concentrated. (CT: 189, see also afterword 'Course Content' by Gros: 352)

This idea of breaking with custom, habit or tradition is also manifested in another important idea from Cynic practices that Foucault tells us stems from the advice given to Diogenes by Apollo, which was change the value of the currency (CT: 226). Foucault points to the connection between *nomisma*, which means currency, and *nomos* referring to the law so that to change the value of the currency can indicate a particular position towards custom, rule or law. If we link this notion of changing the currency to *parrhesia*, we can see that political *parrhesia* involves the courage to speak the truth which is contrary to established and accepted views even though this could be dangerous for the speaker. Equally in ethical *parrhesia* focused upon truth concerned with care of the self, changing the value of the currency evokes local epiphanies through which new modes of existence and their respective novel values may emerge. In this Cynic manifestation, we find this courage of the truth to be concerned with an interrogation and rejection of established customs and principles. The Cynic scandal of the truth is demonstrated not necessarily through speech or discourse but through the way in which one lives. Changing the value of your currency is therefore regarded as an important principle throughout life alongside that of caring for the self and others that facilitates the former task to produce an 'other' life (see footnotes CT: 245–6). Changing the value of the currency amounts then to striving for a life or a practice that tries to be alert to injustices, corruption, repression, prejudice, intolerance and exploitation, to construct a life which is 'other', a life that is not yet known but which expands modes of practice and convivial relations. The militancy of Cynic practice is to try to 'shock' people by attacking

> not just this or that vice or fault or opinion that this or that individual may have, but also the conventions, laws, and institutions which rest on the vices, faults, weaknesses, and opinions shared by humankind in general. It is therefore a militancy which aspires to change the world, much more than a militancy which would seek merely to provide its followers with the means for achieving a happy life. (CT: 284–5)

The underlying theme of Cynic practice is that through the care of the self and others, a general process of betterment and human flourishing will emerge – a continual practice of transformation of people and their world (CT: 316).

> Now – and this is the new aspect of the work of the truth – the aim of this supervision of self which is also the supervision of others, or of this supervision of others which is also supervision of self, is a change, and there are two aspects to this change as it appears in Epictetus: a change in the conduct of individuals, and a change also in the general configuration of the world. (313)

In his archaeology Foucault is pointing to the importance of the subject's relation to self and to others, to ethical transformations of the subject and new configurations of the world. The practice of care and its modes of being are central to such transformations and thus the transformation of *ethos* and *bios*. The existential principle of ethical differentiation is thus important in relations with others, particularly within governmental relations, as for example, with pedagogical relations between teacher and student. But operating or facilitating this ethical differentiation is not concerned with the moral quality of say a teacher; rather it concerns the difference of the truth in the construction of relation to self, the truth as difference from custom or habit (see Gros, 'Course Content' in CT: 345–6). This construction of the relation to self, viewed as a process of the difference of the truth, that is to say, truth event which may open up new possibilities against the backcloth of established relationalities, concerns the idea of the self as a processual assemblage as discussed in the previous chapter. The difference of the truth precipitates changing the 'value of the currency', that is to say, those values structuring the becoming of *ethos* and *bios*. This constitutes for Foucault a reciprocal correlation of veridiction, governmentality and subjectivation (Gross, afterword: 346) – a binding together of *parrhesia* and *epimeleia*, a truth-telling that involves an ongoing care for self, others and the world. The event of truth then is 'other'; it is the scandalous disturbance that opens up possibilities for other worlds to be imagined or constructed, but equally it also exposes limitations or acts as a criticism of prior existence and values prior to its event. This notion of otherness, that the truth is other, takes us back to Foucault's words quoted at the beginning of this section:

> *What I would like to stress in conclusion is this: there is no establishment of the truth without an essential position of otherness; the truth is never the same; there can be truth only in the form of the other world and the other life (l'autre monde et de la vie autre)*. (italics in original; CT: 356)

Jan Patočka and the Scandal of the Other

I now turn to the work of the Czech philosopher Jan Patočka (2002) to extend the Cynic notions of *parrhesia*, the scandal of the truth and changing the value of the currency. Foucault makes reference to Patočka in the fourth of his final lectures (CT: 127) in his introductory comments on Plato's *Laches*, claiming at the time of his last lectures that Patočka's *Plato and Europe* was the only book among modern texts on the history of philosophy to recognize the importance of the place of the notion of *epimeleia* in Plato. Patočka refused to join the Communist Party and suffered years of persecution and was banned from academic appointments and publication except for a very brief time during the Prague Spring in 1968. He was constantly intimidated by the authorities and died of a heart attack during extensive interrogation.

The philosophical work of Jan Patočka emphasizes the importance of the 'other' or 'otherness' (the scandal of the other) to the process of subjectivation and also the collective. His work on the care of the soul from Plato, Socrates and others parallels Foucault's in-depth investigations of the care of the self and techniques of the self, emerging in Greek culture and then in later historical contexts, in which the notions of courage, detachment, equality and openness are deemed to be crucial for developing the 'good life'.

Rodolphe Gasche (2018: 393) argues that Patočka's exploration of the 'care of the soul' involved not simply the life of an individual but also an approach that is tied to 'the life in community'. Gasche quotes Patočka:

> The open soul is in its essence, a soul that has been put in contact; it is not a being that is closed upon itself ... it is possible to say that in a way its essence is to be outside itself', outside itself in the world whose horizon it actively opens up. (2007: 239)

It is this idea of openness and relation (contact) to the other and the ensuing possibilities for opening new worlds that is so important for the care of the soul that for Patočka constitutes the 'embryonic form of Europe' and not the later ideas concerning rational science and its universality (Gasche: 393, note 6). Following the theme of scandal, we might argue that it is the event of 'the scandal of the other' that opens up the horizon of potential (*dunamis*). Patočka traces the transformations of the care for the soul from its Greek origins and notes that in sixteenth-century Europe, the 'care *for the soul*, the care to *be*' is overshadowed by 'the care to *have*, care for the external world and its conquest' (italics in original; Patočka 1996: 83). Thus, the universal idea of care for the soul is lost in this care to have and its manifestations of individualism, property/possession, objectivism, conquest and imperialism. For Plato, as we have seen, the care of the soul was indissoluble from reason and universality and concerned the soul as the site of knowledge that enabled transformations in human being, a process of reflective renewal that led to a reforming of individuals and collective existence: the political nature of existence (Patočka 2007: 236).

This focus on objectivist and physicalist reason and universality towards the world marginalizes the universal theme of care of the soul in terms of individual and collective renewal. Equally the scientific concern for objectivism involved a conception of the human subject as an imperialist entity 'from which the world in its entirety can be drawn' (Gasche: 397), and it stifled the community of self and other that was central to the early Greek notion of care.

Patočka's political concern is the idea of 'post-Europe' following what he sees as the political failure of Europe during the twentieth century up to its current epoch. The term 'post' does not denote an overcoming but the struggle to develop a more insightful interrogation of Europe's ongoing crises and conflicts in order to construct a more humane and convivial future. Although this political project is not my focus, I intend to transpose the idea of 'post' in this critical sense to consider the notion of 'post-education' in the light of an educational project that, over the last forty years, has been driven mainly by economic concerns and which, for many, has failed in that many children and students have not benefited from it. The political emphasis upon economic prosperity and ambition, whereby education is conceived mainly as the production of human capital, can be conceived as 'an addiction to things', involving the primacy of the objective over subjective experiences (care of self) and pursuing the homogenization of differences according to a template of economic ambition and competition. These are the key effects of the techno-scientific rationalism driving the economics of corporate capitalism that has produced what Patočka calls a 'supercivilization', a kind of social flattening, massification, industrialisation and administration. Francesco Tava, commentating upon Patočka's political work (2016: 245), writes, 'The effort to fix any social conflict by erasing every element of political and intellectual diversity within society is at the basis of supercivilization.' We might relate this political idea of a supercivilization to an educational supercivilization in the sense that our current system of education is governed by a reduction that prioritizes particular curriculum subjects and, by implication, their students, over other subjects and their students, thus reducing the values and diversity of learning. Equally the pan-European concern for a narrow set of measurable learning outcomes (PISA TIMMS, etc.) is another manifestation of this reduction and homogenization as well as the belief that by more monitoring, more effective data or information, education will be improved (but only with particular subjectivities and practices in mind).

Patočka (2002, 2007) recovers the ancient Greek notion of the care of the soul (*epimeleia*) to argue for a personal and collective idea of responsibility and care that values difference and communal participation in working through problems and crises together. This would be a move that counters the existential inauthenticity that has developed through the sclerotic tendencies of the supercivilization of Europe and the West. Therefore, an important political and ethical responsibility for this new existential condition would be one that takes care of those who are marginalized, or 'othered', those who have no part. This 'post' perspective and its immanent responsibility to otherness when focused upon the idea of subjectivity requires an ability to detach and question those situations when that which is other 'interrupts' those practices and values to which we have succumbed and been subjected. Can we extricate ourselves, for example, from the totalising grip of capitalist economics or the rationalism of techno-science and their respective shaping of subjectivities? Can we disengage from the current structures and values of education and their particular pedagogizing forces that are largely driven by economic imperatives? Can we detach ourselves from pedagogical processes or models in which some subjectivities become marginalised or are awarded less value that others? Can we do this and promote more authentic modes of practice and becoming for each participant? Patočka's reference to early Greek ideas is not so that we return to them, but to take the idea of care, for example, and to construct its relevance for our historical situation. Tava (2016: 249) hints at this problematic of existential inauthenticity which for Patočka can be overcome through the existential authenticity of thinking:

The mistake of European knowledge involves the belief that thinking means defining. On the contrary, according to Patočka, thinking is the action by virtue of which humans come to possess themselves, realizing all their potentialities. What Patočka has in mind while drawing this new paradigm of knowledge is the Socratic lesson. In light of this conception, Socrates' knowledge of not-knowing takes the form of an open enquiry that must lead humanity to this new post-European field, allowing it to look back at its past as well as to imagine a possible future.

If we relate these ideas of open enquiry to the field of education, we might see that the disposition of not knowing is an important dimension of pedagogic work. If this is taken on board, then pedagogic practice cannot be conceived solely in terms of prescribed methodologies, competences or standards, which is indicative of much school and other forms of education today and which anticipate particular pedagogized subjects but as an open and speculative adventure in relation to each particular pedagogic task. Such tasks are ones which do not attempt to control the future and in doing so marginalise or obscure existential practices and potentials that do not subscribe to the dominant agenda. Pedagogic work therefore has to contend with both a heterotopia and a heteroglossia. It is grounded upon the idea of being-with (*Mitsein*) in its historical existence and a notion of equality that Patočka compares to Hegel's notion of 'mutual recognition' (*Anerkennung*). Tava (250) points out that this notion of equality differs from the flattened or homogenised notion that the supercivilization strives for and which eliminates differences between people in order to attain social cohesion and control. Rather it requires an active dialectical process of recognition and negotiation between members of the collective. Such equality, in valuing difference and divergence, between individuals allows them to value each other as equals, but it also enables them to detach themselves from each other and also from collective or social values whenever this valuing of existential difference is threatened. Patočka (1988) writes:

> Only from this perspective of equality and on its ground can the detachment arise that urges each individual to show what he really is, as an active subject, i.e. what he is able to accomplish.

Such equality in difference seems to involve a paradox similar to that discussed earlier between *parrhesia* and democracy, whereby values necessary for functioning collectively are always at risk of being disturbed by authentic detachment. Such equality in difference therefore rests upon a notion of trust.

We might see the value of adopting these notions of equality and detachment in pedagogical work when confronted with the 'otherness' of learning practices that do not conform to established modes of practice. Patočka argues that these notions of equality and detachment demand a particular kind of courageous subject that he terms the 'open soul', one who is able to stand back from, or rise above, their sociopolitical conditioning as subjects and to be receptive or open to what is other to such conditioning. Being open to and experiencing such otherness may allow the ability to transcend the limitations or problematics of existing situations that frame subjects and to imagine new modes of subjectivation. The subject, in its openness to otherness, comes to see not only its finitude but also its lack. An approach to reality that embraces an active openness suggests that the subject 'becomes out of itself' and indicates a problematic existential position, a metastable ontology, whereby in trying to maintain ethical stability remaining open to otherness demands that it is constantly 'out of her or himself' (Tava: 253). If we adopt a pedagogy of taking care, then by implication pedagogical work involves an ethics of otherness, exposure to others, whereby a teacher is always required to be 'out of him or herself'. The implications for pedagogic work are profound. Is such work to be controlled by a closed paradigm of practice, method, standards, competences and so forth that produces a flattening or marginalization of difference and an educational supercivilization, or is it to enable a being-with that remains open to difference and divergence whilst at the same time acknowledging that such differences will require prescribed knowledge and skills but whose acquisition will be existentially iterated?

Paradoxically then the development of a pedagogy of taking care emerges from its outside, its otherness, on the initiative of teachers who are willing to detach themselves from their established practices and identities when confronted with situations that challenge these. Can we conceive of education that is not grounded in an economic ambition grounded in the 'addiction to things' (having rather than being), nor grounded in a marginalization of difference or otherness in the sense of following prescribed methods of learning and teaching that presuppose particular pedagogized subjectivities? Can we develop a pedagogy of equality and detachment, a pedagogy that moves out of itself, a disobedient pedagogy, that is open and responsive to otherness? Put in Patočka's terminology, this would be a post-pedagogy of care.

The idea of lack arising from an encounter with otherness may engender a sense of detachment that is fundamental to the transcendence of becoming. Here transcendence can be viewed as detachment that generates an ability to imagine new possibilities. This kind of detachment and subsequent invention is central to art and other forms of creative practices, including scientific, philosophical and mathematical practices. Arnason (2007: 16), following Patočka, argues, 'The distance from given reality and the anticipation of other possibilities are inherent in human activity as such.' We might see that this notion of transcendence as detachment is involved in the constitution of experience, whereby experiencing involves 'the opening to horizons beyond the given [and this] makes it possible to consider the given itself as an open-ended totality' (Arnason: 16, my bracket). These ideas on transcendence and detachment seem crucial for developing a pedagogy of taking care and hope, encouraging and facilitating learners to open their being to horizons of possibility that will extend their capacities for thought and action and in doing so also extend the capacity and conviviality of the collective.

Patočka's work in the 1970s traces how the Greek notion of *epimeliea* that involved examining one's conduct and values in order to manage one's life in relation to others evolved in later Christian forms of care grounded in the practices of shepherding as developed in pedagogic, medical and religious institutions that interpreted care according to their respective forms of knowledge. These transformations constituted a weakening of care in relation to the autonomy of the self (Suvak 2019: 31). Suvak (34) writes:

> Europe invented taking care of the soul – taking care of one's being, says Patočka in his fourth heretical essay. The first turning point came as late as in the sixteenth century, when taking care of the external world established itself, associated with controlling the world and caring about possessing things. Taking care of the soul was gradually replaced by a new form of knowledge and learning, which was defined by Francis Bacon's claim that 'knowledge is power' or Rene Descartes's demand that nature become man's property.

As mentioned earlier, Patočka's task was not to effect a return to the Greek notion of care for the self or the soul but to examine how this notion might be manifested today. What enables such care and examination for a flourishing of life, and what suppresses or controls it? This is directly relevant today in those situations and contexts where people's freedom is restricted, where speaking out against governments can lead to imprisonment, where power is abused to control, condition or subjugate. Equally the modern tendency to self-monitor does not recall the Socratic sense of care and examination throughout life, an intellectual and vital practice, but rather a self-monitoring that is governed by the values and practices of modern capitalism and democratically administered societies, in order to produce particular forms of subscribed conduct.

In the last section, I will draw together some of the major points regarding *parrhesia*, *epimeliea*, truth, detachment and otherness as discussed above, and show how these are directly relevant to what I am advocating as a pedagogy of taking care. This will be developed further in the next chapter that deals with the work of Ivan Illich and its relevance today for pedagogical work.

Education and Care: The Scandal of the Truth Aligned with the Importance of Experience in an Epoch of Stupidity

How might we utilize these writings on truth and care from Foucault and Patočka to consider pedagogic practices in an epoch that is dominated by *homo economicus*, the administered subject, and its particular logos of truth in the field of educational practices? Prioritizing economic prosperity, competition and modes of production have marginalized an aesthetics of *bios* in relation to others, to civic and collective values and the worlding of the world together. But is it possible to draw upon these ancient Greek ideas discussed above and apply them to current educational contexts, policies and practices? Is it possible to implement a pedagogy of taking care where priority is given to facilitating and supporting each student's or child's pathways of experiencing and learning?

Patočka's notion of a 'post-idea' can be adopted as a means of advocating an alternative to educational policies driven by economic imperatives that place emphasis and value upon STEM subjects and marginalize other disciplines such as the arts and that regulate pedagogic work according to prescribed standards.

A pedagogy of taking care, in contrast, does not function by fitting learners to a prescribed curriculum agenda, teaching methods and modes of assessment, in other words by operating towards already formulated outcomes. Though it may operate within an established curriculum framework, which I would argue requires a radical rethinking in our current epoch, it prioritizes trying to develop, in response to the haecceities of each child's or student's learning encounters, commensurate modes of address and articulation. Such modes cannot be predicted in advance or simply follow prescribed routes but grow out of the teacher-learner assemblage (*agencements*). Pedagogic practice, in this mode, becomes a process of collective adventure rather than rigidly following prescribed routes and their anticipated subjectivities – an adventure that extends both the teacher's and the student's frameworks of practice and comprehension.

This adventure involves a fusion of politics, ethics and aesthetics in the attempt to ground pedagogic work on a practice of *alethurgy*. This term concerns a truth-telling but one that is not to a knowledge that is useful for those who govern and their pre-planned agendas for education, for example but to a process of bringing to light and supporting differing and divergent pathways of learning that emerge for each student's learning encounter. This emphasis upon differing and divergent pathways to the truth of learning, not grounded in agendas for the production of *homo economicus*, but upon civic values, conviviality, difference and respect, seems close to what Isabelle Stengers (2005a: 995) calls Cosmopolitics. Stengers uses this term not to denote a 'particular cosmos, or world, as a particular tradition may conceive it'; rather she uses the term 'cosmos' to 'refer to the unknown constituted by multiple, divergent worlds, and to *the articulations of which they could eventually be capable*' (my emphasis).

This emphasis upon the articulations of divergent worlds is directly relevant to the politics, ethics and aesthetics of pedagogical practice, a pedagogy of taking care, in that such practice requires paying close attention to modes of articulation emerging from their respective worlds. And paying close attention to such articulations may enable new forms of pedagogical co-existence (being-with and becoming-with) to emerge. This state of 'attention' thus prevents what we might call a closure of pedagogy that closes down divergence and difference and exposure to their truths (otherness). Pedagogical alethurgy, central to a pedagogy of taking care, has a concern for the otherness of each learner's *ethos*, their form of life (*bios*), the truth of each learner's pathways of becoming. Foucault tells us:

> For the Cynics, the function of philosophical teaching was not essentially to pass on knowledge but, especially and before all else, to give both an intellectual and moral training to the individuals one formed. It was a matter of arming them for life so that they were thus able to confront events. (CT: 204)

Can we say that today education is successful in preparing all students for their lives so that they are capable of dealing with events they encounter? I suspect that this would be difficult to maintain. In its current form and organization, we can ask who benefits and who does not? Is it the case that some receive legitimation whilst others are marginalized? Can we address the same question to educational structures such as competences or standards that determine pedagogical subjects? What I am leading to here and hinted at earlier is the truth of the existential function of learning being placed at the centre of a pedagogy of taking care. Earlier I quoted Stuart Hall who maintained the importance of *parrhesia*, 'speaking the truth' in his approach to teaching, and for students to take responsibility when faced with the complexities of life, for speaking 'the best truth that they know or can discover'. Though Hall was addressing the notion of truth more generally to political contexts, his words are relevant for pedagogic practice and the task of drawing alongside and trying to ascertain the existential nature of each student's learning. This involves responding effectively to a diversity of ways of learning, whereby some encounters may challenge pedagogical habits and demand new ways of thinking and thereby trying to articulate new alignments and possibilities for both teacher and student. Teaching and creating sense become indissoluble. Pedagogic work thus involves continual transformations of self, others and the institution of pedagogy. It becomes a process of invention and experimentation as the task of articulations between teacher and student precipitate new or modified subjectivations and relations. The different existential contexts of learning involve both political and ethical challenges for the teacher in the task of trying to forge responses that are commensurate to each learner's context of practice.

A pedagogy of taking care involves a pedagogy of encounter with 'the other', in which affect is primary, in that the encounter is an event of affect, an affective event. Such affects are, following Deleuze (1994, 2004) and Massumi (2002: 23–45) best comprehended as impersonal virtual forces that exceed existing forms of articulation. Andrew Lapworth (2013: 8) states, 'As a thoroughly relational force, affect is also that which connects us to the world; it is the matter within us responding and resonating with the matter around us.' This captures something of the existential relationalities of learning, how something matters for a learner in a learning event viewed as an encounter. This primary aspect of affect in experiencing an encounter, a learning encounter, introduces the notion of *importance* as developed in his last book *Modes of Thought* by Alfred North Whitehead (1938).

For Whitehead the idea of importance is not limited to human experience but is a 'term for the expression of every centre of experience' (Debaise 2018: 25). Whitehead's notion of importance sprang from his rejection of the bifurcation of nature (a primary nature devoid of values and a secondary category of nature that is the projection of human values onto this pure state) in which the 'sense of importance' was excluded from nature and attributed only to human experience. For Whitehead 'experience' is not limited to human dimensions but is applicable to all nature, and importance is a primary category of the experience of nature. Importance then, as already stated, is inherent to every centre of experience. It is not 'pre-scribed' but contingent to events of encounter.

In pedagogic work we can apply this notion of events of importance and their affect to children, students and teachers whom we can conceive as different centres of experiencing. It is from the primacy of such events, from their sense of importance, how they 'matter' in a particular situation or learning encounter, that a sense of coherence can emerge. It is not 'experiencing' alone that has to be evaluated – this would be difficult – but the importance of the ways of thinking and other practices that emerge and articulate experience. When faced with the diversity of articulations or expressions and their senses of value, the task for the teacher then is not a matter of judgement, which might marginalize, ignore or silence some articulations, but to develop what Isabelle Stengers terms a 'diplomatic' scene that tries to respond to the differences as *contrasts* and where such differences constitute an ecology of practices. This accommodation of an ecology of practices through the construction of a diplomatic scene would be central to a pedagogy of taking care, where alterity is not required to conform to prescribed agendas or practices but, we might say, whose scandal provokes an ongoing realignment and accommodation of practice, avoiding the stupidity that seizes hold of certain forms of political and educational administration in our current epoch that pre-define what is important and disqualify what is not (what Whitehead 1967: 197, called 'minds in a groove'). Stengers puts it like this in her book, *In Catastrophic Times* (2015: 117):

> What I will name stupidity cannot be reduced to a type of psychological weakness. It will not be said that 'people are stupid' as if it was a matter of some personal defect. Stupidity is something about which it will be said instead *that it seizes hold of certain people*. And in particular it seizes hold of those who feel themselves in a position of responsibility and who then become what I call our guardians. (italics in original)

Perhaps an illustration of such stupidity is that which seized hold of the political control of education in England and elsewhere in order to make schools in the mid-1970s and beyond responsive to increasing socio-economic-technological-scientific developments – the drive to produce human capital in the form of *homo economicus* that initiated a centralized curriculum with an emphasis upon those curriculum subjects that are required for this purpose and a marginalizing of subjects that are deemed secondary. It is an educational project, we might argue, that prioritizes particular centres of experience whilst paying less attention to others – a project that emphasizes what is deemed to be relevant for its success whilst that which is situated outside is deemed peripheral. Writing in *Modes of Thought*, Whitehead (1968: 111) states, 'We have no right to deface the value of experience which is the very essence of the universe.' This statement might be employed as a leitmotif for a pedagogy of taking care in which the experience of different practices that have been developed through human endeavour and which constitute different ways of knowing should not be defaced or downgraded, but equally they have be able to evolve as and when situations call for this to happen. The adventure of pedagogy concerns the task of responding effectively to the variety of ways in which learning encounters matter and the possibility of opening up new worlds of experience, of changing the value of the currency as appropriate to the emerging values of each learner and each teacher. For the teacher this would entail an 'awareness of the present' whose affect may require a modification or transformation of the abstractions he or she employs to interpret a learner's practice. Abstractions (theories, concepts) are lures that for the teacher vectorize her experience of a learner's practice, but the crucial task is to modify our abstractions when they do not meet the reality that confronts us (not to force reality into abstractions), and in doing so, this facilitates the emergence of new ways of thinking appropriate to such reality. Put in terms mentioned earlier, the exposure to otherness and its values, its *importance* in a pedagogy of taking care involving the creation of a diplomatic scene, may facilitate the expansion of such work, an exposure that constitutes a scandal of the truth of otherness and which subsequently changes the value of the currency of pedagogic practice, which, for many years, has succumbed to the values of capitalist economics. Brian Massumi (2018: 3) makes the point:

> It is time to take back value. For many, value has long been dismissed as a concept so thoroughly compromised, so soaked in normative strictures and stained by complicity with capitalist power, as to be unredeemable. This has only abandoned value to purveyors of normativity and apologists of economic oppression. *Value is too valuable to be left in those hands.* (italics in original)

3

Pedagogy, Conditions and Value

In this chapter I will continue to offer some thoughts towards a re-evaluation of education and pedagogic work in order to exit the practice of education that functions almost exclusively as the production of human capital for economic ambition and competition. After a brief introduction highlighting some of the issues raised by questions pertaining to conditions and value, I will consider the work of Ivan Illich, particularly his books *Deschooling Society* and *Tools for Conviviality*. I will also draw upon a recent book by John Baldacchino (2020), *Educing Ivan Illich*, in which he provides a scholarly and discerning deliberation of the notions of disestablishment, contingency and reform through which he interrogates Illich's opus covering the domains of education, healthcare, religion, technology, the environment and more. My purpose therefore is to show how the writings of Illich aided by Baldacchino's text still have relevance for education and pedagogical work and continue to offer radical alternatives to our current systems of education that are largely grounded in the values of economization. Though there are those who regard Illich's proposals for education and other services as being too radical, utopian or impractical, I believe the writings I discuss still contain profound lessons for developing what I have called a pedagogy of taking care, although, perhaps, it is not a term that Illich would employ. The discussion of Illich's work and its relevance for a pedagogy of taking care that seems inherent to his notion of a convivial society is followed by a brief engagement with Isabelle Stengers's idea of the cosmopolitical proposal that I believe has some resonance with conviviality.

Introduction

There is a contrast between pedagogic practice that is conditioned and regulated by controlled curriculums, knowledge, methods and disciplines and pedagogic work that is obligated to responding effectively to the emerging conditions of a pedagogic relation, for example, a teacher responding empathetically to the existential and divergent conditions of children's or students' responses to their learning encounters. In the latter scenario, the conditions inform and anchor the pedagogic response, such as the existential vectors of affect, sense-making or mattering, of a student's practice, as well as those that inform the teacher's response, which would include established knowledge and method but not to the extent that these dominate. Such conditions then involve not only assimilated ontological and epistemological framings but also what we might call *ontologies of the not-yet*, the kinds of potential that constitute part of the student's and teacher's vectors of experience in relation to a learning encounter, something that is not yet conceptualized or given form in language or other media. Out of such conditions may emerge forms of expression that precipitate new realities, new modes of practice for the learner and the teacher. Allowing the localized and existential conditions the space to flourish and evolve involves both teacher and learner in a process of co-creation, a process of becoming-with (*mitsein*). This process involves a fluidity in which both the universality of formal knowledge and local processes of experiencing intermingle; it is a convivial spatio-temporal relation, involving known and not-known and not simply a space in which separate characters interact with blocks of established knowledge but an evolving assemblage of practice. Yet if existential conditions are dominated by institutionally prescribed agendas, methods and evaluations, the convivial relation, which will be discussed in more depth below, is replaced by a relation of manipulation.

Paying attention to the conditions of practice, the flows of becoming-with, brings with it a concern for an ethics, politics and aesthetics of such becomings and their respective practices. Working with and responding to such becomings would imply, on the teacher's behalf, an awareness of frameworks of identity and their attendant tropes, such as in processes of assessment that may view a learner's practice in terms of established forms that may be incommensurable to its evolving or mutating conditions. Established methods and their values may be incompatible to the existential conditions and coordinates of a learner's practice and may be better approached through Guattari's practice of metamodelizing as discussed in Chapter 1. This is because the process and subsequent outcomes of a learning encounter may spiral in different and divergent directions and may produce a multiplicity of expressions that proffer multiple entry points for a teacher to engage with and respond effectively to their immanent potentials. The difficulty is that such entry points are sometimes unclear, and the task is to work together to create them.

Changing the conditions and values of pedagogic practice in order to respond effectively to each child's or student's conditions and rhythms of learning, or put another way, changing the value of pedagogic currency, would be required in a pedagogy of taking care. But this is not so easy when pedagogic work is regulated by government policies that anticipate the production of those pedagogized identities that fit their educational agenda whereby some forms of learning (and teaching) are valued over others. Policing pedagogic practice in this way perpetuates what Ivan Illich called a 'schooled society'. The security of established frameworks of practice produces a policing legibility that will tend to marginalize those practices and their outcomes that 'do not fit' prescribed pedagogical agendas. We might say that such frameworks protect from the scandal of the gift of the other and its existential 'illegibility' and singularity.

If we adopt a pedagogy of taking care, then this requires a state of openness to the diversity and divergence of students' conditions of learning, their existential learning pathways. In other words, it requires an openness to the potential of learning and, by implication, the potential of teaching. Put in other terms, it requires a receptivity towards the actual and the virtual ontologies of learning practices, to their local capacities, interests and proclivities. When education is driven by economic ambition and its values, it is as though the die is already cast as regards available or possible futures, which involve the production of human capital according to the values of market capitalism. Such predetermined structures may deny the diversity and divergence of capacities and potentials of some learners as learners in general are conceived in Massumi's term as 'quantums of capital'.

Is it possible to change the value of the currency on which education today is grounded in order to re-evaluate the principle and ideals of education? Massumi (2018: 58–9) argues:

> When the metrics associated with profit and capitalist surplus-value are reapplied to the field of life, the regulatory effect is the formatting of life as 'human capital', or of the individual as entrepreneur of himself. Life activity is maximally channelled in keeping with the demands of capitalism's self-driving. Life activity becomes maximally subsumed under the capitalist process. The reductive effect is to convert the individual into an embodied *quantum of capital*, living to appropriate its own punctual profits (predominantly in the form of a yearly salary or an hourly wage). (italics in original)

Can we re-evaluate education so that whilst aiming to develop those knowledges and skills for social integration and employment, we are also concerned to extend each learner's capacity of and for learning that embraces the different capabilities, proclivities, interests, abilities and potentials that each learner embraces. Such a project would be enabled through the advocacy of a pedagogy of taking care. Massumi (20) states:

> But what of life's in-the-making proper, considered as such, vitally instead of economically? What of the creative advance of life as it complexly plies its field of emergence, that immanent outside of the capitalist system whose qualitative differentials capitalism data mines for conversion to its own ends? Vital process too is self-driving. It too self-iterates, turning over on itself across its punctual expressions to continue apace. It too runs on excess, serially fed forward.

The intensity of a learning encounter can be viewed as an existential singularity pregnant with potential for creative advance that phases between the differentials and conditions of the encounter, which involve testing, puzzling, noticing, reflecting and acting. These qualitative phases are likely to be different for each learner, and such difference is likely to be reduced or factored out in the processes of objectification, calibration and quantification according to prescribed outcomes that may cast aside the singularity of the composition of different affective states and their conditions. The initial differences of intensity and affect that constitute an encounter for each learner tend to be annulled for the purposes of assessment and educational achievement, but such differences still exist in the experiencing of life beyond its capture by economization. In effect, the institutionalizing of education in which existential singularities are converted to a quantifiable register and its criteria of measurement or assessment constitute a kind of disjunctive articulation (Massumi: 48) whereby the same grade subsumes different existential experiences and respective matterings under its umbrella, 'systematic quantification always generalises' (Massumi: 48).

In order to unpack some of the issues raised in this introduction coupled with a concern to advocate a pedagogy of taking care, I will consider some of the writings of Ivan Illich, particularly his texts *Deschooling Society*, and his later remarks on this text, and *Tools for Conviviality*. Illich is regarded by some as being too radical or totally impractical in his views on education, but he has, I think, been misunderstood by some, particularly regarding schools. He does not advocate that we get rid of schools but rather that we try to escape from the inherent manipulation of a schooled society, which is manifested through institutional education which conceives and determines what knowledge is and what kind of knowledge is valued. Equally, it determines what learning is and what kinds of learning and teaching are valued so as to create a situation in which knowledge, teaching and learning are conceived only through its institutionalized forms and parameters. This schooled form thus ignores or marginalizes those forms of knowledge and ways of knowing and teaching that lie outside institutionally schooled boundaries. Throughout his work, Illich argued against the manipulative forces endemic to a schooled society and advocated their disestablishment and replacement with what he called a convivial society.

Ivan Illich: Advocating Conviviality

In his book *Tools for Conviviality* published in 1973, Illich argues for a reform of tools/technologies so that they are of use to all, not just for some, whilst others are excluded. In effect, though Illich tended to refrain from engaging in political debate, in the sense of advocating the ideology of one party against another, his call for a redesign of tools and technologies does seem to imply transforming both political and ethical relations. Like others in his generation as well as earlier and later thinkers, he was critical of education that was mainly conditioned by economic forces and industrialization. Tools for Illich involved not simply hand or automated tools but also social apparatuses, institutions such as education in schools and universities, healthcare, legal, bureaucratic and industrial professions and systems. In our modern world, the development of such tools has evolved into a situation whereby we have become manipulated by them. In his later writing, Illich replaces the focus on tools with a concern for systems, which seems close to the Foucauldian notion of dispositif (also extended by Agamben) – apparatuses that capture and determine, model and control behaviours and practices, demeanours and discourses of living beings (see Agamben 2009: 14). *Tools for Conviviality* was/is therefore an advocacy for convivial tools in contrast to those that manipulate for social and civic systems that are not grounded on scarcity, where some succeed and others are excluded. We might view institutionalized education, for example, as a system in which some benefit but others do not, where particular kinds of knowledge are valued over others and where the production of particular pedagogized subjects are valued over others. Such education, as mentioned earlier, fails to nurture every person's development and prioritizes the production of human capital for the capitalist machine. Illich (2009: 6) states, 'A society, in which modern technologies serve politically interrelated individuals rather than managers, I will call "convivial".'

> I choose the term 'conviviality' to designate the opposite of industrial productivity. I intend it to mean autonomous and creative intercourse among persons, and the intercourse of persons with their environment; and this in contrast with the conditioned response of persons to the demands made upon them by others, and by a man-made environment. I consider conviviality to be individual freedom realized in personal interdependence and, as such, an intrinsic ethical value. (18)

Value is placed upon creative intercourse amongst people and with their environment rather than the increasing demand for products and the mantras of productivity, consumption and profit. Illich seeks to replace industrial tools and tools of control with convivial tools, a retooling of society and the political and social systems that are nurturing for all. The implications of such a shift away from hyper-consumption and production will not be straightforward in a world that is interconnected and organized according to capitalist production/consumption relations.

> As an alternative to technocratic disaster, I propose the vision of a convivial society. A convivial society would be the result of social arrangements that guarantee for each member the most ample and free access to the tools of the community and limit this freedom only in favour of another member's equal freedom. (19)
>
> Alternate political arrangements would have the purpose of permitting all people to define the images of their own future. New politics would aim principally to exclude the design of artifacts and rules that are obstacles to the exercise of this personal freedom. Such politics would limit the scope of tools as demanded by the protection of three values: survival, justice, and self-defined work. I take these values to be fundamental to any convivial society, however different one such society might be from another in practice, institutions, or rationale. (19)
>
> Turning basic institutions upside down and inside out is what the adoption of a convivial mode of production would require. Such an inversion of society is beyond the managers of present institutions. (23)

Can we retool education? Do all schools need to look alike? Can we develop a local politics that determines the educational tools required by a particular society? Is this idea crazy?

> Increasingly, institutions have not only shaped our demands but also in the most literal sense our logic, or sense of proportion. Having come to demand what institutions can produce, we soon believe that we cannot do without it. The invention of education is an example of what I mean. (25–6)

The schooled society is one in which education becomes a kind of production line in which people become graded according to their grasp of prescribed knowledge, in which some achieve great benefits, whilst others do not. This establishes a schooled process whose authority is acknowledged and accepted, a process that becomes endemic to society and is manifested across social and institutional relations – a process of instruction and monitoring. Thus, the 'commodity called "education" and the institution called "school" make each other necessary' (27); the structure of institutional schooling and its mode of production make it difficult to imagine other more convivial modes.

> A convivial society should be designed to allow all its members the most autonomous action by means of tools least controlled by others. People feel joy, as opposed to mere pleasure, to the extent that their activities are creative; while the growth of tools beyond a certain point increases regimentation, dependence, exploitation, and impotence. I use the term 'tool' broadly enough to include not only simple hardware such as drills, pots, syringes, brooms, building elements, or motors, and not just large machines like cars or power stations; I also include among tools productive institutions such as factories that produce tangible commodities like corn flakes or electric current, and productive systems for intangible commodities such as those which produce 'education', 'health', 'knowledge', or 'decisions'. I use this term because it allows me to subsume into one category all rationally designed devices. (28)
>
> Tools are intrinsic to social relationships. An individual relates himself in action to his society through the use of tools that he actively masters, or by which he is passively acted upon. To the degree that he masters his tools, he can invest the world with his meaning; to the degree that he is mastered by his tools, the shape of the tool determines his own self-image. Convivial tools are those which give each person who uses them the greatest opportunity to enrich the environment with the fruits of his or her vision. Industrial tools deny this possibility to those who use them and they allow their designers to determine the meaning and expectations of others. Most tools today cannot be used in a convivial fashion. (29)

Education as a convivial tool is for the use of everyone to develop their aspirations, their potentials and so forth, without impinging on those of others. This does not mean the absence of institutions but a balance of such tools that flatten and homogenize with those enabling tools that support individual aspirations, proclivities and potentials.

> What is fundamental to a convivial society is not the total absence of manipulative institutions and addictive goods and services, but the balance between those tools which create the specific demands they are specialized to satisfy and those complementary, enabling tools which foster self-realization. The first set of tools produces according to abstract plans for men in general; the other set enhances the ability of people to pursue their own goals in their unique way. (32)

A schooled society is one in which, for example, those who learn outside school may be viewed as 'uneducated'. Education becomes a standardized product that constitutes a form of social control for achieving particular specified ends. Can we revise education as an institutional tool so that it does not function exclusively as a mould with pre-specified outcomes for the service and production of capital but as a creative process through which each individual is given the opportunity to grow and develop their capacities, potentials, visions and interests? Can we imagine and develop an education system in which schools are not subject to an imperialism of knowledge as determined, for example, by economization?

> A convivial society does not exclude all schools. It does exclude a school system which has been perverted into a compulsory tool, denying privileges to the dropout. (32)

Illich argues therefore for a more just society in the name of conviviality:

> A just society would be one in which liberty for one person is constrained only by the demands created by equal liberty for another. Such a society requires as a precondition an agreement excluding tools that by their very nature prevent such liberty. This is true for tools that are fundamentally purely social arrangements, such as the school system, as well as for tools that are physical machines. In a convivial society compulsory and open-ended schooling would have to be excluded for the sake of justice. Age-specific, compulsory competition on an unending ladder for lifelong privileges cannot increase equality but must favour those who start earlier, or who are healthier, or who are better equipped outside the classroom. Inevitably, it organizes society into many layers of failure, with each layer inhabited by dropouts schooled to believe that those who have consumed more education deserve more privilege because they are more valuable assets to society as a whole. A society constructed so that education by means of schools is a necessity for its functioning cannot be a just society. (51–2)

He contends that schooling is a particular mode of production in tandem with the industrialization of the people. Education is a commodity to be possessed and consumed, whilst learning as a diverse existential process seems to recede into the background.

Disestablishment, Contingency and Reform

Having discussed Illich's advocacy for convivial tools to work towards a convivial society, I will turn to other aspects of his work that articulate a philosophical (political and ethical) grounding which underpins the idea of conviviality. These are dealt with in depth by John Baldacchino (2020) in his book *Educing Ivan Illich*, which provides a deeply philosophical engagement with Illich through an insightful unpacking of the notions of contingency, disestablishment and reform. Taken together as a dynamic process, we might view the process of becoming as one that emerges from the contingencies of events of encounter that precipitate, in principle, numerous possibilities for disestablishing established values and practices that lead in turn to diverse and diverging possibilities for re-forming. A key aspect of establishing conviviality is to interrogate the ways in which institutions and their apparatuses of capture have produced subjectivities that conform to their modes of practice and organization. This would be close to Foucault's earlier work on institutions. To move beyond institutionalization towards convivial relations in Illich's sense involves, as Baldacchino (16) puts it, 'exiting-into a wider world of possibilities'. Illich's approach to this exit is to develop strategies that embrace history, historical texts, for example, to view the relation between the past and the present not in terms of a linear temporal sequence but as a constant iteration of possibilities for disestablishment and reform. A medieval text is continually re-formed within the contingencies of the present, which are also in turn re-formed; the text gives Illich a way to exit the present and reconceive it, thereby re-forming both. Baldacchino (15) writes:

> Rather than *own*, we *belong* to history, which far from indicating a passive sense of being within it, we are encouraged by Illich to embrace it as a perennial point of departure. By its immanent nature, history's departure is never fixed; thereby implying that by belonging to its iterative potentiality, history is an indicator of where we *are*. (italics in original)

If we apply this sense of iterative potential and re-form to the contingency of pedagogic work, it offers a possible way to exit the institutional forces that execute a kind of governmentality of pedagogic practice. Is it possible to find or even to risk an 'outside space' or device that would allow pedagogic practice to engage more effectively with the difference, the gift of otherness and thereby reconceive pedagogic practice? Such a space of exit would imply that pedagogical ethics emerges from the singularities, contingencies and iterations of practice. Erich Fromm (1969-70) in his introduction to Illich's book, *Celebration of Awareness*, regards this emancipatory aspect of Illich's works as crucial and

> lies in the fact that they have a liberating effect on the mind by showing entirely new possibilities; they make the reader more alive because they open the door that leads out of the prison of routinized, sterile, preconceived notions. (10)

Commenting upon the current functionality of university programmes and the subsequent hierarchy of knowledge, Baldacchino (45), in a paragraph quoting Illich from *Deschooling Society*, writes:

> 'The modern university has forfeited its chance to provide a simple setting for encounters which are both autonomous and anarchic, focused yet unplanned and ebullient,' says Illich. Instead, modern universities choose 'to manage the process by which so-called research and instruction are produced' (DS 36). With hypotheses dismissed for being ungrounded, and for measured predictability to enjoy almost exclusive recognition, knowledge and creativity give up their autonomy to a dogma of functionality. This is best illustrated by how knowledge and creativity are now ranked against hierarchies of 'need' in an effort to justify the existence of certain disciplines in academia.

This functionality can be levelled also against the current organization of schools, the way the curriculum is organized and how it is taught and assessed, placing emphasis upon measuring achievement that leads to a marginalizing of visioning, imagination and experimentation. The arts have become marginalized and viewed by some as an expendable luxury. Can we reverse this process in terms of new visions for education as a convivial tool – a vision that disestablishes long-held views that see education purportedly (but failing) as a democratic process for human progress? The tool of education now governs our *idea* of progress; we no longer are able to *use* education according to our different interests but are subjected to its current ruling ideology, *homo economicus*.

The ideas of iterative potential, contingency and reform are also important to bear in mind in relation to tradition and inheritance often conceived in terms of established form. Such conceptions have implications in education and pedagogic work not only for the application of standards and competence but also, equally, for established practices and values. Illich (1969–70), echoing his notion of history as a constant iteration of possibilities, regards tradition not in the sense of fixed or enduring practices or meanings but in terms of what it could mean when considered from different and evolving perspectives, in terms of potential seeds for new growth. Here tradition is not opposed to the new and set in some timeless warp but is always open to iterations in terms of the new. Taking a Spinozan attitude, it is important not to be entrapped by established norms but to evaluate according to the matterings and contingencies of experience, to what is or might be possible to think or to make – not always to judge according to schooled established categories or methods but to respond to the thisness (haecceities) of experiencing. Within a schooled version of education and pedagogic practice, the diverse possibilities of existential practices are often constrained and channelled by institutional agendas that determine learners as well as teachers as particular forms of human resource. Baldacchino expresses this form of social control:

> In a schooled society the primary concern is not that of the child per se, but the learner who is expected to follow an agenda by which the child becomes a resource and the teacher an instrument that manufactures it. Those who are 'left behind' in the schooled paradigm of society are likely to be considered as irrelevant to the economy. (58)
>
> Far from the school per se, a schooled society is characterized by the identification of interests by which human beings become quantifiable units: kids to be counted and measured in their ability and contribution to a set agenda. (58)

The agenda here then is to deliver a curriculum that is aimed at economic ambition, efficiency and a society that is governed by such criteria and their underpinning values. Illich is not proposing to abolish schools but the manipulative system of a schooled society. In other words, he proposes to disestablish both schools and society, but as Baldacchino argues, 'This would mean nothing unless there is a serious critique of how teaching and learning have evolved into a form of administration' (61). Rather than teaching and learning perpetuating a manipulated and administered society, the task is to work towards education as a tool to forge a convivial society in which all lives may flourish, where teaching and learning are not suborned into the production of human capital nor controlled by established canons. This is not to argue that the skills and knowledge required for the world of work should be ignored but that these should be only part of an educational programme which allows learners to develop their individual capacities, aspirations and potentials across a range of practices. Such a programme is not premised on the idea of manipulation towards a fixed agenda and particular interests whereby some benefit whilst others do not but upon its convivial use. It is crucial to acknowledge that Illich is not dismissing the practice of education or in fact schools but rather the institutionalization of these practices whereby the tool of education manipulates (schools) teaching and learning to specified ends that privilege particular curriculum subjects and therefore particular learners and abilities.

A convivial society is an interdependent society that embraces contrast, difference, otherness, disagreement, care and understanding. It is a community in which convivial tools enable capacities to act that do not impinge upon another's capacity to do so. In order to fulfil this pursuit, a constant process or spirit of disestablishment is crucial when we are confronted with otherness that disturbs, an otherness that can change or modify tradition and certainty. Tradition is not an unchanging entity but a mutating and evolving process that involves a 'letting go' and a re-forming, a process which involves a propagation of acting-noticing-reflecting, a process of questioning, curiosity and action. It is a continual process of iteration from which diverse possibilities and horizons may emerge, an iteration that emerges within different forms of expression (maths, art, science, ethics, politics, etc.) that construct new possibilities and new worlds. In a sense this flow of tradition in a micro sense *is* the process of becoming, applicable to each person in their social milieu. A convivial educational space is therefore one in which the potentials of each learner are subject to a rigour of taking care and support, where no one's capabilities or potentials are placed above those of others. This idea is encapsulated, as Baldacchino (81) suggests, by Etienne Balibar's notion of *equaliberty*, the fusing of liberty with equality, and can perhaps be viewed as a key imperative for a convivial pedagogic space as well as wider social relations. Such a space of *equaliberty* would lie in sharp contrast to the schooled spaces of education that are premised upon an academic prioritization and production of particular kinds of knowledge and learners which thereby marginalize or fail those who for whatever reason do not achieve such knowledge and are therefore seen as of less value. This would be a dispositif or apparatus of education that is grounded in scarcity and failure. Expanding Foucault's notion of a dispositif (apparatus), Agamben (2009: 14) writes:

> Further expanding the already large class of Foucauldian apparatuses, I shall call an apparatus literally anything that has in some way the capacity to capture, orient, determine, intercept, model, control, or secure the gestures, behaviors, opinions, or discourses of living beings. Not only, therefore, prisons, madhouses, the panopticon, schools, confession, factories, disciplines, judicial measures,

and so forth (whose connection with power is in a certain sense evident), but also the pen, writing, literature, philosophy, agriculture, cigarettes, navigation, computers, cellular telephones and – why not – language itself, which is perhaps the most ancient of apparatuses – one in which thousands and thousands of years ago a primate inadvertently let himself be captured, probably without realizing the consequences that he was about to face.

This institutional capture raises the complicated issue concerning not only the relationship between subjective experience and the bestowal of meaning, particularly the bestowal of meaning by institutional criteria upon the existential experiences of learners, but also in relation to the values imposed by the selection of those forms of knowledge and learning deemed to be important in contrast to other forms that are not. This imposition suggests that some pedagogized subjectivities are deemed more valuable than others.

Apart from this institutional bestowal of meaning, the tension between experiencing and meaning within local experiences of learning is important in terms of how something comes to matter, for example, in a learning encounter. We might view this tension as crucial for the transduction of creative practice, an idea I discuss in the next chapter. Take the practice of painting: the application of paint on a surface generated by a kind of thought/feeling process sets up a transduction, or a propagation, in which initial application of paint generates processes of noticing and reflection upon what emerges on the surface which in turn precipitates further forms of application, a continuous entanglement of forming-noticing-reflecting-reforming. Painting practice is therefore an evolving assemblage in which its constituent 'members' (body, mind, affect, canvas, brush paint, etc.) proposition each other in its dynamic flow.

The idea of a convivial educational space as mentioned above is extremely difficult to advocate in our current epoch of schooled education, its proposal almost seems like a *non sequitur*. But Baldacchino (89) offers a possible 'way out' through reference to Immanuel Kant's text *On Education* (1900: 14).

> One principle of education which those men especially who form educational schemes should keep before their eyes is this – children ought to be educated, not for the present, but for a possibly improved condition of man in the future.

The crucial point is that this future does not, for Kant, follow on sequentially by adapting present conditions to the future, of mapping the future according to established conditions, but of transcending present conditions to meet the requirements of the future and thus introducing a speculative dimension to education and learning. This returns us in a way to the difference between experiencing and how this becomes bestowed with meaning; such bestowal should not only rest upon or within established parameters but also, when necessary, on our further capacity to speculate and construct new imaginings, conceptions, visions or theories that transcend present circumstances and lead to a transformation of established modes of practice, thus improving its conditions. Our current administered and managed forms of education may not be compatible with what the future holds (the current school curriculum in England is based upon the subject curriculum devised over a century ago) and the new forms of practice, values and sensibilities that may be required. The task therefore in Illich's terminology is to disestablish those systems and modes of practice that do not facilitate convivial relations. For example, the idea or the fiction that 'every child matters, no child left behind' does not ring true when set against educational systems that perpetuate inequality, failure and scarcity.

The myth of planning is brought to our attention by Baldacchino (162) as he refers to Illich's recounting of a conversation with his mentor Jacques Maritain. When we consider the administered and schooled nature of education, we might see that children/students are not really placed at the centre of learning. This idea is a popular and recurrent myth; rather they have become objects of learning as formulated and managed by the school, which in turn is responding to the dictates of government that demand particular forms of human resources. Planning in this context is therefore concerned with the production and management of such resources for particular ends. Illich's philosophical problem with planning was with this administered and controlled form, and he sought advice from Maritain who asked him, 'Is not planning, which you talk about, a sin, a new species within the vices which grow out of presumption?' (Illich 1992: 221–2). Illich reflects, 'He made me understand that in thinking about humans as resources that can be managed, *a new certitude about human nature* would be brought into existence surreptitiously' (Illich 1992: 222; emphasis added by Baldacchino: 162). Such planning is thus a form of conscription of human resources, and in education, we can interpret this production of certitude in education manifested in the economization agenda and also in the production of standards and competences according to which practice is measured, regulated and controlled.

Baldacchino (164) asks, 'What does disestablishment mean in an age of systems?' How can we square Maritain's comment on the sin of planning with disestablishment? He elaborates upon disestablishment with reference to the importance that Illich places upon the parable of the good Samaritan, more specifically upon the *outside place*, that place outside established orders and values, that the encounter with the Samaritan symbolizes. We might view the Samaritan in terms of the gift of otherness, or even the scandal of the other as discussed in the previous chapter, whereby established values are punctured, disestablished and then re-formed. Put in other terms, the gift of a contingent encounter with otherness may inaugurate an open set of potential. The emphasis upon planning in an administered world ignores or occludes the diversity of possibilities, but it may not prevent disobedient or disestablishing practices. We can experience forms of disestablishment not only in the challenge of encounters with the work of artists but also in pedagogical encounters with the art practices of children.

Another way which Illich (1969–70: 106–16) finds to provide a contrast to the planned and administered society in which people and their values and desires become planned is to give emphasis to the idea of Epimethean *hope* that provides an opening to diverse potential and possibilities. And this idea can be inducted into pedagogic work and educational sites that are not governed by the production of 'promethean beings' for the economy but by convivial spaces in which learners are not viewed instrumentally as planned resources for economic life but themselves as creative sites of growth and potential. Value in this latter space of conviviality is not derived from planning towards specified subjectivities and practices but is as yet unknown, evolving and intrinsic to each person's experience of becoming. Brain Massumi (2018: 25) puts it this way:

> What is a quality of life, construed as a value? The answer is simple: a qualitative life value is something that is *lived for its own sake*; something that is *a value in and of itself, in the unexchangeable 'currency' of experience*. (italics in original)

In much of his writing, Illich is arguing for a change in the value of the currency according to which institutions, social dispositifs, such as education, have been organized through which people are produced as human resources largely for economic life. Are our current values of education benefiting all children and students? Do the current values, structures and organizations of teaching and learning 'work' for everyone in our current world? Do the values informing our current mode of politics work for all? Is our mode of politics outdated? Do we need to change the value of the currency of our politics to find a more convivial way of conducting politics?

Illich completes *Deschooling Society* by arguing for hope above expectation which he defines as 'reliance on results which are planned and controlled by man', whilst 'hope centres on desire on a person from whom we await a gift'

(1969–70: 106). He calls for a people who 'love people more than products', and, quoting from Yevtushenko's poem *People* (1962), those who believe that

> No people are uninteresting,
> Their fate is like the chronicle of planets.
> Nothing in them is not particular,
> And planet is dissimilar from planet.

Our current emphasis upon 'teaching' within institutionalized education, that is to say, with teaching as the *delivery* of a curriculum that children and students should consume, fails to acknowledge the crucial pedagogic practice of *listening and observing*, of listening to and observing the particularity of the vernacular and its heteroglossic expressions, not teaching an obedience to the monoglossia of set and prescribed agendas that perpetuate what Friere calls the passive banking system of education and hierarchical relations between teacher and learner. A convivial pedagogic relation is one that recognizes and values learning-*with* but does not ignore the practice of learning *from*.

Cosmopolitics: Vernacular Potential, Pedagogies of Unlearning and Ecologies of Practice

Baldacchino (112–16) draws attention to the importance of 'vernacular potential' in terms of the potential that may emerge from the diversity of actualities (haecceities) of practice. The vernacular thus lies in contrast to established modes or norms of practice that may operate a constraining, habituating or schooling force. Baldacchino (116) states, 'In its establishment of learning, education practically suppresses the vernacular possibilities of human artifice.'

The importance of the vernacular is also brought to our attention by Joe Gerlach (2014: 3) through his notion of vernacular mapping:

> Vernacular mappings are cartographies that in their ethos and practice are more vulnerable and susceptible to change and perturbation; cartographies that perform the unsettling of epistemological and representational certainties while affirming spaces for inhabiting and navigating the world otherwise.

Could we try to engage with what we might call the 'vernacular immanence' of a learner's practice so as to make such immanence accessible? I use the term 'immanence' to refer to local relations and values of modes of existence, to those flows of experiencing through which someone makes sense, conceives, feels or develops particular capacities to act. I will come back to this notion in relation to the idea of local ecologies of practice. Obviously, a teacher initiating learning encounters with their students will proceed from particular inherited practices (in art education these could be drawing, painting, 3-D work, video, performance, collage, printmaking, digital work, etc.) to tackle the encounter, but the pedagogical task, from a non-doctrinal perspective, 'without criteria', would be to try to engage with how a particular learning encounter matters for a learner in their situated specificity of learning and how this mattering becomes inherited by the teacher. Equally, extending this point on inheritance in the context of art and design education, we can ask how might teachers adjust their pedagogical practices through their inheritance of the disturbance of new forms of art practice, the scandal of art, that in turn disturbs how such practice is understood. I will develop this issue in a later chapter. We might then consider a pedagogical site in the term employed by Blaser and Cadena (2018) as an *Uncommons*, as a heterogeneous collective that values working together whilst respecting difference and divergence.

In passing but in a related vein, Lauren Berlant's article, 'The Commons: Infrastructures for Troubling Times' (2016), raises the notion of infrastructure as 'the patterning of social form, the living mediation that organises life' (393). Infrastructures, for example, those that apply to institutions such as education, include conceptual and affective processes. Berlant is interested in those glitches, disturbances or troubling times that reveal infrastructural failure and how we might proceed with the ensuing 'messiness' to repair such failures and what that repair might look like. This has some resonance with Illich's concern with institutional failure. What kind of conceptual infrastructures do we require to construct an imaginary that allows us to manage troubling times? She writes:

> Rather than thinking of the 'freedom from' constraint that makes subjects of democracy value sovereignty and autonomy, and rather than spending much time defining the sovereign-who-is-never-a-sovereign (Agamben 1998; Mbembe 2003), this project looks to non-sovereign relationality as the foundational quality of being in common. (394)

Such non-sovereign relationality of being in common seems very close to Illich's advocacy for convivial societies. Berlant seeks to 'extend the commons concept's pedagogy of learning to live with messed up yet shared and ongoing infrastructures of experience' (395). In querying the notion of the commons, she:

> asks visceral questions about how the commons as an idea about infrastructure can provide a pedagogy of unlearning while living with the malfunctioning world, vulnerable confidence, and the rolling ordinary. (396)

Berlant's notion of a pedagogy of unlearning as a means of trying to deal with the disturbances and messiness of living together with infrastructural shortcomings, and then trying to find convivial resolutions, is important if we adopt a pedagogy of taking care in relation to the heterogeneity of ways in which children or students experience learning encounters. It involves the possibility, if required, of rolling back norms of inherited practice and their forms of expression so as to be able to respond to the vernacular potentials or mappings of learners that, in Gerlach's terminology, may 'navigate the world otherwise'. In learning-with such different navigations, pedagogical practice involves not only phases of unlearning but also phases of expansion.

At this point, Isabelle Stengers's (2011a) idea of practice is also important to consider in relation to institutional education and its modes of practice and forms of assessment. In the article 'Comparison as a Matter of Concern', she argues against the imposition of a 'comparative' criterion that is applied across practices so as to define practice. For Stengers, the notion of practice,

> denotes any form of life that is bound to be destroyed by the imperative of comparison and the imposition of a standard ensuring equivalency, because what makes each practice exist is also what makes it diverge. (59)

Each practice has its distinct way of paying 'due attention', of how something matters; each practice has its own existential line of divergence.

> Divergence is not between practices; it is not relational. It is constitutive. A practice does not define itself in terms of its divergence from others. Each does have its own positive and distinct way of paying due attention; that is, of having things and situations matter. Each produces its own line of divergence, as it likewise produces itself. (59)

Taking a more provocative and speculative stance, in contrast to those regulatory forces of comparison in education manifested through the imposition of competences or standards, can we view the practice of pedagogic work as a process of adventure? Can we conceive it as a process of experimentation *without criteria*, which attempts to draw alongside the immanence and difference of ways in which learners learn, some of which often lie beyond or are disobedient to our established parameters of pedagogic and artistic practice? It seems to me that the challenge when facing such uncertainty is to view it as an opportunity to experiment, to try to develop what I have called *pedagogies against the state* (Atkinson 2011), that is to say, the state of being, the state of knowledge and the state of political control. Another way of conceiving this is to think of such pedagogies as *speculative* pedagogies – speculative in terms of adopting an experimental mode of practice/thinking that through the invention of imaginative propositions seeks to challenge and thus create a transformation of a learner's (and thus a teacher's) experience. In other words, speculative pedagogies in the form of imaginative and experimental propositions or questions (propositioning) aim to *construct a future* whose efficacy and relevance will have to be negotiated. We can think of speculation as a kind of wager, propositioning or mode of questioning on an unfinished present whose potential is the invention of strategies, operations or ideas, which are capable of provoking a child, student or teacher, to transition into a future and into novel situations.

Without directly contradicting the idea of a pedagogy 'without criteria', a valuable guiding light to such a speculative pedagogy might be to adopt as a pedagogical imperative the advice given by Alfred North Whitehead (1938: 116) from his last book *Modes of Thought*. He writes:

> Our enjoyment of actuality is a realization of worth, good or bad. It is a value experience. Its basic expression is – *Have a care, here is something that matters!* Yes – that is the best phrase – the primary glimmering of consciousness reveals, something that matters. (my emphasis)

We might employ a little adjustment and ask, '*How* is it *here* that something *matters*?' This deceptively simple question contains a deep complexity on many levels. How is this 'how' constituted? How is this 'here' (local time and space) constituted? How is this mattering (actual and potential) constituted? And how do we begin to 'have a care' for the situated specificities of mattering so that how a learner responds to a learning encounter comes to matter?

I am not speaking here about 'situated knowledge' as developed by Donna Haraway and in education by Jean Lave and others. The idea of the situated specificity of learning refers to relationalities that arise prior to knowledge, relationalities that generate an ecology of affects and feelings or 'matterings' prior to the formation of knowledge. In other words, when directed at practices of learning and teaching, these questions about mattering are concerned with local etho-ecologies of practice, what Stengers (59) calls their *ethos* (the way of behaving of a particular being) and *oikos* (the habitat of that being and the way in which the habitat satisfies or opposes the demands associated with the ethos or affords an ethos to risk itself). Spinoza argued, 'We don't know what a being is capable of or can become capable.' We might view a learning encounter as a 'proposition' that confronts the etho-ecology of each learner, and therefore, pedagogic work demands a thinking, feeling and experimenting 'in the presence' of such ecologies.

This raises the point Michael Hampe (2018: 14) makes concerning *homogenizing the interpretation of experience* in discourses that construct general schemas or concepts to *capture* concrete experience in order to produce a system of understanding. The interpretation of a learner's experience through a particular pedagogical system constitutes therefore a transcendent form of inheritance which might be considered dogmatic if priority is given to the conceptualizing structures that act as a hylomorphic forming of experience. However, if we can set aside this form of inheritance and attend to and inherit instead those disturbances, those experiences, those differences, that do not fit our interpretational frameworks, and/or if we can enter into a critical dialogue with the way in which we frame our experiences, we may be able to reconfigure or invent new, perhaps more insightful, modes of interpretational practices that invoke ethical, political and aesthetic reconfigurations.

But speculative practice, or to borrow a term from Martin Savransky (2017: 32), 'speculative pragmatism', involves more than critical reflection in that it requires a *speculative sensibility*, which, on encountering or feeling a problem, or feeling a need to comprehend a situation in more depth, attempts to cultivate imaginative propositions that invoke a future that itself depends upon the propositions that can be constructed for it. Savransky states, 'Speculative pragmatism, then, designates an experimental mode of harnessing experience such that new intelligent connections among things may become possible' (30). We can view speculative thought therefore as a 'pragmatics of thought' where thought invents a future when such a future, that of a student's learning encounter or a teacher's practice, demands thought. To speculate is therefore to make a wager on the incompleteness or the uncertainties of the present based upon what confronts us, the material for speculation, a wager that detects a possibility for creative experimentation and transformation. This would involve 'a pragmatics of the suddenly possible' (Buck-Morss 2013).

Though it is important for pedagogical practices to introduce learners to established forms of practice and knowledge that constitute the 'known world', how such traditions are inherited and iterated by students suggests that both students and teachers are viewed as both *critical inquirers* and *speculative innovators* enabling potentials for a world to come, a world that is not yet known and which cannot, in the didactic sense of prescription, be fully controlled or predicted nor fully accommodated by established orders.

Ecology of Practices

I turn now to consider some of the above points through the idea of an *ecology of practices* in the work of Isabelle Stengers (2005b). She uses this term as a tool for inquiry, a tool to make us think and explore what might be happening in a specific situation, particularly when confronted with something that does not fit but also as a device not to take things for granted. She writes:

> Approaching a practice means approaching it as it diverges, that is, feeling its borders, experimenting with questions which practitioners may accept as relevant, even if they are not their own questions ... rather than posing questions that precipitate them mobilising and transforming the border into a defence against the outside. (184)

In order to approach a specific practice and feel its borders, processes of 'recognition' or 'habit' that exert a commonality with past experiences may have to be resisted in order to avoid homogenizing the interpretation of experience. Rather, *we need to give to the situation the power to make us think*. As a tool for thinking an ecology of practices functions in a minor key, not from a model or established concept, criteria or theory that judges or determines practice. (I am thinking of such structures as competences, standards and methodologies.) The point is not to renounce such arbiters of value but rather to soften their power to structure and capture experience in contrast to allowing the power or the *force of experiencing* a situation to provoke thought or other forms of expression. Here the different temporalities of 'experience' and 'experiencing' seem important in that the former *has been given a form*, perhaps conceptualized, whilst the latter *is dominated by forces of affect prior to conceptualization*. Perhaps the difference is illustrated by standing and looking at a waterfall, giving it a form, in contrast to standing inside a waterfall, experiencing the chaos.

Hopefully, our pedagogical practice facilitates learning, but, perhaps unconsciously, it can also impose values that might disqualify or marginalize forms of learning that 'do not fit', so as to 'bully' such practices into its frame

(Stengers 2005a: 1,000; Bell 2017: 187). This is not to argue (Stengers 2010) for trying to think in the place of others but to 'look to a future, [to create the possibilities] where they will take *their* place' (italics in original; see also Bell: 192). It is developing a case for modes of attentiveness to the potential violence of our questions, our pedagogical orientations and values that may prevent or disqualify 'other' modes of practice, a case for a speculative ethics in pedagogic work. The notion of looking to the future or thinking and acting pedagogically **for** a future, and not **about** the future, is central to the notion of speculative inquiry with which I am concerned. The difference in thinking for a future from thinking about the future concerns inventing modes of thought that *construct* a future as opposed to applying established modes of thought to *re-present* the future. It may be that if the notions of 'learner' or 'teacher' are tied too closely with the idea and representation of a prior world, then we need to find another term that embraces both the inheritance of practice and equally a potential for invention. Here perhaps, in a speculative mode, we might then see learning and teaching in this light as an aporia, a process that undermines or is disobedient to its own inheritance, its own established premises – a practice of internal insurgency.

Speculative practice is inherent to art practice in the sense of inventing new relationalities, sensibilities, materialities, spatialities, temporalities and collectives. We might think of speculative pedagogies as processes in which new futures and new modes of becoming are invented and explored. Viewed in this light, art practices (or other practices) in schools and elsewhere are therefore not concerned with the representation of a world but with *the invention of worlds*, the ontogenesis of worlds as they emerge within the situated specificities and matterings of practice. Equally then, pedagogic work becomes an aesthetic process in which life itself is conceived as an ethico-political challenge.

How might we conceive an ethics and politics of speculative pedagogies that are devoted to trying to negotiate and inherit how something matters for a learner in the singularity of an event of a learning encounter? By engaging in a process of negotiation with the immanence of each singular case of learning/practice, we are in a sense inventing a future which is not yet known. Although we may consult, we cannot *rely* upon a kind of static inheritance of established codes or institutionalized apparatuses such as competences or standards by imposing these upon the singularities of practice. This would be to resort to homogenizing the interpreting of experience that Michael Hampe warns us against. Such negotiations and inheritances 'in practice' give rise to aesthetic, ethical and political questions as such negotiations approach the boundaries and divergence of each student's practice and its potentialities that potentially may evoke new questions, uncertainties and possibilities. Such negotiations in the here and now of diverse matterings of practice evoke an ethics of practice in its situated specificities, an ethics that is conscious of its fallibility, as suggested by William James (1956: 209):

> The highest ethical life – however few may be called to bear its burdens – consists at all times in breaking the rules which have grown too narrow for the actual case.

To echo James's words, we might argue that pedagogical ethics has to be prepared to put aside forms of practice that are too narrow for responding to the situated specificities of a student's learning encounter. It involves an ethics of the not-yet-known open to the situated and virtual potentialities of becoming, not a prescribed code for action. In pedagogic work therefore a teacher has to acquire, in Donna Haraway's terminology, a *response-ability* to local events of learning. This suggests, in relation to pedagogical relations, an ethics that is cultivated in the process of learning how to think and act in a particular pedagogical situation. These ethical considerations also involve or require a politics close to what Isabelle Stengers develops in her cosmopolitical proposal in which initially she draws our attention to the reference made by Deleuze and Guattari to the idea of the idiot found in Dostoyevsky.

Idiotic Events and the Cosmopolitical Proposal

Stengers (2004) tells us that in ancient Greek, the idiot is the one who does not speak the Greek language or share established customs. For Deleuze and Guattari, the idiot, as a conceptual character, is the 'one who slows the others down' by resisting or interrupting established orders and customs, not because these are wrong but because there is something more important (which they do not know). This idea of 'something more important' resonates with Whitehead's advice, 'Have a care, here is something that matters.' The idiot, or more appropriate for my pedagogical purposes, an idiotic event, produces a gap, an interstice. We might say that the idiotic event is a provocation for thought and practice, a questioning presence. It does not tell us how to proceed but confers on a situation the power, the challenge, to make us think, as do some art practices produced, performed or orchestrated by artists, or some art practices of children or students.

An idiotic event is one that may have the power to make us think or act differently, but it does not offer criteria or guidance by which to do so. It punctures established procedures and produces the potential for a space of speculation in which we might conceive practice beyond the rules and grammars of established practices, a speculative space in which practice can be reimagined and reconstructed beyond the borders of established thinking and making.

Stengers's notion of the cosmopolitical proposal is aimed at giving priority for the power of a particular situation to provoke thought into new ways of thinking or making and how we might inherit such provocations. It does not seek general solutions or prescriptions and reduces the transcendence of authority or authoritative discourse. It refers to the creation of a space or process, a conjunction, in which each person has particular attachments and respective constraints. We are thus concerned with the idea of an etho-ecology with no transcendent position but an equalization of presence and voice. This equalization does not suggest that everyone is equal but respects the notion of divergent attachments, diverging morphologies of becoming and belonging. There is some affinity here with John Dewey's democratic project that values and depends upon difference and responsibility, where all who participate develop a confidence in their individual abilities to be discerning and insightful. The term 'cosmos' does not refer to the universe but to the unknown as constituted by divergent worlds and what they may be capable of. In pedagogic work, it refers to the not-known constituted by the divergent worlds of learners and teachers and to what they may be capable of. A cosmopolitical proposal for pedagogic work therefore suggests an ethics, politics and aesthetics by which such work is informed by a feeling that it cannot 'master' the situated specificities of a learner's experience but nevertheless faces the challenge of how it might inherit from such situations. This 'insistence' of the not-known is part of pedagogic work and research. Do we allow it to 'matter', or do we anaesthetize it away (e.g. through what Hampe terms homogenizing the interpretation of experience in the form of assessment criteria and competences)? The cosmopolitical proposal as relating to pedagogic work concerns how we deal with the *insistence of the not-known*, how we inherit from it. This raises the inseparability, mentioned earlier, of the *ethos* from its *oikos* and the point that we don't know what a being is capable of or can become capable of.

The cosmopolitical proposal is the one that is 'idiotic', that disturbs our foundations by a presence that invokes an etho-ecological 'question' and which demands a new etho-ecological signification that disturbs our stable acceptance of established orders. It asks us to consider and reflect upon how, in our domains of practice, we might or can inherit such disturbances and questions. Here, taking a cue from Stengers, we might consider both politics and ethics as an 'art' in the sense that art, *not* Art, or research, *not* Research, has *no ground to demand compliance from what it deals with*; it has to *create the manners*, to artefactualize, that will allow it to deal with what it deals with. How can we artfully 'become-with' and *create the manners* in pedagogic practice or in research practice that allow us to respond effectively and commensurably with those encounters that confront us?

The cosmopolitical proposal is thus concerned with the becoming of relationalities in their various domains of practice, a process of *composing and learning-with* others without imposing established orders, a proposal that implies no transcendence but one where the need to pay due attention is crucial.

4

Gilbert Simondon: Transduction and Pedagogic Practice

Introduction

In this chapter I give an account of Gilbert Simondon's work on the process of individuation all the while trying to view it in relation to pedagogic practice and processes of learning. I draw mainly from discussions of Simondon's text *Psychic and Collective Individuation* (*L'individuation psychique et collective*) given by Muriel Combes, Anne Sauvagnargues, Didier Debaise and Alberto Toscano. This will form a substantial part of the chapter. My task is to introduce some of Simondon's key concepts that he elaborates in order to develop his notions of individuation and ontogenesis and then apply these to pedagogic practice and practices of learning. Then I will apply the notion of individuation and concomitant notions, particularly the idea of transduction, to consider the practice of children's drawings. Finally, I will give a very brief account of some contemporary art practices viewing these in turn through the lens of Simondon's theory of transduction. Simondon's work on individuation and ontogenesis was influential upon the work of Gilles Deleuze and Felix Guattari. In recent years his work on technical objects and on ontogenesis, social and psychic individuation, has generated much interest across the domains of philosophical and social inquiry.

How does an encounter with Gilbert Simondon's thought on individuation help to inform the encounters, transformations, transitions, vicissitudes and the ups and downs of pedagogic practice? A practice that is fundamentally concerned with the ontogenesis, but also the heterogenesis, of teaching and learning that aims to generate expanded capacities for feeling, thinking and acting; for generating new modes of sensibility and sociality; for innovating new potentialities for future practices and relations? The following enquiry into Simondon's work will try to tackle such questions. Put simply, for Simondon, a particular entity, human or non-human, comes to exist through a series of operations of individuations, and this ongoing process is what he calls ontogenesis. However, we are asked not to consider the individual as the starting point for thinking about individuation because this would institute the individual as a predicate to the process. We need to think about individuals *beginning with individuation*, and in doing this, we are encouraged to think about what an individual actual is and might become. By focusing upon individuation, we have to consider the unfolding of becoming rather than the substance of being

Andrew Lapworth (2016) engages with Simondon in order to theorize bio-art encounters, and he draws three implications of his work for 'theorising the constitution and transformation of subjects': first, Simondon asks us to rethink subjectivity by discarding the notion of a unified, autonomous being and to replace this by focusing on its processes of becoming, described in terms of a *transductive* emergence from what Simondon calls pre-individual reality, arguing further that subjectivity is to be conceived as a *metastable* process open to ongoing transformations. Second, to replace voluntarist notions of thought and the autonomous individual by prioritizing an 'involuntarist primacy of material *encounters* as the conditions for novel individuations' (123; italic in original). Placing emphasis upon the relationalities and affects of material encounters means that we move from positing the idea of an already-existing 'subject who experiences the world' to prioritizing relation and becoming as productive (or not) so that experience (as a relational process of becoming) is an attainment, a construction or composition that may precipitate new individuations, modes of practice or thought. Third, to rethink the ethico-politics of an art encounter (though Lapworth is concerned specifically with bio-art encounters) as an ontogenetic process through which a material production (not a representation) of new sensibilities, subjectivities and worlds may emerge.

This chapter is concerned with applying the notions of individuation and ontogenesis to pedagogic practice and its relations, particularly in the domain of art education but also to other educational domains. Such relations between what we call 'teachers' and 'learners' when thought of in terms of individuation are themselves, in Simondon's terms, operations of individuations and not autonomous individuals – operations that involve material and incorporeal (Grosz 2017) *encounters* that may precipitate new modes of feeling, thinking and acting. The ontological privileging of 'the individual' is replaced by a concern for the ongoing entanglements of *machinic* material and incorporeal relations consisting of affective, cognitive, embodied, environmental flows. The emphasis then is upon ongoing encounters (events) of individuation, or perhaps more precisely, *events of individuating*, within material processes that lead to the ongoing production of a subject as a metastable state. Put another way, the function or meaning of a body, an individual, does not reflect or depend upon an interior identity, an already-constituted being, but rather on the particular assemblages (affective, cognitive, practical, embodied) it forms with other bodies, objects, technologies, environments or milieus.

If we dramatize a pedagogical situation through Simondon's philosophy of individuation, we cannot think of such a situation as consisting of relations between a teacher and a learner or bodies of knowledge, as though these were already-existing subjects/individuals or entities. Instead, we have to think of this situation in processual terms, as a series of relations involving operations of individuation on different levels occurring within specific milieus, where operational processes, which will be discussed below, may individuate new relationalities of knowing and practice out of which emerge what we call 'learner', 'teacher' and 'knowledge', terms that mask their processual nature.

For Simondon then, the idea that being *is* relation is paramount (Debaise 2012), and he draws upon a number of concepts to explicate the processes underpinning a relational ontology: modulation, singularity, information, metastability, disparation, transduction and affectivity.

An important principle of Simondon's work on individuation is, as he puts it, 'to know the individual through individuation, rather than the individuation through the individual' (2009: 5). A simple way of grasping the prioritizing of processes of individuation rather than individuated beings or entities is not to consider the human subject as already constituted as, for example, when we speak of 'the child who experiences' or 'the artist who expresses' (subject-predicate), as though the experiencing or the expressing stems from a pre-constituted being. In contrast, by prioritizing individuation, we have to begin with the assemblage of functional processes and relations in their particular milieus.

For Simondon, these processes operate on many levels including what he called the pre-individual and the transindividual that involve potential and actual (individuated) realities. In pedagogic work therefore we might ask how a learner or a teacher emerges. The task of knowing the individual through individuation casts us into deep complexity in that we have to acknowledge that 'individuals' are in fact ongoing processes of relation, both internal and external, that operate on many levels, psychic, biological, physical, collective, cultural and historical, as well as on actual and virtual planes.

When we turn to the domains of pedagogic work, to begin with individuation means that we do not begin with individuals (e.g. learners or teachers) but with an acknowledgement that these ontological or epistemological 'entities' are in fact dynamic relational assemblages that function within their respective and evolving milieus. Therefore, in order to comprehend learners from the orientation of individuation, we have to begin with their singular modes and practices of functioning in order to extend these and their potentials. This approach contrasts with a process driven by premeditated pathways towards the acquisition of particular skills and knowledge that are congenial to (external) government mandates or directives, which tends to be the case not only in current state education systems but also within the more confined subject domains when subjected to taxonomies of competence.

In order to grasp how pedagogic work might be conceived through a philosophy of individuation and ontogenesis, I will consider some of Simondon's concepts and try to apply them to the functioning contexts of learning and teaching. This application entails abandoning substantialist and hylomorphic modes of understanding and replacing them with processual notions of modulation, disparation and transduction, which I will develop shortly.

In passing, if we apply the notions of relation and events of individuation to the domain of research in education (or other domains), we are encouraged no longer to think of the research process as involving a pre-existing researcher and a separate, pre-existing 'object' or field of research from which the researcher collects existing 'data' which is then interpreted according to established methodologies and their respective theoretical principles. At the risk of repetition, such a stance assumes a pre-constituted researcher and object of research, the collection of existing data and existing principles for interpretation of data. In general terms such research is therefore predicated upon pre-established individuals, premises and principles. Such a stance may ignore or marginalize actual functioning operations and relations and their milieus (psychic, affective, social, spatio-temporal intensities, operations and materializations) that actually constitute *research-in-practice* out of which emerge what we call researcher, object of research, data, analysis and so on. A common modus operandi of postgraduate research in education frequently consists of the formulation of clear research questions prior to engaging in research, often without an appreciation of the ensuing constraints relating to requirement and obligation that such questions invoke. How might such questions 'constrain' what is being researched or the researcher? Equally, there is often a demand to produce a coherent and preconceived research methodology, but is this demand aware of the hylomorphic force of a preconceived method and its constituting power for the focus of research, the researcher or the research 'data'?

Hylomorphism and Modulation

Anne Sauvagnargues (2012) provides a clear exposition of Simondon's conceptual apparatus when she discusses Deleuze's appropriation of his work in *Difference and Repetition*. She presents her account of Simondon's contribution to Deleuze's work in six 'logical and physical propositions' (1). I will draw on some of these. For Simondon, as we have seen, the problem of individuation involves thinking about the processes and relations that condition the emergence and ongoing differentiations of assemblages that constitute 'individuals' in any domain. We might see how this concern is of direct relevance to the domain of educational practices and the ongoing differentiations of learners and teachers. He argues that the history of Western metaphysics, from Aristotle to Kant, was captured by a static and abstract representation of being that prevented it from investigating the dynamic processes involved in individuation. A key postulation developed by Aristotle was hylomorphism, which established a relation between form and matter whereby an active form imposes itself upon passive matter – the imposition of an anterior and active principle of form upon formless or unstructured matter. The pervasive nature of hylomorphism may include conceptual forming, aesthetic forming or technological forming, whereby in each case, such forming involves the imposition of a particular form upon the amorphous fluctuating matter of experiencing. Hylomorphism therefore constitutes a relation between a transcendent principle or an enunciator which impresses itself upon passive matter, but it fails to acknowledge the immanent and dynamic forces, operations and relations of 'actual' processes of individuation. Simondon (2009) provides the notion of *modulation* to elaborate his idea of individuation and consider 'the entire progression of its reality' and its continually evolving plane of forces and materials that facilitate a continuous constructing.

Modulation

As an immanent force, modulation involves a series of dynamic flows, vibrations, intensities and material interactive processes that constitute individuation. There is no separation of an active form imposing upon a passive matter. Simondon takes the practice of brick making to contrast hylomorphism with modulation. A hylomorphic interpretation would view the brick mould as impressing form upon the shapeless and passive substance of clay. But viewed through the notion of modulation, the process of brick making is not the simple imposition of form upon matter, the mould upon the clay, but, as Sauvagnargues (2012: 3) tells us, it involves three different energies acting on the plane of forces. First, a 'strong energy of the amorphous substance in a metastable state' (the clay prepared by the brick maker). Second, 'the weak energy borne by the mould that functions as a continuous modelling energy and acts as information that guides the transformation of the clay'. Third and most important, a 'third energy, a "coupling energy" … the one that brings about the taking-form between the pre-individual substance and its modulating form', brought about extrinsically by the brick maker. The flow of intensities and energies rather than 'object' relations constitutes the actual (and virtual) morphogenetic components of individuation.

Sauvagnargues (2012) mentions the importance of Simondon's concept of modulation to Deleuze:

> As Deleuze gradually realised, what makes Simondonian analysis of modulation so powerful is that it permits us to finally get rid of the ancient and contemporary vicissitudes of hylomorphism and to propose a material and intensive analysis of form in continuous variation. Matter and form no longer need to be abstractly opposed; form is a becoming of material forces, an immanent and fluctuating standard. (4)
>
> The analysis of modulation therefore consists in replacing the abstract confrontation of form and matter with a new analysis of form as intensive variation of forces and materials – as information – that presupposes the existence of a system in a state of metastable equilibrium with the potential for individuation. (5)

These quotes have some bearing upon processes of learning and teaching in pedagogic work. Adopting this idea of modulation, both learner and teacher are viewed not as separate autonomous entities acting on materials but as immanent intensive and fluctuating processes of becoming. We might say that both learner and teacher exist in their respective states of metastable equilibrium that contain potential for individuation

The Pre-individual

Muriel Combes (2012: 1) suggests that there is a difference between being as such and being as individual; the former precedes or is a prevailing condition for any individual being, and this is why Simondon calls it *pre-individual*. We might view the pre-individual as an evolving field of potential, whereas the individual is the result of an operation of individuation (2, 46). The pre-individual is a domain of potential energy, a metastable energetic field, where there is no relationality, individuality or identity as such but a composition of tensionalities, intensities, vibrations, incompatibilities and disparations existing in a metastable state.

Debaise (2012: 3) tells us that in formulating the pre-individual, Simondon returns to the Greek idea of *apeiron* postulated by Anaximander, as an infinite and indeterminate ground that is constantly producing new forms of existence, the source of all creation. Debaise quotes Simondon:

> We might call nature the preindividual reality that the individual carries with him, in seeking to rediscover in the word nature, the meaning that the pre-Socratic philosophers gave it; the Ionian philosophers found the origin of all the species of being, prior to individuation: nature is the reality of the possible, under the kinds of this *apeiron* from which Anaximander created all forms of individuation: nature is not the opposite of man, but the first phase of the self, the second being the opposition of the individual and the milieu, complementing the individual in relation to the whole. (Simondon 2007: 196; translator's translation)

We might conceive this *apeiron* as an infinite reality of the possible. Out of this metastable order of tensionalities and potentialities that *is* the pre-individual, and which is neither in equilibrium nor in disequilibrium, emerge potentials that may lead to individuation. But it is important to bear in mind that an individuation from pre-individual reality does not, as Debaise (2012: 6) states, produce:

> a completely autonomous individual, which would exclude the nature from whence it came – this preindividual nature, source of the possible – but a hybrid shape, half-individual, half-preindividual. As an individual, it is the result of an individuation and, as a bearer of preindividual dimensions; it is the actor of new individuations, of new possible actualisations of the possible.

This hybrid of half individual and half pre-individual seems very close to the distinction made by Deleuze and Guattari of actual reality and virtual reality. The individual is the result of an individuation or a series of individuations but is also a field of potential for further individuations which in turn impact the field of potential. This hybridity also helps us to understand the metastable nature of what we call not only an individual as composed of individuated states of being but also pre-individual potentials. The affects of a disturbance experienced in an encounter with that which is unfamiliar or incomprehensible may disrupt the spatio-temporal stability and precipitate change or transformation. A learning encounter can be thought of in this sense as a disturbance to a learner's assimilated modes of functioning which precipitates a change that expands its capacities, what we call learning. That which disrupts or disturbs can be viewed as a germ of information, to be discussed shortly, that acts as a catalysing force for transformation. We might see then that an individual is always metastable in that it is always 'more than itself', in the sense that it contains potentials for self-transformation that may be activated by a combination of germs of information and affective tensionalities that arise in a particular encounter.

Commenting upon these processes involving the pre-individual, metastability, potential and transformation, Muriel Combes (2012: 3) writes:

> A physical system is said to be in metastable equilibrium (or false equilibrium) when the least modification to the parameters of the system (pressure, temperature, etc.) is sufficient to break the equilibrium of the system. ... Before all individuation, being can be understood as a system that contains a potential energy. Although this energy becomes active within the system, it is called potential because in order to structure itself, that is, to actualize itself according to certain structures, it needs a transformation of the system. Preindividual being and, in a general way, every system that finds itself in a metastable state, harbours potentials which, because they belong to heterogeneous dimensions of being, are incompatible.

We might consider 'events of learning', as moments of disequilibrium, that arise in a learning encounter as composed of such tensions, heterogeneities, intensities and incompatible potentials for transformation. Such events include the intensities of struggles, uncertainties, disappointments, frustrations and illuminations that might lead to new individuations. What I take from the ideas of the pre-individual and metastability with respect to human becoming is the importance of a kind of vital background and immanent potential that is continually constructed as new encounters are experienced. In practical terms this relates to the event of a learning encounter that precipitates new sensitivities, new modes of thinking, making, acting, seeing and feeling (as well as unresolved potentials) from those prior to the event that transform both individual and environment. For Simondon, individuation always carries with it 'unresolved' aspects of the pre-individual that remain as a source for future individuations, what Toscano (2006: 138) calls a 'primal surplus of being'. When thinking about learning encounters in pedagogic work, the notion of a surplus of potential may be useful to bear in mind when responding to the different 'expressions' or outcomes that learners produce within their specific situational encounters. Approaching different learners, learning with them, involves exploring, paying due attention to and negotiating different 'boundaries' between zones of mattering, not overcoming or transcending these boundaries by trying to impose prescribed values but seeing what might be exchanged (Stengers and Savransky 2018). Isabelle Stengers, in conversation with Martin Savransky, discusses the notion of 'thinking together through boundaries' that does not incur an erasure of boundaries but an exchange through them. Prosecuting erasure may often entail blindness to the specific value and demands of a particular learning space.

But how does transformation arise from a metastable system so that inherent potentials might become actualized? To provide an answer to this question, we need to consider Simondon's approach to disparation and transduction.

Transductive Disparation

In this section I draw upon the article by Anne Sauvagnargues, titled 'Simondon, Deleuze, and the Construction of Transcendental Empiricism', published in the journal *Pli* (2012). In essence the process of disparation produces a new dimension that resolves a disparity between two (or more) disparate levels or dimensions of reality between which there is not yet any interactive communication. In other words the coming together of disparate entities produces a new dimension from which emerges a novel entity. It emerges through a resonance between disparates, a resonance not based upon similarities or identity but difference. In practical terms we might see an encounter, a learning encounter, for example, involving a disparation between a student's established modes of practice and understanding that are confronted by something that challenges and cannot be assimilated – two heterogeneous realities. In the book *Psychic and Collective Individuation*, Simondon gives the example of binocular vision to illustrate the process of disparation. The different images produced by left and right retinas create a metastable problematic field or tension that is integrated by the brain producing three-dimensional depth perception. In other words a new dimension is created that the two retinal images do not themselves possess. It is the problematic incompatibility, the incompatibility between the two retinal images, that Simondon calls disparation. As Sauvagnargues (6) states, this process of disparation is extended by Simondon to a 'general logic of becoming'; it 'serves as a model for the creation of the new'. It is important to acknowledge that the emergence of a resolution to disparation is not a resolution of an initial contradiction but 'the creation of a new dimension not contained in the initial problem' (7). Sauvagnargues summarizes:

> Disparation becomes the determining category of individuation. It names the process of all real genesis, addresses the problem of the actualisation of the virtual, and accounts for what Simondon calls the metastable character of being. (7)

Sauvagnargues (11) turns to Simondon's physical description of crystallization to illustrate further the process of disparation, or what she terms *transductive disparation*, in order to introduce the key notion of *information* employed by Simondon to refer to the structural germ that sparks or triggers individuation. I will turn to the notion of information shortly. In crystallization, disparation arises between the pre-individual mother liquid existing in a metastable state and the 'seed' or 'impurity' that, as Sauvagnargues puts it, 'causes the crystal to "take" abruptly and initiates individuation'. The problematic tension, or state of disparation, arising as a consequence of the introduction of the seed (a singularity) in the pre-individual mother liquid precipitates the creative individuation of the crystal. And each formed layer of the crystal becomes the organizing ground for the next layer which is an illustration of transductive process in operation.

The seed or singularity that triggers the process of individuation is conceived as 'the bearer of information' (12). But the singularity emerges 'in a pre-individual environment whose metastability may resonate disparatively with the introduced singularity' (12). The compatibility between the singularity (the seed in this case) and the pre-individual setting is not based upon 'identity' but upon difference. It is the tensional difference that facilitates individuation. So this resonance of heterogeneous elements, the seed and the pre-individual environment is crucial for individuation to occur. Sauvagnargues (13) summarizes again:

> Transduction thus involves creation and differentiation; structuration by heterogeneous disparation leads to a complete reconfiguration of the field, which may then serve as the point of departure for a new type of transductive structuration that works by putting in tension two disparate realities, here, the mother liquid and the seed, the pre-individual environment and the singularity that provides the transformation. It therefore consists in a problematic tension that is resolved by the appearance of a new dimension, the formation of an individual-crystal. *Individuation thus appears at the same time as 'the solution to a conflict, the discovery of an incompatibility, the invention of a form'.* (my emphasis)

When we are affected by the force of a new concept, a new structuring element, this is a little like a seed that grows and restructures our inherited modes of thinking or practice as the concept becomes more embedded. The embedding system and its pre-individual potentials will initially affect how the concept is propagated, and they in turn will individuate forming a modified pre-individual ground. We might apply this idea of transduction or transductive structuration through heterogeneous disparation to the practice of painting when a particular series of marks or an accidental mark (like the crystal seed) results in new possibilities that transform the direction and structuring of practice. They become new structuring elements that modify or change the painting practice and the form of the painting. Equally, we might acknowledge such disparation as something which in a sense is anticipated and underpins the rationale of participatory art practices where contingent events (seeds) occurring during the process of the work change and transform its direction. Furthermore, we can consider encounters with 'otherness', as discussed in previous and later chapters, precipitating transductive disparations that propagate new structurations and individuations.

Simondon (1964: 30–1) states:

> By transduction we mean an operation – physical, biological, mental, or social – by which an activity propagates step by step within a given domain, and founds this propagation on a structuration of the domain that is realised from place to place: each region of the constituted structure serves as the principle and the model for the next area, as a primer for its constitution, to the extent that the modification expands progressively at the same time as the structuring operation. A crystal that, from a very small seed, grows and expands in all directions in its supersaturated mother liquid provides the most simple image of the transductive operation: each already constituted molecular layer serves as an organising basis for the layer being currently formed. The result is an amplifying reticular structure for the next region.

Equally, in those art practices mentioned above or indeed other forms of practice we might want to consider, we can envision their evolution as a transductive process of propagation through which the practice evolves as new structuring elements affect the direction of practice and its values. Each phase of practice serves as an organizing basis for the emerging phase which is not necessarily a smooth process but one which can and usually does involve phases of disturbance, frustration, surprise and so on. We can perhaps see how events of learning constitute a transductive process through which new operations, propagations and structurings emerge (or do not) as a result of 'germs of information' (an event of encounter) that then serve as a structuring platform for further operations and restructurings from a pre-individual reserve of potentials. This process of transductive propagation brings to mind Guattari and Deleuze's notion of the ritornello, an initial structuring element/process that precipitates territorializations, which I will come to shortly.

By taking on board these notions of metastability, disparation, individuation and transduction, we are encouraged to think in terms of the relationality of being and becoming. As Sauvagnargues (13–14) states:

> In reality, there is no unitary individual, but only *multiple processes of individuation*; furthermore, the individual involves no unity or identity, for it requires the heterogeneity of the heterogeneous phases from which it appears by means of differentiation. It necessarily follows that there must be a perpetual interdependence between the individual and the environment in which it is constituted. (my emphasis)

Disparation and Signs

We can consider the tensional disparation between heterogeneous components as generating a 'signalling' and what emerges from this disparate coupling is called a 'sign' as discussed by Deleuze in *Difference and Repetition* (12). Alberto Toscano (2006: 142) puts it this way, 'A sign is what individuates a system on the basis of an initial disparation.' In a learning encounter, we can take this as the coupling of a germ of information, the spark of otherness, with its embedding system from which a new or modified sign emerges. A young boy is able to respond effectively to the task of solving $5 + 6 = ?$ But when confronted with $8 + ? = 17$ he struggled. His father, pointing to the $=$ figure tells him, 'This can mean "the same as".' With that the boy was able to complete his task. The father's remark seems close to a structural germ, a sign, that allowed the tensional disparation, between the boy's established understanding and the encounter with the otherness of the 'odd' form of the addition problem to be resolved and facilitate a new individuation of practice.

A sign for Deleuze is not the representation of a prior reality but something that resolves the conflictual tension of disparation through the invention of a new form. Sauvagnargues (15) puts it succinctly, 'Disparative becoming is substituted for mimetic resemblance.' By viewing individuation as a process of 'disparative becoming', involving disparate orders or heterogeneous realities 'between which a problematic field is formed according to the difference between them' (16), this involves a simultaneous co-productive individuation of individual and environment. Out of the tensions, intensities, singularities and incompatibilities of pre-individual reality may emerge potentials for what Toscano (146) terms the 'presence of a germ of structure' that enables a resolution of disparation.

Putting things more simply and trying to avoid the technical complexity of these terms, we might think of the notions of the pre-individual, disparation and germ of information that are required for individuation to occur, in relation to events or epiphanies of learning when something happens that 'resolves' the instabilities and uncertainties of how to proceed. Sometimes the outcome of such events produces a new or modified structure of practice and thought. I have just provided an illustration of this process in a home environment involving a boy and his father. The processes of art practice are frequently full of uncertainties and tensions, a not-knowing how to proceed, of experimenting, and these phases are sometimes resolved through the emergence of a form that 'in-forms' and restructures practice and thought, such structurations then becoming the ground for future restructurings. The emergence of structural germs in such situations is frequently contingent and unpredictable. In early childhood drawings, we can witness the emergence of particular forms from the adventures of practice, forms that are repeated but then extended in the here and now of practice, in-formation in the making, extending the relations between self and world. We might equally apply this description to pedagogic practices which frequently involve moments of uncertainty when confronted with an obligation to respond effectively to the different ways in which a learning encounter matters for a child or student.

As mentioned earlier, emerging from these explorations of Simondon's work on ontogenesis and individuation is the conviction that when we consider learning events or the relations of pedagogic work, it becomes redundant to think of these in terms of pre-constituted individuals, principles or objects, learners and things learned. Rather we have to think in terms of relationalities and events, of individuals as a 'theatre of individuation' functioning on many levels. Toscano (149–50) writes:

> If we can indeed speak of any 'primacy of the organism' here it is certainly not of the organism qua agent, but only of the organism as a local resolution of disparation, as the invention of a compatibility between heterogeneous domains and demands: ... the organism denotes a site of becoming and not an agency that determines its outcome.

The notion of a learner or a teacher conceived in terms of sites of local resolutions of disparation and becoming provides a challenging counter to substantialist notions of agency as it prioritizes such resolutions in terms of an ongoing inventive (informational) process – a transductive propagation. This seems to have important implications for an ontogenetic ethics and politics in that these processes will not be viewed in terms of established principles for action or relation but will emerge from local resolutions of disparation, in other words from the actual tensions, intensities and incompatibilities of living together in particular environments. These issues will be tackled in the final chapter.

Toscano, echoing Simondon, points out that the event of information, the structural germ, which is key to individuation, does not disappear with an initial morphogenesis but rather contributes to the continuous becoming of further individualizations so that individuals are to be seen as constant sites of invention. He writes:

> The living individual is not just the local invention of a resolution to the heterogeneity of being, but must persist in being the site of inventions, with regard both to its environment and to itself: the individual is that being which functions upon itself, transforming its potentialities and inventing new structurings, in turn requiring new relationships to the preindividual component. (150)

He concludes this passage with a key statement:

> In this sense, we could even say that the living individual is *its own problem*. This problematicity is crucial if we are to entertain the idea of the individual as a 'theatre' rather than an 'agent' of individuation. (150; italic in original)

This is an intriguing statement whereby the individual is viewed as a site or an assemblage of problematicity or metastability of ongoing inventions of itself and its environment denoting a never-ending struggle in-forming (or not) new relationalities, the invention (or not) of relation. This struggle is not driven by teleological principles but emerges in the immanence and non-identity of disparation, the tensions and intensities of the pre-individual and the possible emergence of a germ of information leading to ongoing local resolutions that transform potentialities or fail to do so. This point is echoed by Debaise (2012) when speaking of the hybrid nature of the individual, half pre-individual and half individual. The challenge of a learning encounter might then be viewed in terms of a disparation or a tension between two (or more) levels of reality, a learner's inherited practices (ontological and epistemological ground) and the immediate affective disturbance of the encounter that precipitates the need to invent new or modified practice.

This tension between levels constitutes a problem of becoming and requires something to resolve the tension, a seed of information (the genesis of a new schema or idea, way of acting or conceiving) that enables a resolution towards new structures and potentials. When reflecting upon practice, I suggest that we usually try to resolve such tension through the process of experiment and investigation, by probing and exploring ways to resolve the encounter. Such exploration is vital and contingent for each learner to be able to work towards a resolution. I will deal with the evolution of new structures and potentials below when discussing the idea of the ritornello in relation to children's drawing practices, but now I turn to Simondon's important notion of the *transindividual*.

Transindividual

We can proceed to consider the structural germ of information that resolves disparation and triggers transductive individuation as a relational and intensive force of *affectivity* (Combes: 31; Lapworth 2016: 133), a dimension of individuation that brings in the idea of the transindividual. A crucial aspect of Simondon's work on individuation in relation to human and social individuation concerns the relation between the subject and the collective that he approaches in *L'individuation psychique et collective* (1989). Muriel Combes emphasizes that this title does not refer to psychic *and* collective individuations but to a single individuation, 'bringing together two terms across the unifying distance of an "and"' (25). The transindividual should not then be viewed in terms of a relation between individuals and the social (pre-constituted entities) but as a relation emerging 'bringing together' or rather 'constituting' and propagating these two (relational) terms, and this has significant implications for the individuating evolution of the psychosocial or psychic and collective being. In a nutshell the transindividual refers to the emergence of a new or modified constitution of the subject and the collective simultaneously; it is not that 'which unifies individual and society, but a relation interior to the individual (defining its psyche) and a relation exterior to the individual (defining the collective): the transindividual unity of two relations is thus a relation of relations' (26). Psychic and collective individuation is the unity of two reciprocal relations that constitute a subject.

Combes (35) tells us that Simondon insisted that the transindividual which is 'the mode of relation to others constitutive of collective individuation, must be discovered and can only be discovered through an ordeal of solitude'. The affectivity of an encounter, its 'bare life' as it were, may trigger a shift from established inter-individual relations that disturbs their affective quality and propagates transindividual (individual and collective simultaneously) relations that facilitate new relational sensibilities. The affectivity of the event disrupts the subject, stripping away both self and established social relations, and invokes a new subject-collective dimension. We might see this process as a *disindividuation* that leads to new transindividual becoming that precipitates new ethical, political or aesthetic relations.

Combes (48) states that the transindividual concerns the 'effects in a subject of the discovery of its more-than-individuality', exposed by the affectivity of an encounter, a discovery that then provides the potentials for new relations with others. This can be experienced in the affectivity of pedagogic encounters when confronted with a child's or student's response that does not fit our expectations, and we try to pass beyond these to try to embrace the 'otherness' that we do not know. Such awareness may lead us to recognize that what we call 'human' or 'teaching' or 'learning' is always *incomplete* and, as a consequence of such incompleteness, Combes (49–50) raises some important points in the following quotations:

> Simondon does not speak of the incompleteness of the human in terms of humans in general, but 'individual by individual', that is, from the point of view of each human insofar as each human is a bearer of potentials, of uneffectuated real possibility. ... Thus it is only in consideration of the real potential that humans carry with them 'something that can become collective' that *a* human, as a single human, can be considered as incomplete. (italic in original)

She continues this line of thought relating to the human and incompleteness, with a Spinozan inflection, referring to Toni Negri's writing on Leopardi (Exil: 12):

> We might say of Simondon's thought that it proposes 'a humanism after the death of man', a humanism without the human to be built on the ruins of anthropology. A humanism substituting the Kantian question 'What is man?' with the question 'How much potential does a human have to go beyond itself?' and also 'What can a human do insofar as she is not alone?'

These questions relating to incompleteness, potential and a humanism beyond the human bring into play the importance of Simondon's ideas on relation, individuation and transindividual for thinking about the invention of practices, in pedagogic work, for example, that draw upon and acknowledge the potentialities of each individual, an individual-in-relation, as a bearer of potentialities for both individual and collective life.

Art Practices

In this final section, I will look at children's art practices and some contemporary art practices through the lens of Simondon's work on individuation. I will do this by considering early mark-making and subsequent drawing practices as transductive processes that lead to an inventive territorialization of worlds. Then I will discuss briefly what we might call an intervention of otherness in encounters with some contemporary art practices when the affectivity of such events may strip away normalized inter-individual relationalities and open up new transindividual possibilities. This stripping away of the constituted inter-individual can be said to constitute the radical and scandalous force of art both in terms of its practice and its encounter.

There is a paradox in art education in that the practices, methodologies, criteria, principles and so forth that constitute this institutionalized mode of practice and its values may be strongly inimical to the scandalous force of art whose effects often puncture such values. Prior to any construction of educational aims, objectives or competences that compose the subject 'art', in schools or elsewhere, lies a more fundamental process of existential practice and its heterogeneous manners that may be occluded or marginalized if restrained or regulated by pedagogical constraints of art education. This requires some qualification. I recognize that the domain of art practice (or that of other domains) is established over time through a body of practices that form traditions that mutate and change. School art education is constituted by a range of art practices and methods of teaching that are deemed to be important for children and students to experience in order to facilitate particular modes of expression and learning that are distinctive to art practice. Difficulties can arise when such institutionalized practices generate criteria according to which art is comprehended, when such criteria demarcate values of 'ability'. The problem then is that some iterations or individuations of practice emerging from their specific existential ground may be discounted or marginalized.

Ritornello and Children's Early Drawing Practices

Felix Guattari by himself and also writing with his friend Gilles Deleuze developed the notion of the ritornello that I employed in a previous publication (Atkinson 2018a: 174). For Guattari (1996a; also O'Sullivan 2006) subjectivity is constituted by a multiplicity of evolving ritornellos, phases within which subjectivity is organized or structured. Deleuze and Guattari give the example of the ritornello of an anxious child humming in the dark to provide a sense of security. A ritornello can be conceived, rather like Simondon's structural germ or seed, as facilitating the individuation of a territory, a spatio-temporal holding form, composed of specific rhythms and repetitions according to which subjectivity is configured. It affords a local individuation and subsequent composition of becoming with a world.

> We call a refrain (ritornello) any aggregate of matters of expression that draws a territory and develops into territorial motifs and landscapes. (Deleuze and Guattari 1988: 323; my bracket)

We can conceive the ritornello therefore as an initial spatio-temporal event whose developing rhythms and repetitions structure different aspects of being and becoming in our different and evolving milieus. The immanence of rhythm to an emerging ritornello is important in that it relates to its repetition, but this is not a repetition of the same but a repetition as differentiation in response to evolving relations and contexts. Following Elizabeth Grosz (2008), Kleinherenbrink (2015: 215) tells us that rhythm is:

> something constituted by the capacities of a being in reciprocal determination with the affordances and events in its environment. Hence, rhythm 'runs through all of life' in connecting living things to both nonorganic and organic entities in a series of contingent encounters (Grosz 2008: 18). If milieus concern what happens where, rhythms are about how and when things within and between milieus happen, and hence the flexibility and survivability of a milieu is a rhythmic concern. If milieus primarily refer to spatial arrangements and the constitution of components, rhythms are the 'particular temporal form' that maintains a certain measure of continuity and coherence. (extract from Grosz 2008: 47–8)

The propagation of this structuration process can be viewed as a transductive operation whereby the production of ritornellos, their rhythms and structuring operations provide the ground for further ritornellos, further structuring

Figure 1

operations that precipitate new dimensions across a domain of practice, thus extending both practice and the domain. For example, in early drawing practices, a child's mark or graphic schema can be viewed as a structural germ, a ritornello, whose developing rhythm generates a territorialization and thus a structural and temporal order along with its respective potentials within the milieu of the child's drawing practice, where practice persists as a continual site of invention and individuation. A drawing practice can be viewed therefore as a particular kind of expressive territorialization that emerges in the flux of practice, a dynamical rhythmic process that constitutes local expressions of practice. In other words early drawing practices can be conceived as being composed of marks that function as stepping stones that structure the temporality of practice and upon which practice and its potentials evolve.

Such early practices consist of lines, rotations, zigzags, dots and other marks that acquire a consistency, consolidation and a repetition as differentiation. These marks, viewed as ritornellos, constitute emerging territorializations and explorations of drawing practice; they can be conceived as local schemas that organize, mutate and amplify as new potentials emerge in the contingencies of practice. Many so-called scribble drawings appear chaotic, but if considered closely, we can detect early marks and schemas as mentioned above, structuring components and zones of intensity that compose a territory. We can see drawings like the one in Figure 1 that contain early formations of lines, spirals and enclosed forms.

And then in Figure 2, we can see a more dynamic orchestration of these early marks that facilitate an expressive territorialization.

In the following drawings (Figures 3 and 4), we see the use of these early graphic forms to produce what we might call a representation of a butterfly and a beetle, though the term 'representation' is problematic because it tends

116   *Pedagogies of Taking Care*

Figure 2

Figure 3

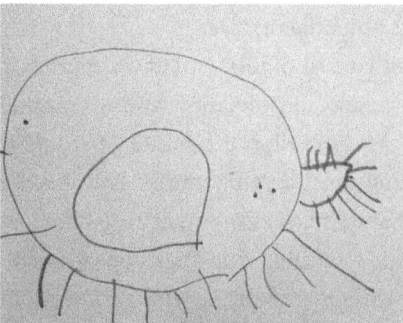

Figure 4

to presuppose a prior reality to be represented. It would be more appropriate to view these drawings as novel productions or *formulations*.

In Figure 5 we see a similar employment of early graphic schemas to formulate two lions.

Gilbert Simondon: Transduction and Pedagogic Practice 117

Figure 5

We can conceive these early marks and their configurations as evolving ritornellos or structuring germs or devices whose evolving rhythms provide a sense of coherence to the territorializing process of drawing. The immanence of rhythm to the ritornellos relates to their repetition and amplification, not of the same but to an ever-expanding differentiation as drawing practices evolve into new or modified ontological and semiotic territories, new sensibilities, which constitute a process of ontogenesis of the drawing and the drawer.

In this discussion of the graphic evolution of drawing practices, I have not mentioned the crucial aspect of the existential ground of practice and its potential, that is to say, the child's affective and cognitive as well as material engagements with practice, which are crucial to the individuations of practice and its ontogenesis. Viewing the evolution of marks and configurations that compose these drawing practices through the notion of transduction allows us to conceive them as *immanent* processes of differentiation and individuation. They are not guided by any transcendent references but by the energetic potentials, affects and structural germs, emerging from the contingent events immanent to practice and which propagate practice from one phase to the next, thereby individuating new materialities, new sensibilities and modes of practice. Practice is thus *actual* and *virtual* in the sense that as well as the actual processes involved in mark-making, there is also a virtual reservoir of potential actualizations and affects, some of which will happen whilst others remain unactualized. We can understand each drawing practice as a passage from an assemblage of emerging marks and configurations coupled with their affective charges to another assemblage still in the process of being formed – a continuous process of differentiation. We can view this cutting edge of practice as a metastable horizon, where new rhythms and tensions arise in the here and now of practice. We might then conceive the drawer (the human body, a complex organism of diverse layers of functioning) and the drawing as an assemblage of dynamic affects and intensities rather than in terms of a more static separation between drawer (subject) and drawing (object). The notions of modulation, disparation and transduction allow us to develop a perspective in which drawings and drawers are individuated simultaneously, thus abandoning the separation of an active subject and passive object (hylomorphism). Paolo de Assis (2017: 698), commenting upon Simondon's notion of modulation in the context of musical performance, which we can also relate to drawing practices, writes:

> Any individual involved in a performance is modulating through a complex set of disparate elements, solving and resolving on the spot diverse disparate inconsistencies of the materials, operating instant synthesis (actualizations) out of a cloud of really existing pre-individual singularities (the virtual).

We can view a drawing practice as a modulating and transductive operation involving a transmission of virtual impulses and tensions from actualized mark to actualized mark – the transmission of forces of felt potential across the field of actualization.

Simondon's notions of modulation and transduction are important therefore for developing not only an analysis of art practices, such as children's drawings, but also the wider domain of art practice or performance. These notions are important because they offer a very different way to problematize practice in contrast to hylomorphic interpretations that presuppose a distinction between active form and passive matter. Transduction and modulation give us a way to conceive practice in which practice and its outcomes as well as practitioners themselves are individuated/individuating simultaneously. Assis (700) writes:

> A more general and broader definition of transduction is to be found in Simondon's collected essays *Sur la Technique* (2014: 452), where – in the context of discussing notions of technical progress –transduction is presented as the passage from a constituted ensemble towards another one in the process of being constituted (Simondon 2014: 452). What is striking in this definition is the fundamental inclusion of time and temporality as quintessential to the transductive operation. Transduction happens in time, it is a process, an operation with a temporal and energetic direction (even if not precisely determinable). And this temporal dimension unfolds from one point to the next, in closest vicinity from one another, but not in a full continuum: 'En ce sens est transductif ce qui se transmet *de proche en proche*, ce qui se propage avec éventuellement amplification' ('In this sense transduction is something transmitted *little by little*,

something that propagates, eventually, in amplified form', Simondon 2014: 452, my translation and emphasis). 'De proche en proche' means 'gradually', 'little by little', 'slowly', 'progressively', 'in succession'. Simondon couldn't be clearer about the essential feature of transduction, namely its *processuality*. <u>This reflection lies at the heart of Simondon's project: more important than discussing what things 'are' is to consider how they come to be what they are, and what futures they entail. Every present, every 'here and now', every event – but also every material construction – is infinitely divided into past and future.</u> (my emphasis)

He continues (701):

The transductive process leads to ever-changing states that are, at the same time and without contradiction, *more* and *less* than their past or future potentials: *less*, because they cannot contain all virtual possibilities; *more*, because they generate new, unpredictable, and unforeseeable new tensions, new potentials that require further processes of equilibrium. If transduction involves a *reduction* of the potential(s) to its ongoing actualization, it also comprises a future increase of tensions (unpredictability), which will reinforce the field of the virtual. (italics in original)

These quotations dealing with the processuality of transduction indicate its energetic dimension composed of not only actualizations and amplification but also, as mentioned above, virtualizations of future transductions and their as yet unknown tensions and potentials. We might say every event of learning is therefore, as Assis puts it, 'infinitely divided into past and future', and the task of pedagogic work is to try to engage with and respond effectively to both the actualizations of practice and their virtual potentials. Pedagogic work is a matter then of employing the notion of an ecology of practices as a tool for inquiry that allows us to explore what might be happening as what happens emerges from the immanence of practice.

In pedagogic work the heterogeneity of practice and its potentials can be viewed as a gift that can extend how we understand and develop pedagogic work, a practice which is thus considered in terms of *learning-with* as well as *learning-from*. Learning-with continually emerges in the here and now of practice, a learning that may modify or even transform prior practice and its forms of comprehension. From this perspective when we approach a child or student's practice, we try, as it were, to 'feel' its borders, experiment with questions, that are hopefully relevant to the learner and their particular ways of paying due attention to the learning encounter which is what makes each practice exist.

The idea of learning-with is grounded upon the heterogeneity and divergence of learning-from which consists of a confluence of each teacher's inheritance of learning and each learner's inheritance of learning. Both inheritances are 'brought' to and iterated in the here and now, to the novel dynamics and contingencies, of each pedagogical encounter so that both learner and teacher individuate simultaneously. Learning-with thus moves from substantialist views of the relations between teacher and learner and sees the pedagogical relation as a dynamic modulation and transduction of actual and virtual domains.

Such an approach to pedagogic work contrasts with one that is governed by hylomorphic forces that constitute a pre-established pedagogical framework through which to interpret and thereby conceive practice. Assessment criteria, competences or standards are all examples of such devices that can easily occlude the 'thisness' of local dynamics of practice, its tensions, rhythms and potentials. In other words these devices impose a particular mode of being which may exclude the haecceities, the heterogeneity, the potentials for possibility and the metastability of becoming. Transduction involves the 'ongoing actualisation or structuring of potential' (Simondon 2013: 77–82, in Assis: 704), a process precipitated by the singularity of a structural germ (in the drawing examples, this could be a particular mark or configuration). It involves a propagation and amplification from the event of an initial singularity and its conditioning ground. Referencing Simondon, a point that is crucial for the process of learning, Assis (705) states, 'Being cannot be reduced to what it is; being is at the same time structure and energy ... sign and potency, longitude and latitude'.

A point made by both Assis and Alberto Toscano is that the structural germ and ensuing event of individuation can be conceived as a process of *dramatization* opening up new spatio-temporalities of practice that sometimes facilitate (as in art or other practices) unexpected directions of travel. This is a crucial function of art that remains beyond any attempt to assess it in that such devices are always behind and therefore fall short of art's eventful capacity to break new ground. Such events that open new possibilities are referred to by Deleuze and Guattari (1988: 260–5) as haecceities. Assis (706–7) appropriates this term for the performing arts which I suggest includes visual and performance practices in contemporary art. He introduces the term 'micro-haecceities', that relate to the here and now of an evolving musical performance and he describes their actual-virtual dynamics:

> The young pianist performing Brahms' second piano concerto ... is navigating high-speed successions of 'prolonged singularities'. There is no time for

contemplation, things must happen in the unavoidable urgency and imperative sequentially of the here-and-now. Micro-haecceities are high-energy-loaded and high-speed-moving singularities that carry a force of potential from one metastable state to the next. They make up the visible or audible part of artistic transductive processes. In their functioning as radical becoming they never appear as stable 'beings', remaining an impulse of virtuality from one actualization to the next. If one thinks, or does, or experiences artistic performances with these operations in mind, the Deleuzian notion of 'capture of forces' becomes more graspable than ever: the virtual becomes actual in order to be instantly dissolved into the virtual again.

Some years ago (Atkinson 2011, 2018a), I wrote about a young boy involved in a painting practice that lasted over fifteen to twenty minutes. The practice, seen as a transductive process, passed through a range of phases or events, micro-haecceities, constantly shifting and evolving. Actions accompanied by the boy's running commentary emerge and evolve through the contingencies, impulses and amplifications of practice, as one energetic and intensive phase becomes actualized and potentialized and passes into another, in the here and now of practice. Each phase seems to 'capture virtual forces' and produce new individuations in the intensive process of becoming whose potential then leads to further individuations. The following edited extract from 2017 (24) tries to capture the boy's practice which I have just 'read' through Simondon's notion of transduction.

> Some years ago I was shown a video of a young boy called Luca (3 years) engaged in painting. Briefly Luca engages in a series of painting processes that involve a number of inventive phases flowing together. He paints a storm, a windmill, a train going backwards and forwards and then coming to a dead end and crashing. He paints around his hand, makes hand prints and then paints his hand and forearm. As the painting continues we witness periods of sustained concentration as well as glimpses of surprise, fascination and uncertainty. The temporality of Luca's practice as it proceeds seems to involve what Susan Buck-Morss (2013) calls a pragmatics of the suddenly possible, a very powerful phrase I think, which has implications for the practice, ethics, aesthetics and politics of pedagogic work. Luca passes through a series of little events of learning, little epiphanies that simply evolve with no clear sense of direction or end point. It is as though there is no commanding plan-leading action, but rather an aspirant imagination (Ingold 2015) feeling a way forward and improvising a pathway through an as yet unformed world. It might be described as an undergoing of action in relation, where there is no separation between the actants but a

kind of correspondence of body movements, imaginings, paint, brush, paper; a becoming-with, a generation and a dis- solution, a process on the edge of the not-yet-known. We might think of the flow of events of learning as being on the edge of time, as consisting of a tension between that which exists and that which-is-yet-to-arrive.

This description tries to capture the transductive evolution of the boy's practice consisting of micro-haecceities that generate new intensities and rhythms, new actualizations and virtual potentials that create the ontogenesis of practice. Simondon writes:

> The individual, by its energetic conditions of existence, is not only inside of its own limits; it constitutes itself at the limit of itself and exists at the limit of itself; it comes out of a singularity. (Simondon 1995: 60)

Can we detect, in this practice, what Sauvagnargues (2016: 16), with reference to Simondon, terms individuation as an event of 'disparative becoming' – an event that triggers new structurations of practice. The transduction of the boy's drawing phases seems to arise from a combination of heterogeneous realities that generate tensions between unactualized potentials of practice, spontaneous narratives and their respective visual manifestations and such manifestations acting as signs that resolve tension through the actualization of new visual forms.

Art as a Rupturing of Sense (The Scandal of Art)

Art wants to create the finite that restores the infinite.
(Deleuze and Guattari 1994: 197)

The role of art turns out to be crucial and paradoxical: it is from art, in so far as it is real experience, that philosophy awaits theoretical renewal, but this renewal is not produced conceptually: it is elaborated on the plane of artistic work.
(Sauvagnargues 2016: 68)

Taking on board Simondon's work on modulation, disparation, individuation and transduction, we learn that the affectivity of an encounter is generated by two (or more) heterogeneous (disparate) realities that trigger a 'disparative becoming' (Sauvagnargues 2016: 16). Such becoming seems relevant both to encounters with some contemporary art practices and to the actual composition of practice. Some art interventions generate problematic fields constituted by disparations where heterogeneous realities are brought together and thus generate affects that provoke a questioning of values, traditions and social interrelations leading to new ways of thinking and making, which in turn effect transindividual individuations that precipitate modified or new ethical, political and aesthetic relations.

I will briefly consider such art interventions here because more will be developed in the following chapter. Duchamp's gesture of placing everyday objects, such as *Bottle Rack* into an art gallery or museum, and his other use of 'readymades', created shock waves whose ripples we still feel today. As Zepke (2011: 33) argues, 'The readymade is one of the foundational strategies of contemporary art.' More will be said on the paradox of readymades in the following chapter. Duchamp's work problematized and troubled the entire regime and apparatus of art practice that at the time was grounded in conceptions of the artist as the 'creative individual': the artwork as the outcome of their unique creativity, the spectator as a passive receiver of this creative impulse, the gallery as a cathedral of creative work and enterprise that established a value system for what constitutes art. The everyday object as a singularity in heterogeneous relation to the entire panoply of artistic traditions and institutions sparked a troubling of established aesthetic values and principles. It also generated a disturbance of ethical and political relations in the sense of an ethics and politics that unsettled what Ranciere (1999, 2010) called the 'distribution of the sensible', which is, roughly speaking, the established system of social relations and positions, its ways of making sense of these and the world – a scenario that establishes who and what is visible (and by implication who and what is invisible) and who is able to speak (and who has no voice). Politics and ethics for Ranciere are concerned with the disruption of established orders and the force of discrimination in the name of those who are invisible to or unheard by these. Duchamp's objects as singularities disrupted not only traditional aesthetic conceptions and values of art practice but also the politics and ethics of established notions of art practice: who is to be considered an artist, what constitutes a work of art and who has the power to make such decisions?

In more recent times, we can consider the works of artists such as Joseph Beuys, Joseph Kossuth, Fred Wilson, Nancy Frazer, Barbara Kruger, Jenny Holzer, Mary Kelly, Marina Abramovich, Cindy Sherman, Shirin Neshat, Kara Walker and many more, whose works make interventions that facilitate new transindividual individuations that rework aesthetic, ethical and political relations. Shirin Neshat deals with the realities of women in Iran, their relation to the totalitarian government and the West's perception of them or their relation to the Western 'gaze'. She explores ongoing conflictual tensions, for example, those generated by 'the veil', and in doing so, the signifier 'woman' is troubled and problematized. We might see the veil in these works titled *Women of Allah* (1997), as a singularity, existing within the tensional relations generated by Eastern and Western perceptions. As a signal the veil does not resolve these tensions but acts as a charged object against the heterogeneous realities of Iranian culture and the Western gaze. Thus, it does not function in the Deleuzian sense of a sign resolving a disparation through the invention of a new form but rather seems to hold the difference, the disparation, in an affective tensional relation, a continuing transductive force, that maintains a problematic field and its continuing affects.

Fred Wilson's intervention in 1992–3 at the Maryland Historical Society is another illustration of creating a problematic field in which heterogeneous realities are brought together. This work titled *Mining the Museum* included an installation entitled *metalwork* which consisted of placing a pair of slave shackles in the middle of a collection of silverware. This intervention created a disparation between the historic collection of silverware produced for wealthy clients and a pair of slave shackles that symbolize the source of their wealth. The tensions and affective currents that are generated by this disparation begin, in turn, to generate questions of value, cultural bias, the politics and ethics of wealth built upon slavery, the legitimacy of museum collections and display (in other words, what this particular display in its normal composition tends to occlude), subjugation, dehumanization and terror. A transductive process of political and ethical issues is triggered by an initial disparation that continues to generate and individuate along transindividual vectors. Though occurring within the institutionalized environment of a museum, the 'readymade' operates not only on a conceptual level generating 'information' but, more significantly, as a generator of affects on a molecular level impacting individual sensibilities and transindividual vectors, affects that may precipitate new sensibilities (affective ritornellos).

5

On the Idea of Speculative Pedagogies

Introduction

In this chapter, which is in part stimulated by the book, *Speculative Research: The Lure of Possible Futures*, edited by Alex Wilkie, Martin Savransky and Marsha Rosengarten, I argue against the current dominance and instrumentalism of present educational policies affecting schools in many countries whereby the purpose of education is aligned closely to economic ambition and competition so that some subjects seen as vital for this purpose, such as mathematics and science, are given priority over others, such as the arts and humanities, which have become increasingly marginalized. Such instrumentalism is manifested through government control of education whereby, in England, teaching and learning have to conform to prescribed curricula content, academic standards and competences, modes of assessment and inspection as manifested in batteries of testing, performance indicators and league tables. The power of this dogmatic approach to educational policy and practice tends to marginalize other approaches, thus disqualifying the potentialities they may have to offer for pedagogic work.

In sharp contrast to this prescriptive approach to education and pedagogic work, I will argue that speculative inquiry, thinking and practice as conceived by Alfred North Whitehead, Isabelle Stengers and similarly by Maurice Merleau-Ponty and Hannah Arendt are crucial to pedagogic work because such inquiry recognizes the immanence of potential that enables a more expansive pursuit of invention and innovation. Though it is important for pedagogical practices to introduce learners to the inheritance of tradition and established forms of knowledge and practice that constitute the known world, it is also crucial to view teachers and learners as innovators enabling potentials for a world to come, a world that is not yet known and which cannot, in the didactic sense of prescription, be controlled or predicted, nor accommodated by established orders. In a trite sense, we can say that if enquiry or learning that occurs on the cusp of a 'developing present' (Savransky 2017, p.37) is not speculative, then it is not learning, but the obviousness of this remark does seem to have been obscured within those instrumentalist approaches to educational practice that dominate many countries.

For Arendt, 'the essence of education is natality' (1977: 174), by which she means the introduction of something new that disrupts present orders or conditions or the determinism of such orders. Crucially for Arendt, in addressing the idea of the political, such disruption, or what I have termed disobedience (Atkinson 2018a), has to arise in the presence of others. Rosalyn Diprose (2017: 44) quotes Arendt on this point:

> Political thinking 'cannot function in strict isolation or solitude; it needs the presence of others "in whose place" it must think', not in the sense of thinking on behalf of others, but thinking that refers to others 'whose perspectives it must take into consideration, and [most crucially] without whom it never has the opportunity to operate at all'. (Arendt 1977: 220–1)

For Arendt, the political is not the exclusive domain of institutions of government but emerges from public relations, in all their diversity, between people. In contrast to Arendt's communal notion of the political, a didactic approach to pedagogic work *does* think on behalf of others, both teachers and learners, as is manifest in government instrumentalist policies today, where the 'other' is a subject whose perspective is already prescribed; to a large extent, the future is already drawn out. The contrary position I take here in adopting a speculative approach to pedagogic work recognizes the importance, the inevitability of inheritance and also the futurity of invention that may open up new, unpredictable ways of thinking and acting that may be disparaged or marginalized within the determinism of didactic pedagogies and their norms of practice.

Diprose (42) tells us that for Merleau-Ponty, 'speculative research and thinking arise with the "dehiscence" of being'. The term 'dehiscence' in botany refers to the splitting of a seed pod to release new life; Merleau-Ponty uses the term to describe the splitting or rupturing of habit whereby something new emerges, a new way of seeing, conceiving or acting, a divergence from instituted habits of thinking, speaking, seeing, listening and feeling. In general terms such events of rupture, or dehiscence, tend to occur through the experiencing of an encounter, when assimilated habits, modes of thinking or modes of acting fall short or are inadequate and also when there is a call to explore, or in Merleau-Ponty's term, to 'investigate'. Investigation for Merleau-Ponty is a speculative venture; it does not refer to systematic exploration or research but rather to a *new impulse*, in experience, close, I think, to Whitehead's notion of a proposition as a 'lure for feeling', which I will discuss below.

My concern then is to advocate what may be termed speculative pedagogies emerging from the ground of inheritance but which try to remain open to potentials for invention when experiencing the dehiscence of learning encounters – encounters when assimilated modes of practice (thinking, seeing, acting) are inadequate for providing a way forward. I will begin by trying to articulate the notion of speculation with reference to the works of Alfred North Whitehead, Isabelle Stengers and Martin Savransky. Then I will apply the outcomes of this articulation to the contexts of pedagogic work with the intention of arguing for a different approach to such work than those determinist and prescriptive models that dominate many educational settings today. This is not to argue for the removal of such models but for a relaxing of their totalizing power affecting pedagogic work and thus to consider the value of speculative modes of practice for opening up potentials for extending capacities of learning and teaching in all domains, which in turn expand the domains themselves and relations between them.

Speculation

In recent years the term 'speculation' has been associated with the practices of financial risk management that have produced unimagined hardship and suffering for many. It is also used generally as a term suggesting wild flights of fancy, 'mere speculation' (Bell 2017: 188). But in the philosophy of Alfred North Whitehead, this term, through his notion of a *proposition*, which will be discussed below, refers to a speculative thought or venture that, although destabilizing, may lead to a new more productive mode of thought or practice.

Vicky Bell (2017: 188) writes, 'Speculation involves an opening toward other presences heretofore ignored, un-consulted or otherwise rendered irrelevant to the scene at hand.' We might say that it arises as a consequence of an encounter that disturbs or challenges and which creates an uncertainty in how to proceed (what I call the gift of otherness). My experiences of responding to children's drawing practices involved some encounters when I struggled to grasp what was produced because I seemed to have no working framework of reference. I was puzzled. The affect of mystery was assuaged or passed over by reading the drawings through cliched responses without engaging in a critical examination of the epistemological or ontological foundations, the constraints, of my practice and understanding. A crucial question therefore is, how is it possible for others such as teachers to 'see' or acknowledge the sense and relevance of these drawings for those who produce them and thereby support and encourage their potential? On a more general level, how might we facilitate a movement from that which appears incomprehensible or strange from our habits of perception and knowledge to a scene of legitimacy and value? Such questions raise etho-ecological issues concerning the development of new modes of paying attention to those practices that 'object' to established orders of practice and, in paying attention, transform the pedagogical space itself. We might say, as mentioned earlier in Chapter 3, that pedagogical work produces particular ways of conceiving that may act inadvertently as a constraint upon practice by advocating values that marginalize some practices that 'do not fit' and so 'bully' such practice into its frame (Stengers 2005a: 1,000; Bell 2017: 187). A pedagogy of taking care would need to be vigilant towards the potential violence of approaches to learning practices and their potential futures that operate such constraints.

Can we conceive pedagogic work in terms of diverse and diverging futures, those concerning future processes of learning and teaching; futures that are not simply extensions or continuations of the present but open onto new vistas? Martin Savransky (2017: 25), in the context of social science research, advises us to take care here because what is being asked when thinking *for* the future invites a different set of constraints (to thinking *about* the future), 'ones that seek not to dispel, but to inhabit, the living paradox that the becoming of a future – one that cannot be reduced to the present – demands thought, it forces us to think, yet by definition is beyond the capture of what thinks it'. Inhabiting this paradox in pedagogic work therefore suggests that when we consider the futures of learning practices, we can't rely absolutely on established modes of practice and thought to guide our actions, nor can we be certain that the actions we do take will be effective. Our tendency is to rely on an *isomorphism between present and future* whereby the future becomes an extension of the present. In contrast can we therefore conceive speculation as a means of conjectural demand, a demand to think pragmatically and creatively beyond the present that holds us but recognizing that such thinking can never capture the future? In this speculative key pedagogic work becomes an adventure or an experiment, one whose success in constructing a future is never guaranteed. For Savransky, the speculative pragmatisms of William James and John Dewey that, in their respective ways, concern philosophies of experience, logics of inquiry and the function of concepts in experience offer a viable mode of inquiry into speculative practice – the demands and responsibilities for a pragmatics and efficacy of practice. Savransky (26) writes:

> Speculation can be conceived as a wager on an unfinished present, whose potential is that of cultivating thinking to lure experience – at once natural, social, cultural, political – to take the risk of opening up to its own becomings.

Regarding pedagogical practice, the notion of speculation tied to a pragmatics, ethics and efficacy of practice, a pragmatics of the suddenly possible (Buck-Morss 2013), has to be key to initiating and responding effectively to learning encounters with the intention of opening and extending the diverse futures of those involved. Such speculative practice is also key to what we might call a politics of pedagogical work, which I will address in a later chapter. Savransky (27) quotes Dewey (2008a: 10) from *Philosophy and Civilization* where the latter makes a plea

> for the casting off of the intellectual timidity which hampers the wings of imagination, a plea for speculative audacity, for more faith in ideas, sloughing off a cowardly reliance upon partial ideas to which we are wont to give the name of facts.

In the context of pedagogic practice and enquiry, the idea of speculative audacity coupled with a concern for efficacy is put to the test in those pedagogical situations/encounters whereby a teacher aims to make an incremental difference in terms of extending the capacities of practice, thought, feeling and values of learners. Such audacity involves taking a risk, not only testing out ideas but also making challenging propositions to a learner. In terms of learners themselves, such audacity relates equally to taking risks, trying things out in order to meet the challenges of learning encounters in order to extend their capacities and sensibilities for acting, making, thinking and feeling. It is worth briefly elaborating the notion of radical empiricism that underpins both James's and Dewey's speculative pragmatism. For both, experience is always 'incomplete'; it can never be fully formulated in thought or indeed in other forms of expression, but it consists of a dynamic process through which practices such as thinking or making can be articulated and also transformed. The unpredictable, contingent or unexpected flows of experiencing can put practice (thinking, making, seeing, listening, valuing) to the test. Experience, according to James, has 'ways of boiling over and making us correct our present formulas' (James 1907: 147). It is crucial to this idea of empiricism that 'experiencings' of thinking emerge from grounds of feeling, that is to say, 'thinkings' emerge from felt experience emerging in the flux of experiencing. This idea is central to Whitehead's process philosophy. It is not that thoughts emerge from a prior thinker but that thinking itself is an experiencing that constitutes the thinker but more fundamental than thought is feeling, or affect, which constitutes the ground for thought. Savransky (29) states that radical empiricism involves:

> an audacious production of a mode of thought that instead of forcing experience to stand still in order to claim cognitive victory over it, could partake in the flow of experience, contributing to the latter's mutating, surprising and novel drops.

The fact that the processual and complex relational nature of experiencing, its affective force, cannot be captured by thought is not to be understood in negative terms or in terms of lack or incapacity but should be conceived as characteristic of the shifting nature of experiencing, of which thought is a part, so that fallibility and error are part and parcel of thinking, and therefore, thinking itself has to be viewed as experimental (Savransky: 28). Perhaps we can view this point in the context of pedagogic work, a practice itself conceived as experimental rather than didactic, where its efficacy is to be found in how successfully it can engage with the immanence of a learner's experiencing mutations emerging through a learning encounter so that the learner 'takes his or her place'. Pedagogic work is therefore constituted as a *learning-with* rather than a *learning-from*. An ethics of pedagogy has to be able to respond effectively to the mutating processes of experiencing that constitute learning. Such an ethics would not rely upon established principles but would itself adopt a speculative key towards the futures of individual learning practices. This is echoed by Savransky (30) who argues that speculation is 'an experimental mode of thinking … that by cultivating its material in the mode of imaginative propositions seeks to create the possibility of an experimental faith in the transformation of experience'. In other words, speculative thinking in the form of imaginative propositions (propositioning) aims to construct a future whose efficacy and relevance will have to be negotiated. I will come to the notion of propositions as developed by Alfred North Whitehead shortly.

For Dewey in *The Quest for Certainty* (2008b: 63), speculative experimentation, when experiencing a problematic encounter, where there appears to be no established scripts that work, is characterized by three aspects:

> The first is the obvious one that all experimentation involves overt doing, the making of definite changes in the environment or in our relation to it. The

second is that experiment is not a random activity but is directed by ideas that have to meet the conditions set by the need of the problem inducing the active inquiry. The third and concluding feature, in which the other two receive their full measure of meaning, is that the outcome of the directed activity is the construction of a new empirical situation in which the objects are differently related to one another, and such that the consequences of directed operation form the objects that have the property of being known.

If we consider a learning encounter of a student or a teacher, these three aspects of experimentation seem apposite and interrelating in the experiencing of a problematic situation which 'makes felt an unfinished present that is incomplete and developing' (Savransky: 31). The *feeling* of an 'unfinished present' acts as a kind of lure into the future of a problematic or an encounter and, as Savransky argues, 'makes the future itself depend upon the propositions that may be constructed for it' (32). For a teacher, responding to the variety of learning practices and their different outcomes, their futures depend upon how the teacher is able to work from the 'facts', that is to say, the particular characteristics of each learner's practice and relations and what they make perceptible for the teacher in the form of propositions that construct a possible future, what James (1996: 65) calls, 'harnessing perceptual reality ... in order to drive it better to our ends'. This attention to the procedures and outcomes of a learner's practice in a learning encounter and the construction of propositions to develop efficacious possibilities are crucial components of pedagogic work in a speculative key. The primary function of a proposition for Whitehead is as a 'lure for feeling' that leads to an intensification and transformation in experience; it is to generate a difference that makes a difference in modes of practice such as painting, mathematics, physics or music, a difference that is a creative response to those impending problems or encounters that confront us. In his last book *Modes of Thought*, Whitehead (1938: 50) writes, 'A thought is a tremendous mode of excitement. Like a stone thrown into a pond it disturbs the whole surface of our being.' We might view the splash as the way a proposition functions (see Sehgal 2014).

The efficacy of a proposition concerns its ability, in Stengers's (2011c: 510) terms, to 'infect' the ways in which the world 'goes on', thus producing those different ways of relating that Dewey saw as the outcome of experimentation. In more practical terms, in a pedagogic context, this refers to the new relations and values with the world that emerge from a learning encounter. In other words, the *splash* and *infection* of a proposition may enable new relationalities to emerge and new potentialities, the construction of a new world, new universes of value. It constitutes an ongoing reciprocal tension in the here and now. Savransky

(2017: 35) also points to what we might call the importance of relevant efficacy, when he writes, 'The test of speculative thought is not performed against a world such thinking uncovers but against the one to which it has already contributed to composing by means of its own addition to it.' This crucial point is also echoed by Dewey (1929: 109) who states that the,

> test of ideas, of thinking generally, is found in the consequences of the acts to which the ideas lead, that is the new arrangement of things which are brought into existence.

These comments on the efficacy of speculative enquiry through the construction of relevant propositions that compose a future have important implications for pedagogic work and the futures of learners and teachers. From a teaching perspective, it is not a case of inventing propositions to reveal a prior reality for a learner to access but of propositions that help in composing a reality for a learner. This brings about, in Dewey's terms, 'new arrangements' or new modes and relationalities of acting, thinking, feeling and valuing that develop gradually, so that the process of infection, whereby the proposition and the reality it helps to compose for the learner begin to respond to each other. Of course, this is not a story of total success, pedagogical work is fallible, sometimes such speculative functioning fails to open up new ground for a learner and the teacher struggles to find a way forward. There is no promise that the future will agree to what is proposed to it. But if we scoff at the kind of speculative mode as discussed above being employed in functioning realities such as pedagogic practice, then we may be in danger of denying or betraying the future, for as Whitehead (1928: 76) wrote, 'to set limits to speculation is treason to the future'. When we consider carefully the nature of pedagogic work and those moments or situations when we feel the precariousness of our grasp, when confronted by a puzzling situation or when we meet something new, often something minor, then sometimes, but not always, we are able to construct speculative propositions that we propose to the future without guarantee but coupled with a faith that those contexts of precarity might respond to our proposals.

The Function of Speculative Practice

Didier Debaise (2017: 210) writes that the function of speculative philosophy is 'the intensification of an experience to its maximal point', in other words, to make experience, or perhaps better, experiencing, *matter*. In making this claim,

Debaise draws upon two key notions from Whitehead, first from, *Modes of Thought* (1938), in which Whitehead refers to that which gives experiencing a *sense of importance*, the value of something experienced, and then from *Process and Reality* (1928), he also cites the *relevance* of speculative propositions, as just mentioned, for the process of the constitution of our actual world.

Debaise (216) states:

> Importance is given. It belongs to all existence in so far as importance embodies a particular perspective on the universe that is expressed in each of the elements of the cosmological dimensions that it inherits. The ways of feeling, of connecting, of grasping, and the importance that these assume are constitutive of nature itself.

We are concerned with how something matters, and the intensification of this mattering, for someone in a particular time and place, to bring into clear articulation and the maximization of its value. The obligation of pedagogic practice grounded in the notions of importance and speculative inquiry is to foster and support the learner's experience to its maximum importance and potential. The origin of importance is not to be conceived in cognitive or even conscious terms but, more fundamentally, as a process of affect or feeling that arises in an encounter and which generates the construction of new ways of thinking and acting. Importance relates directly not only to a sense of what matters, to the experiencing of what matters, but also, perhaps more significantly, to the potentialities beyond this event of mattering in terms of how they might produce new sensibilities and capacities to act and think. We might say that the event of a learning encounter can produce a sense of mattering (importance) that generates a new perspective on the world that in turn produces new relationalities and values.

If pedagogic practice is to try to intensify how something matters for a learner and thereby bring about an extension of capacities, then how can this be achieved? How can we generate this 'feeling' of a sense of importance for a learner? Debaise (213) turns to Whitehead's use of propositions in *Process and Reality* whose aim, according to Debaise, is to precipitate an intensification of experience. He writes, 'The making of a proposition is, essentially, the luring of a multiplicity of feelings.' A lure in Whitehead's work does not refer to something that might trick or fool someone but to something that precipitates or incites a change that could lead to positive or negative outcomes. It might alter or interrupt an encounter so as to generate a possibility for new openings. Turning to an incident I mentioned earlier in the previous chapter involving a father and his son who were tackling some arithmetical problems such as 5 + 6 = ? The boy had no problems solving this arithmetical format, but when confronted with 7 + ? = 15 he was puzzled. He approached his father with his problem, and his father pointed to the '=' sign and proposed, 'This can mean 'the same as.''' With that said, the boy's demeanour was positively transformed, and he ran off to complete his work. We might argue that the boy was lured as a consequence of the affect of the proposition made by his father to take the imaginative leap into a new relationship with his work. Such situations are not uncommon, I believe, in the daily practices of pedagogic work when the deployment of propositions by teachers that lead to imaginative leaps by learners may often go unnoticed. Propositions in Whitehead's terms have the capacity to link actual feelings (of worry, anxiety, puzzlement, curiosity, excitement, etc.) to possible worlds. The obligation to develop *relevant* propositions for the constitution of worlds and experiencings inhabited by learners is crucial to pedagogic practice. This becomes more difficult, we might argue, when such practice has to operate from predetermined agendas and methodologies that impose particular pathways for teaching and learning. Thus, the efficacy of a proposition employed in a speculative pedagogy concerns its relevance to the ongoing construction and value of *how something matters* for the actual worlds of learners and their respective potentials. The task is made more complex when we ask, 'Is what we are offering learners going to be relevant for their future whose challenges we cannot know?'

In passing, I am not downplaying the importance of acquiring established forms of knowledge and skills and the iterations of inheritance but that speculative propositions are *inherent* to facilitating teaching and learning. The pedagogical task rests in 'making thought and other practices creative of the future' (Savransky 2017: 36). Working with learners involves enabling their experiences to face the challenge of their becoming and negotiating this becoming into existence with its surrounding milieu. The inherence of speculation in pedagogic work therefore demands a concern for multiplicity in the sense of developing an openness towards experiencings whose outcomes may be ignored or deemed irrelevant from within prescribed scenarios or methodologies of pedagogic practice. Vicky Bell (2017: 188) puts this point in a different way alluding to phases of disturbance or puzzlement in practice; the task is 'how to "sign" such events, how to inherit from them', coupled with the task of interrogating established practices in the light of that which disturbs or puzzles or simply appears a little different. Bell (189) refers to Stengers's paper on *The Cosmopolitical Proposal* (2005a) where Stengers discusses scientists involved in the practice of experimenting upon animals. Bell (189) comments that if such scientists were

> to be exposed, to be obliged to hesitate and to attempt to decide "in the presence of" those that may turn out to be the victims of that decision, [this would likely] put at risk the ethos of one's way of being. It [would] allow the truths by which one lives to be suspended.

Perhaps we might transfer this dilemma across to educational practices where the decision made by government to 'educate' children and students in a particular way is often not taken with the full 'presence and difference' of those to be educated in mind. If such differences were to be acknowledged, then a change in policy, which is in fact not negotiable, would follow. The current policy in England of teaching reading only through the technique of synthetic phonics is an illustration of a uniform approach that may exclude particular presences and differences that we might inherit and which would benefit from other teaching strategies.

It is in the interstices, gap or phase of hesitation when confronted by something different that Whitehead's notion of propositions may intervene in order to provoke thought to slow down and invent, to quote Judith Butler, 'scenes of recognition', relevance and obligation for 'presences that were heretofore ignored' (Bell: 188). Such invention suggests that we may need to try to develop new modes of paying attention beyond the boundaries of established practice to facilitate 'other becomings', other ways of experiencing, thinking and acting, other sense of importance. This point introduces the issues of politics and ethics in pedagogic practice, and we can turn to Isabelle Stengers's idea of a cosmopolitical proposal to develop such issues relevant for pedagogic work.

Speculation, Ethics, Politics and Cosmopolitics

What might an ethics and a politics that attempt to prevent 'ignored presences', those that exist in the dark, look like – an ethics and politics that might be mutable in order to pass beyond existing frameworks and so pay attention to that which is different, to the gift of otherness, and in doing so remain open to contesting those narratives and structures that may constrain? This would be an ethics and politics that focus not only upon the 'here and now', the haecceities of becoming, but also upon its proposing and creating a future to come into existence. Looking awry, Maurice Blanchot (1989) writes enigmatically about otherness and its gift:

> In the night, everything has disappeared. This is the first night. Here absence approaches – silence, repose, night. ... But when everything has disappeared in the night, 'everything has disappeared' appears. This is the *other* night. (163)

How might we develop a productive or convivial relation to this 'other night' that appears beyond the fading of the day when everything has disappeared into the night – an otherness, a gift, that is already present? Isabelle Stengers (2004: 1) writes:

> How can I present a proposal intended not to say what is, or what ought to be, but to provoke thought; (*the provocation of otherness*) one that requires no other verification than the way in which it is able to 'slow down' reasoning and create an opportunity to arouse a slightly different (*other*) awareness of the problems and situations mobilizing us? (*my insertions*)

She continues:

> The 'cosmopolitical' proposal, as I intend to characterize it, is not designed for generalists; it has meaning *only in concrete situations where practitioners operate* ... practitioners who have learned to shrug their shoulders at the claims of generalizing theoreticians that define them as subordinates charged with the task of 'applying' a theory or that capture their practice as an illustration of a theory. (my emphasis)

Cosmopolitics is not connected to the Kantian renewal of the ancient theme of cosmopolitism that advocates a 'worldwide civil society, in accordance with citizens' rights' so that one is a citizen of the cosmos rather than a particular state or religion. Stengers's notion of cosmopolitics does not advocate a common civil world but interrupts this notion of the common or consensus, to create a space for hesitation in order to question values that are taken for granted.

I think it is important to bear in mind that the term 'proposal' should be read in the sense given to the notion of proposition by Whitehead, as a 'lure for feeling' that may incite a change, good or bad, something, as Debaise (2017: 81–2) writes, that might 'modify the course of an event, and make it go in a new direction'. To shed more insight into the cosmopolitical proposal's application and relevance to the 'concrete situations where practitioners operate', Stengers recalls a literary figure, turned into a conceptual character by Deleuze and Guattari in their last book, *What Is Philosophy?* This is the character of the 'idiot', which I extend to include the notion of an idiotic event. We might call such an event an event of otherness. In ancient Greek, the idiot is the one who does not speak the Greek language and is therefore excluded from 'civilized community'. Deleuze and Guattari, borrowing the term from Dostoyevsky, describe the idiot as a conceptual character who slows everyone else down and resists convention and consensual practices. The idiot does this not because he thinks normal practices, ways of thinking and valuing are wrong but because he thinks (or perhaps senses) there is something more important, but he does not know what this is (an emerging presence?). He therefore acts as a 'gap', an interstice, a questioning presence that 'asks' us to slow down and question our assumptions, our ways of knowing, particularly in situations in which we find ourselves perplexed or disturbed. An idiotic event is one that interrupts normal procedures and may, therefore, open up directions for action and thought. For Stengers, the cosmopolitical proposal can be viewed as 'idiotic' in the sense that it addresses those who have perhaps been able to slow down and 'shrug their shoulders' at the assumed authority of knowledge and theory but who have not as yet been able to provide alternative resolutions yet recognize the need to compose them, to engage in speculative enquiry. *Cosmos* in the term 'cosmopolitical' does not refer to our universe in all its complexity as conceived in different cultures and traditions but to the 'unknown constituted by multiple divergent worlds and to the articulation of which they could eventually be capable' (Stengers 2004: 3). It is therefore conceived as an emergent individuating process.

A politics and ethics that might try to embrace such as yet unknown capabilities cannot begin from a position of transcendence but more from a feeling of wary uncertainty, of not knowing how to proceed. It asks how we might inherit from those as yet unknown presences and events we experience, which disturb our modes of thought and practice that try to 'pull' us back into their normalcy.

Referring back to Blanchot, the notion that when 'everything has disappeared', an 'otherness of disappearance' appears seems to resonate with the conceptual notion of the *idiot* or the idiotic event. This constitutes an interruption that 'dis-appears' established values and frameworks that hold us, or more precisely, slows them down, as the dark of night covers the light of day – that behind the light of knowledge lies a dark presence, an otherness whose effect can disturb and unsettle. The idiot or idiotic event effects a 'dis-appearance' of 'reality' to invoke an 'other' reality, one whose *insistence* demands that we try to recompose our modes of practice in the here and now, which is the aim of speculative enquiry. How might we conceive ethics and politics in the 'uncertain' process of the recomposing of the here and now? That is to say, an ethics and politics that confer upon the specificity of a situation or a presence of the power to make us think, not to impose the force of established frameworks of thought to explain a situation.

For Stengers, the insistence of unknown presences and the fact that we do not know with certainty how to proceed in their presence call us to speculate, to invent new modes of thought and action, and this constitutes her cosmopolitical proposal. It is a call for an etho-ecological approach to the presence of divergent worlds and to their as yet unknown potentials. *Ethos* refers to a being's way of behaving, whilst *oikos* refers to the habitat of a being and how it either supports or opposes the requirements of an ethos or allows the ethos to take risks. How might a teacher respond in an *oikos* that demands that they think 'in the presence of' divergent *ethea* in a pedagogical situation? Can a teacher remain open to the different etho-ecologies that compose each student? Might a pedagogical site require the 'presence of the idiot' to prevent the totalizing effect of established modes of practice that define learning and teaching through the prescription of standards or competencies?

Vikki Bell (2017: 188) comments on the importance of speculation when faced with difference that disturbs, when we are not sure how to proceed.

> Among the first things to insist upon in relation to discussions of speculation, therefore, is the necessity that it be accompanied by a concern for multiplicity, where multiplicity becomes the prompt and the justification that prevents the 'mere' forever accompanying the practice. In order to be something more than 'mere speculation', from which nothing follows, speculation involves an opening toward other presences heretofore ignored, un-consulted or otherwise rendered irrelevant to the scene in hand. It is not the ruminative practice that takes place in contemplative comfort, but that which follows an interruption and a consequent re-orientation. For Isabelle Stengers, that re-orientation results when self-assurance falters. When actors are faced with an indeterminacy concerning how to proceed following an intervention, be that a shout, a murmur or a newly imposed constraint, they are forced to consider how to 'sign' that event, how to *inherit* from it. For this reason – that there is a hesitation that will not be resolved through the presentation of argument – the question of the cosmopolitical is precisely 'speculative'. (Stengers 2011b: 356)

A cosmopolitical ecology would therefore be concerned with the immanence of the emergence of difference rather than imposing transcendent criteria in its attempt to respond to the situated specificity of events. It is the power of such situations, such events, to induce thought that might produce 'other' kinds of questions that lead to transformation. It means giving voice to those who do not fit, whose modes of practice/thought appear aberrant; it means being open to idiotic events and then trying to 'artfully' invent commensurate ways of functioning. For Stengers (2004: 11), the cosmopolitical question asks:

> How, by which artifacts, which procedures can we slow down political ecology, bestow efficacy upon the murmurings of the idiot, the 'there is something more important'. Which is so easy to forget because it cannot be 'taken into account', because the idiot neither objects nor proposes anything that 'counts'.

The cosmopolitical proposal (remember a proposition is a lure for feeling) is thus one that is 'chaotic' in that it disturbs our foundations by a presence; we might say a 'splash' that invokes an etho-ecological question, demanding a new etho-ecological signification beyond our established orders, and recomposes the political and ethical ecology. It requires developing sensibilities to presences and their potentialities that as yet have been marginalized or ignored but, when heard, may constitute a difference that 'make a difference'. Here politics and ethics cannot work from or impose established parameters, the point being, so well put by Stengers (11), that we have to see politics and ethics in terms of an art and, 'an art has no ground to demand compliance from what it deals with … it has to create the manners that allow it to deal with what it has to deal with'. The task then is to try to artefactualize in response to the force of an encounter whose affect makes thought think. Cosmos, as meant by Stengers, and cited earlier, refers to an 'unknown constituted by multiple, divergent worlds, and to the articulations of which they could eventually be capable'. This unknown indicates that *cosmos* prevents any ethico-political or aesthetic closure.

The cosmopolitical perspective attempts to accommodate all presences without subjection to 'general interests' or transcendent criteria. Here ethics and politics are always emergent. The immanence of emergence has to be 'artfully created'. How do we artfully gather around the situated specificity of events of learning? This requests that in pedagogic work we pay attention to the situated specificities of events of learning/teaching, the etho-ecologies of events of learning and teaching, but also that we slow down and take time to artfully invent the manners and propositions that allow teachers and learners to deal with what they have to deal with – to develop sensibilities to potentialities that may be present but as yet have no voice as well as propositions that will facilitate and extend capacities of understanding.

Vikki Bell (2017) comments on Stengers's counsel to slow down:

> Rather than imposing 'cosmopolitics' as a solution, Stengers offers her speculative notion in order to propose attending differently in order to allow different perceptions and thus different possibilities. As such, she wishes that it be understood as both pragmatic, insofar as it is concerned with what is possible, and as a tale that is full of wonder. Indeed, Stengers suggests that cosmopolitics requires the creation of *obstacles that allow wonder*. Such obstacles presumably promote a requisite interruption, the slowing down Stengers insists is needed in order that we wonder about conditions that may arrive from elsewhere, the instigators of which she suggests we will not know before they put 'us' at risk. (193; italics in original)

The notion of artfulness (see Manning 2016) encapsulated within the term 'artfully create' introduces a speculative creative practice to pedagogic work that may enable a politics, ethics and aesthetics of worlding, 'concerned with the processes through which a world is being brought into existence' (Blaser 2016). Such practice lies in stark contrast to the notion of politics, ethics and aesthetics that assumes an already-existing world (a common world) whose codes and values predetermine those who are included and by implication, excluded, as well as defining acceptable differences. A speculative creative approach to pedagogic work posits the possibility of an 'uncommon world' or 'uncommon worlding' whereby difference and divergence need to be foregrounded – difference, that, in the words of Eduardo Viveiros de Castro (2004), is approached through a process of 'controlled equivocation' that does not anticipate working towards a common referent or ground but respects the equivocation of different worldings. The work of Viveiros de Castro will be discussed in Chapter 7. This links with what Stengers refers to in her notion of cosmos as the 'unknown constituted by multiple diverging worlds and the articulation[s]' that may be possible.

Artfulness and Speculation

The process of artfulness as discussed by Erin Manning (2016: 46), in contrast to the art object, refers to the *manner* of practice, to its ways of becoming that emerge from an experiencing germ, understood as a relational event. This seems close to Simondon's idea of information as a structuring germ that precipitates individuation. Manner, for Manning, is allied to the notions of intuition and concern, referring to 'the relational movement through which the present begins to co-exist with its futurity, with the quality or manner of the not-yet that lurks at the edges of experience' (47). Intuition refers to a fold or an incipient moment of experiencing that precipitates or agitates a lure towards that-which-is-not-yet, at the edge of experiencing, whilst concern refers to the forming of a mode of expression sympathetic to the intuiting moment and its potential for becoming.

Artfulness can be viewed as a speculative process described above by Savransky as a 'wager on an unfinished present whose potential is that of cultivating experience ... to take the risk of opening up to its own becomings'. In pedagogic work this includes the practice of artfully inventing manners that allow teachers and learners to cultivate experiencing that may lead to new or modified ecologies of practice. Artfulness gives expression to that 'not-yet that lurks at the edge of experience', a process that opens up inherent potentialities that may transform current ecologies of practice. For Whitehead (1978: 105–6), 'life lurks in the interstices', suggesting the possibilities of new forms of coherence yet to be constructed; we might say awaiting new forms of expression and subsequent experiencing. Manning (59) writes, 'Artfulness emerges most actively in the interstices where the world has not yet settled into subjects and objects.' Artfulness is therefore concerned not with that which already exists in terms of objects, concepts, relations, practices and ecologies but with ways of becoming emerging from the edges of experiencing that may extend capacities to act or think into new cartographies of being. In the context of this chapter, the notion of artfulness is allied closely to Whitehead's ideas on speculative inquiry as described in a key statement from *Process and Reality* where he comments on the 'true method of discovery':

> The true method of discovery is like the flight of an aeroplane. It starts from the ground of particular observation; it makes a flight in the thin air of imaginative generalization; and it again lands for renewed observation rendered acute by rational interpretation. (1978: 5)

This statement does not simply refer to a requirement for empirical observation followed by a process of imaginative construction (speculative flight) which is then confirmed or denied by a return to reality. It implies that when we leave the reality of practice or thought that constitutes the ground for the imaginative flight and then return, the *efficacy* of the flight, our speculation or proposition, is not addressed or evaluated according to the world from which we departed but to a world-in-the-making so that on return, our understanding and the world will have been changed. This is the test of speculative inquiry. A pedagogical speculation will therefore not return to the same ground from which it 'took off' but, if successful, will contribute to the artful construction of a new pedagogical reality and its relations, objects and subjectivities that did not exist before.

The leaps that we take in speculative inquiry, for example, in pedagogic work, do not mean that we transcend such work. Stengers, following Whitehead, encourages us not only to extract ourselves from established grooves of thought and action when these prove to be inadequate or limiting but also to have faith in the very ground from which we leap. Taking a leap, forming a proposition, by a teacher in pedagogic work is not a matter of formulating a choice of what to do or to be *in* a particular situation, but it is *a choice for the evolving situation* to which the leap is a matter and manner of contributing. It is not only a case of such choices contributing to a world in the making but of realizing that the very assemblages that constitute a world, in this case, teachers, learners, pedagogical 'objects', knowledge, skills and values, are themselves indeterminate, that is to say, always 'incomplete', and whose ongoing processes of individuation depend upon the teacher's faith and risks to speculate and engage with them. Stengers puts it like this:

> We can and we may, as it were, jump with both feet off the ground into or towards a world of which we trust the other parts to meet our jump and only so can the making of a perfected world of pluralistic pattern take place. Jumping off the ground … transmutes the question of choice. It is no longer a worldly choice – what should one choose to be or to do in this world? – but a choice for the world to which it is a matter of contributing. This choice doesn't only imply a world in the making; it affirms a world whose components are themselves indeterminate, whose 'perfectibility' depends on the jumper's trust that he may connect with 'other parts' that may become an ingredient in its fabric. (Stengers 2009b: 11)

The speculative leaps that we take will be justified (or not), not according to our 'return' but by a recomposing of a world, by the creation of new ways of thinking and acting, through new relations within an emergent pluriverse to which we have contributed.

I will conclude this chapter on speculative pedagogy with a long quotation from Didier Debaise (2017: 216–17). His focus is upon the function of speculative philosophy, but the text I have chosen has deep resonances with what I have called speculative pedagogy. I have inserted italicized parentheses and underlinings to the text, in order to draw attention to this resonance.

> It is now possible to return to my initial definition of the function of speculative philosophy (*pedagogy*) the <u>intensification of an experience to its maximal point</u>. Importance is given. It belongs to all existence in so far as importance embodies

a particular perspective on the universe that is expressed in each of the elements of the cosmological dimensions that it inherits. The ways of feeling, of connecting, of grasping, and the importance that these assume, are constitutive of nature itself. There are not primary qualities on one side and secondary qualities on the other. Rather, <u>there are the specific articulations of each existent that are the affirmations of what matters here and now</u>. But even if importance is everywhere, it is nevertheless up to speculative philosophy (*pedagogy*) to intensify it (*a learner's practice*), to give importance (*as far as is possible*) to all the dimensions that it requires. In a word, <u>to establish its value.</u> Even if this question has been posed in terms of a historical event, it is clearly not limited to the realm of history and its legacies, as it concerns our contemporary experience and the possibilities that animate it. The duty of speculative philosophy (*pedagogy*) is to devise some tools that allow to increase all aspects of (*a learner's*) experience (physical, biological, technical or social) to their maximal importance. This is why speculative philosophy (*pedagogy*) is inherently a moral and political activity whose maxim could be: 'our action is moral if we have thereby safeguarded the importance of (*a learner's*) experience so far as it depends on that concrete instance (<u>what matters here and now</u>) in the (*learner's*) world's history'. (Whitehead 1938: 20)

I could not summarize as eloquently or as succinctly these crucial points made by Debaise as they apply directly, from the perspective I am taking, to pedagogic practice as manifested in a pedagogy of taking care. The pedagogical task is to give due attention to the *importance* of each learner's experience and its particular perspective in a learning encounter, to establish its value for a learner, how it matters. This task thus requires pedagogical tools that will increase and expand the learner's experience in relation to the immanence of its evolving importance.

6

The Scandal of the Truth of Art and Its Implications for Art in Education

Part One

Introduction

This chapter is composed of two parts. Part One considers what I call the scandal of the truth of art, taking the notion of scandal from Foucault. Part Two looks at the implications of this scandal for art in education. In a previous book chapter (Atkinson 2018b: 3–16), I employed the term 'poietic materialism' to consider the nature of the dynamic force of art. The early Greeks employed the word *poiesis* to denote a process of appearing, a coming into presence, a movement from non-being to being, from concealment to full view. It denotes a notion of truth as unveiling (*alethia*), and its materiality is immanent and processual in contrast to the production of a prior will or idea. The force of art therefore in terms of its poietic materiality is not directly concerned with an object, painting, film, performance or installation but with its *poietic event* and what this might precipitate in terms of its potential for invention or transformation: the invention of new worlds, new subjectivations, new or modified modes of practice and value. Implicit to the poietic force of the event of art is not only its affective power to generate new sensibilities but also forcing thought to think. The *vital* significance of the force of art and its poietic materiality lies therefore in its encounter.

David Burrows and Simon O'Sullivan (2019) in their collaboration, *Fictioning*, employ the term *mythopoesis* to refer to the production 'of worlds, people and communities to come, often drawing upon residual and emergent cultures' (1). They investigate the mythopoetic power of art and literary practices to generate such production and in doing so employ a variety of conceptual tools, such as

Deleuze and Guattari's concept of the 'war machine' and Burrough's use of the 'cut-up' to do so.

In this chapter the force of art will be regarded from the notion of the scandal of art, a term that was introduced in Chapter 2, which I draw from Foucault's final lectures at the College de France titled *The Courage of the Truth* (CT), when he discussed the scandal of the truth in Cynic practices and which he argues characterizes an important aspect of art practice since the nineteenth century. I quote at length from these final lectures. Foucault states:

> After religious movements, throughout the Middle Ages and over a long period, [after] political practice since the nineteenth century, I think there was a third great medium of Cynicism in European culture, or of the theme of the mode of life as scandal of the truth. We would find it in art. (Foucault 2011, CT: 186)
>
> But I think it is especially in modern art that the question of Cynicism becomes particularly important. That modern art was, and still is for us the vehicle of the Cynic mode of being, of the principle of connecting style of life and manifestation of the truth, came about in two ways. (CT: 187)

Foucault suggests that the first way rests on two principles:

> First: art is capable of giving a form to existence which breaks with every other form, a form which is that of the true life. The other principle is that, if the artistic life does in fact have the form of the true life, then this in turn guarantees that every work which takes root in and starts from this life truly does belong to the dynasty and domain of art. So I think that this idea of the artistic life as the condition of the work of art, as authenticating the work of art, as work of art itself, is a way of taking up again, in a different light, from a different angle, and with a different form of course, that Cynic principle of life as manifestation of a scandalous break by which the truth becomes clear, manifests itself, and becomes concrete. (CT: 187–8)

Secondly, Foucault suggests:

> There is another reason why art has been the vehicle of Cynicism in the modern world. This is the idea that art itself, whether it is literature, painting, or music, must establish a relation to reality which is no longer one of ornamentation, or imitation, but one of laying bare, exposure, stripping, excavation, and violent reduction of existence to its basics. This practice of art as laying existence bare and reducing it to its basics stands out in an increasingly noticeable way from the mid-nineteenth century. Art (Baudelaire, Flaubert, Manet) is constituted as

the site of the irruption of what is underneath, below, of what in a culture has no right, or at least no possibility of expression. (CT: 188)

As the 'site of the irruption of what is underneath', as that which 'has no right or possibility of expression', art can be thought of as a site of otherness and as a gift of otherness.

These ideas of art as a practice that operates a scandalous break through which a truth becomes clear and simultaneously makes visible 'what has no right' to expression is thus summed up:

> And art thereby establishes a polemical relationship of reduction, refusal, and aggression to culture, social norms, values, and aesthetic canons. This is what makes modern art since the nineteenth century the endless movement by which every rule laid down, deduced, induced, or inferred from preceding actions is rejected and refused by the following action. In every form of art there is a sort of permanent Cynicism towards all established art. (CT: 188)
>
> Modern art has what could be called an essentially anti-cultural function. The consensus of culture has to be opposed by the courage of art in its barbaric (*scandalous*) truth. Modern art is Cynicism in culture; the cynicism of culture turned against itself. And if this is not just in art, in the modern world, in our world, it is especially in art that the most intense forms of a truth-telling with the (*scandalous*) courage to take the risk of offending are concentrated. (CT: 188–9; my emphases)

Foucault's reference to modern art as 'Cynicism in culture', opposing consensus, social norms and values, routines and established traditions, denotes the courage of art, the scandal of art, to risk exposing forms of difference that are ignored or marginalized. It is a practice that challenges traditions and established values and in political matters making visible what Ranciere called 'wrongs' that lead to ethical and political revaluations which call forth a new people and new collectives – new transindividual subjectivities. Equally, beyond such political or ethical issues, art is a site of invention that opens up new sensibilities, new coordinates for becoming.

In this chapter, therefore, I will explore art practice from this perspective of scandal, exposure and potential before considering some implications of this disruptive and transformative function of art practice for art in education.

Turning briefly to the psychoanalytic work of Jacques Lacan, particularly his Seminar XXIII titled *Le Sinthome*, we might say that the scandal of art arises from a lack or perhaps a deficiency in the Other, the existing symbolic order, its values and its desires; it involves an exiting, a breaking free from established practices and creating new forms of expression that Lacan calls 'sinthomes'. In their chapter, 'Lacan's Analytical Goal: "Le Sinthome" or the Feminine Way', Verhaeghe and Declercq (2002: 15) tell us:

> At the end of the *Encore* seminar, Lacan had already evoked this idea – the creation of a new signifier – *(a sinthome)* in talking about poetry. A new knowledge can be created only at the place of the lack of the Other. As long as one stays under the umbrella of the Other, there is no new knowledge possible. (my bracket)

Referencing the work of James Joyce that influenced Lacan, Verhaeghe and Declercq (16) continue:

> The seminar on Joyce demonstrates that it is possible for a *sinthome* to take the role of the signifier of the Name-of-the-Father. Lacan invites everyone to follow Joyce's example and to create an own *sinthome* at the place of the lack of the Other; the aim of this creative act is to be able to function without the signifier of the Name-of-the-Father, that is, the Other.

The sinthome, like an art practice, is highly individual, heterogeneous, not something whose 'Real' can be directly transmitted to others but whose affective force may lead to new imaginary/symbolic productions, transindividual subjectivities, that rupture established orders and practices. The sinthome can thus function in a similar way to Simondon's structuring germ, as a body or event emerging in the place of the lack of the Other; it reforms relations between the Real, imaginary and symbolic, the established orders, and creates a new expressive form.

Readymade-making

An important strategy of modern/contemporary art is the 'readymade', first introduced, we might say scandalously, by Marcel Duchamp. This strategy can be regarded as the source of the conceptual turn in contemporary art. For Duchamp, it is the *conceptual decision* 'this is art' that, as it were, precedes, and the readymade object is therefore merely information (Duchamp 1973: 32). The decision is free from the forming and manipulating of any art medium and from aesthetic conditions; it is, as Stephen Zepke (2017: 761) puts it, the production of "grey matter" and of the concept of art that it instantiated'. However, in contrast to Duchamp's conceptual grounding of art, Deleuze and

Guattari in *A Thousand Plateaus* (1988: 345–9) argue that rather than being simply information that manifests an initial conceptual decision, the readymade is both material and aesthetic and can be conceived as an event of non-conceptual thought – thought that is composed of affective forces and material sensations. The readymade *event* can generate what Guattari (2013: 206) calls a 'problematic affect' that may in turn generate a complex of sensible affects of becoming. Zepke (762) writes:

> Here we have the beginning of a genealogy of contemporary artistic practice that incorporates the readymade as its foundational moment, but rather than being post-conceptual involves, instead, producing material sensations through a sublime thought.

Zepke points out that the idea of the readymade is not only applicable to objects but also to the body or other entities. Before commenting upon particular artists and their work, Zepke's writing on the readymade is helpful to consider in that I think his interrogation of this particular strategy of art practice extends and explores what Foucault termed the courage and scandal of art and its 'permanent Cynicism'. We might argue, following Foucault (2011: 188), that the readymade constitutes 'the site of the irruption of what is underneath, below, of what in a culture has no right, or at least no possibility of expression'. Its affective force therefore is a crucial aspect of it functioning.

Guattari (1996a: 206, 209) argues that Duchamp's *Bottle Rack* (2013) produces a 'problematic effect', what we might call a scandalous affect, that generates a chaotic mixture of components (an eruption of nonsense) whereby established orders of understanding are disturbed and other unpredicted possibilities may emerge and crystalize. Zepke (2017: 762) puts it like this, 'The readymade is first a sublime moment dislocating experience from its conceptual conditions and allowing it to receive the aleatory forces of the event.' This disruption, which in Simondon's terminology would constitute a transductive disparation, constitutes the expressive vectoral force of art, in terms of its actualities and virtualities. Such force in relation to the readymade, or indeed other forms of practice, produces an 'aesthetic rupture' (762) of established modes of practice which becomes actualized in new individuations of practice and, in Simondon's terminology, the possibility for new transindividual sensibilities.

The readymade, rather than being viewed as the outcome of a conceptual decision, generates an excess of affect that escapes the limits of conceptual understanding; it generates a sublime event that, as Zepke (753) puts it, tears 'apart the veil of representation in an explosion of the real'. In disrupting representational orders, the affective force of the readymade may open up new possibilities and sensibilities. Zepke (754) writes:

> Art, then, can cause explosions that destroy the structure imposed upon perception by the understanding (i.e., conceptually organized cognition), and its representational image of thought (most significantly, recognition). This would be art's politics, to explode the representational clichés that dominate our thought and sight, and to offer alternatives to the underlying cognitive structure that supports this.

Thought here is not just a product of mind but also involves a virtual mind–body entanglement that can be deterritorialized through contact with other bodies and forces of affect.

The problem with conceptual art according to Deleuze and Guattari is that it focuses upon *information* rather than the dynamic, intensive and transductive forces of affect (see Deleuze and Guattari 1994: 198). The consequence of this emphasis on the concept and information is, as Zepke (760) points out, that 'contemporary art therefore risks becoming the mere "propagation of information"' in an era when, as Deleuze says, 'information is exactly the system of control' that the force of art would want to subvert (Deleuze 2006: 320–1). In a more forceful statement condemning this emphasis upon information, Deleuze writes, 'A work of art has nothing to do with communication. A work of art does not contain the least bit of information' (Deleuze 2006: 322).

It is the force of art, in this case the force of the readymade, that constitutes its power of political resistance through ethico-aesthetic affects, through the force of transductive disparation, as when an object's or body's normal spatio-temporal functioning is disrupted so as to function 'otherwise'. This ontological disruption (by the gift of the other) is the catalyst for affective forces that may generate new or modified existential territories and transindividual sensibilities. This force of affect constitutes, as Zepke (2011: 36), after Deleuze and Guattari, argues, a war machine of a politics of sensation.

In passing, but an important point to which I will return, we might argue that the entire apparatus of assessment of art in education is based upon a 'representational image of thought', that is to say, upon a hylomorphic process in which conceptual devices such as assessment criteria, competences or standards are employed as conceptual tools to assess the art practices of children and students. Little emphasis is placed upon the affective or the sensible force of art practice in this domain; how can you assess affect or sensibilities that exist ontologically beyond such conceptual frameworks? This question raises the more general issue of the production of pedagogized subjectivities and the homogenization of subjectivity by state and corporate apparatuses that control and regulate pedagogic work according to the forces of capital. It points to the fact that these educational conceptual frameworks become complicit with what Deleuze called the control society.

Following Zepke (36), we might enquire into which art practices utilize 'affectual readymades' and act as war machines of sensation. In the following descriptions of artist practices, we might alter the notion of the readymade to 'readymade-making' which captures more a sense of ongoing mutation and production. One artist's work that Zepke refers to is the early performance practice by the black American woman Adrian Piper titled *Catalyst IV* (1970). In this work the body acts as a readymade-making. Piper travelled on public transport with a bath towel stuffed into her mouth. In an interview in 1972 with Lucy Lippard, Piper states:

> I dressed very conservatively but stuffed a large red bath towel in the side of my mouth until my cheeks bulged to about twice their normal size, letting the rest of it hang down my front, and riding the bus, subway, and Empire State Building elevator. (76)

Piper also performed this event with a white hand towel stuffed into her mouth. The practice can be read against the background of racism, social stereotyping, social minorities and the pervasive force of whiteness. Her intention was to exit the gallery or institution in order to 'let art lurk in the midst of things' (1996a: 37). As Zepke (2011: 41) states, 'Piper's readymade is "bio-aesthetic"' involving her body and its social milieu, but her actions and the subsequent affects attempt to disturb by making an intervention of radical difference that questions and disrupts 'normality' and existing social conditions. Her practice cajoles us to consider 'normal' social conditions that are in effect forms of social constraint or regulation that can be questioned. For example, the 'hidden persuaders' and the generation of desire by contemporary capitalism grounded upon repressive and exploitative work conditions for many, 'how capitalism works on us and through us' (1996b: 27), the hidden, as well as overt faces and practices of racism and other forms of victimization.

The act of radical otherness manifested in her work exits her body not only from the social dispositifs that have produced it but also, significantly, from the institutions of art that would remove her practice from its life world and view it as an artificial 'performance'. For Piper for her practice to have its radical impact on those encountering it, they must not be previously informed that 'this is art'.

This would dilute the radicality of the practice – its force of affect that might engender new sensibilities. Piper (in Lippard and Piper 1972) tells us:

> One thing I don't do is say: 'I'm doing a piece', because somehow that puts me back into the situation I am trying to avoid. It immediately establishes an audience separation – 'Now we will perform' – that destroys the whole thing. As soon as you say, this is a piece, or an experiment, or guerrilla theatre – that makes everything all right, just as set-up and expected as if you were sitting in front of a stage. The audience situation and the whole art context makes it impossible to do anything. (78)

Piper's body, as readymade-making, according to Zepke (2011: 43):

> brings into existence an aesthetic paradigm in which the political efficacy of art is achieved in those humble and yet singular events that invent new possibilities for life. In the readymade life becomes a work of art.

We might think of Piper's radical act as breaking free from the symbolic and its desire in order to create new or alternative imaginary worlds, an act that not only exposes or problematizes current socio-political, economic and moral frameworks of what Deleuze calls 'societies of control' but also opens up potentials for different subjectivations, social collectives and their political and ethical relations.

A central question of the work performed by Tehching Hseih is 'how is art different from life?' jan jagodinski (2019, 2020) explores his strangely compelling but difficult-to-comprehend durational performances in which the artist's body functions as a mutating readymade-making in which life and art become indissoluble. In contrast to seminal figures of performance practices, jagodinski (2020: 8, draft provided by author) argues:

> Hsieh presents an anti-psychological and anti-subjective mode, quite different from the usual autobiographical subjective staging of performance artists such as Allan Kaprow, Chris Burden, Vito Acconci, and Marina Abramović, ... In the cases of these artists, 'art as life' prevailed as happenings and performances of all kinds were framed under the institution of art despite attempts to go beyond gallery and museum walls by staging performances in studios.

Hseih completed five durational performances, each lasting one year between September 1978 and July 1986. Some of these have resonance with ancient Cynic practices discussed in Chapter 2, an ascetic life free from all possessions and material goods except for food and drink and a rejection of social conventions, manners and behaviour. This relates particularly to Hseih's first one-year performance when he was locked in a cage constructed in his loft except, unlike the Cynics, he had no one to communicate with, nothing to read and nothing to do except exist and think. This ordeal was documented each day by making marks on a wall much like a prisoner in their cell and taking a photograph of themselves. An assistant brought him food and disposed his waste. This is a disturbing performance and not easy to fully comprehend. It raises issues of identity and how this might be constructed and normalized. It is as though Hseih existed outside the normal symbolic orders that structure and regulate life and that provide identity. He had to give his cage a structure, so the corner of his cage where his bed was placed became 'home' and the other corners as 'outside' (jagodinski 2019: 63). The performance also points towards political incarceration and the deprivation of human contact.

His second performance consisted of punching a time clock, similar to entering and leaving work in earlier epochs, but he did this every hour twenty-four hours a day for a year. This was verified by an observer. Hseih also shaved his head at the beginning and then let his hair grow so that every time he punched the time clock, a movie camera took a single frame. The completed film recorded the whole year performance in around six minutes.

In his third performance, Hseih travelled on foot around the streets, alleyways and other spaces of Lower Manhattan. He remained outside for the entire year, sleeping rough. He maintained contact with friends either by pay phone or meetings in the streets. His roamings were recorded on a map that documented where he slept or ate. There is some resonance again with Cynic practice in the sense that Hseih abandoned the material comforts of a home and in doing so raised the notion of 'home', its symbolic as well as its cultural and material significance. What does it mean to be without a home; how does this affect our identity and security? There are obvious resonances here with the plight of refugees, the massive exodus of people from Syria, Africa, Myanmar, South America and elsewhere who have left their homes, often by force or by other threats to life, and in doing so, lose their material and psychological sense of security.

In the fourth performance called *Art/Life*, Hseih explores the nature of human relations and, in particular for me, the affect of otherness – not only how it might be viewed as a gift but also how it can be exploited, ignored or persecuted. Hseih worked with Linda Montano; they did not know each other before the performance. They were tied together for a year by an eight-feet rope but tried to avoid touching so as to maintain their own space. The performance was documented by taking photographs and audiotapes. It raises issues relating to how one can survive with the 'other', of the contingencies, desires and ongoing negotiations of living together.

In a fifth and final one-year performance, Hseih did not involve himself in any 'art' practice or had any connection with the art world, but when set alongside, the other four performance questions begin to emerge, such as what is the relation between art and life? How is art different from life? Can anything be viewed as art, and if so, why do we have the category or term 'art'? Hseih's final project called 'Earth' lasted for thirteen years (1986–99). During this time he made art but only in secret; there is no documentation of what he produced.

Throughout these performances, Hseih is challenging or disrupting the various spatial, temporal and symbolic orders that normally structure our lives as well as our everyday psycho-social relations. We are left with a feeling of synchronicity between art and life. The point is that art is part of life, life as *apeiron* (as boundless), not a reflection upon it; it posits a way of experiencing that is life and in doing so reveals life's cosmological infinity whilst also exposing the limitations of the finite orders and dispositifs that try to capture and regulate life. Steven Shaviro (2008) summarizes Hseih's eternal struggle as manifested through his performances:

> Whether Hsieh was concerned with solitude and isolation, with the self's boundaries and its relationships to others, or with the way our lives are embedded in time and space, he always sought to grasp the issues as concretely as possible. He did not just think about these fundamental dilemmas. He also lived them, in their full existential density, joy, and terror. Doing this required an incredible force of discipline and dedication. But it also required an extraordinary willingness to let go: to give oneself over to time and chance and materiality. The stubborn excess of the real, its refusal to be contained within the ideas we have of it: this is the true substance of Hsieh's art.

The photographic work of Ingrid Pollard titled 'Pastoral Interlude' (1987) and the postcard image titled 'Wordsworth Heritage' (1992), a billboard poster commissioned by the BBC displayed in various locations in the UK, also raise the issue of the presence of the body – the alterity of the 'other' body in a particular setting. The work raises the issue of the presence/absence of the 'other', depicting a group of black ramblers in the settings of the Lake District in northwest England. These images have a rather uncanny but poignant effect of bodies seeming to be 'out of place', and yet they are *there* and therefore of this place. The English countryside idyll is disrupted, and all of its historical associations with landscape, ownership by middle and upper classes, the links to colonialism and slavery seem to circulate. In a text linked to the 'Pastoral Interlude' (1987), Pollard herself tells of her anxiety as a black person in these rural areas and comments:

> It's as if the Black experience is only lived within an urban environment: I thought I liked the Lake District where I wandered lonely as a Black face in a sea of white. A visit to the countryside is always accompanied by a feeling of unease, dread.

The countryside idyll of rolling hills and the uplands and valleys of the Lake District are disrupted by an unfamiliar bodily presence that simultaneously reveals issues of ownership and its colonial past.

Regina Jose Galindo also uses her body (a mutable readymade-making) often as a means to raise issues of power relations. Her performance, *Who Can Erase the Traces?* (2003) took place on the streets of Guatemala City in order to expose political tensions surrounding a controversial political election. The performance was documented by video which shows Galindo walking through the streets of the city from the courthouse to the presidential palace. She walked barefoot whilst carrying a bowl of human blood, stopping periodically to dip her feet in the blood so that her red footprints were left on the pavement. She left the bowl of blood in front of the palace. The performance was a form of protest against the permission granted to the former military dictator, Rios Montt, to run for president after being prevented from doing so initially by the Supreme Court. He had been accused of a number of human rights abuses including torture and massacre of indigenous communities during the civil war (1960–96).

In the films and photographs of Zarina Bhimji, there is an absence of the body, but in her explorations of historical spaces in Africa, India, the UK and elsewhere, we find subtle, even poetic, images of 'other' places such as abandoned factories and objects that are part of the troubled histories of colonial repression and violence (Love 1998–2006; Waiting 2007). In *Waiting* the interiors of sisal factories and their tools in Mombassa and Voi were filmed without people. In an interview with Chika Okeke-Agulu (2010), Bhimji states that the absence of people is deliberate in that the work is specifically not about historical fact. Rather, through her concerns with spaces, plays of light, mood and other compositional details, the aim is to refuse 'obvious' socio-historical narratives and through the composition of other images (e.g. in the film *Out of*

Blue (2002), the transition from a peaceful and misty early morning landscape of Ugandan countryside into a violent raging fire) and to point to an unspoken acknowledgement of the historical realities of exploitation, brutality and torture of Idi Amin's terror. Through her particular compositional treatment of difference, of other spaces and their ghostly absences, issues of ethics and politics are raised through a medium of poignance. In relation to this point Bhimji (in Okeke-Agulu 2010: 71) states:

> My work is about learning to listen to difference, the difference in shadows, microcosms, and sensitivity to difference in its various forms. It is about listening with the eyes, listening to changes in tone and difference of color. It is not a personal indulgence; it is about making sense through the medium of aesthetics. It is a question that is close to my heart, since the significant ethical issues have a resonance for me. In some of my work I register these issues, to mark what has happened: elimination, extermination, and erasure, whether in Kampala, Kigali, or Kosovo. Within the broader questions of difference, an important part of my work is the possibility of creative difference. Such a combination of personal and public aspects holds a particular resonance for me.

Speculative Practice and the Non-philosophy of Francois Laruelle

In *A Thousand Plateaus* Deleuze and Felix Guattari discuss the concepts of the minor and the war machine. Deleuze describes the concept of the war machine not in terms of war but in terms of revolutionary movements, such as in art practice, that invent new spatio-temporal relations (Deleuze 1995: 172). We might connect art as a war machine with the notion of the scandal of art, an event of rupture that pushes boundaries of established practice and thought and opens up new possibilities, new rhythms, new compositions for a people to come. The breaking of boundaries may involve the production of new forms of expression, challenging socio-political or economic orders, questioning established or traditional values, raising environmental concerns or proposing new social realities and subjectivities. Such practice can be conceived as a speculative venture, the spark of a transductive disparation, that opens up new vectors for a future yet to emerge – a practice whose speculative mode invents new methods, ideas, values and practices that lead to novel individual and collective outcomes. Wilkie, Savransky and Rosengarten (2017: 4–5) capture both the risk and the importance of what we might call creative speculation for an openness towards as yet unknown possibilities:

> It matters how we enter the future, what senses of futurity we bring into play, which modes of relating to the not-yet we enable knowing and thinking practices to nurture. Thus, rather than objects of knowledge or thought to be captured by a backward-walking present, possible futures are here engaged as vectors of risk and creative experimentation. It is futures themselves that, whenever one takes the risk of cultivating them, can escape the impasses of the present, and lure our own practices of thinking, knowing and feeling to unforeseen possibilities. (4–5)

We might consider art practices as generating 'vectors of risk and creative experimentation' in order to lure and cultivate 'unforeseen possibilities'. The importance of *how* we enter the future and develop new sensibilities cannot be underestimated. And entering a future through art practice is as much ontological as aesthetic, where art and life become indissoluble in the creation of the new, a creation in which, to use a phrase from Deleuze, we become 'cosmic artisans' constantly creating and re-creating the world anew. Art practice does not consist of a separation between artist and artwork but a synthesis of an immanence of becoming.

Combining the idea of a war machine, the cultivation of futures through vectors of creative experimentation that 'lure our practices of thinking, knowing and feeling to unforeseen possibilities', I want to begin to consider what we might call the speculative and experimental practice of non-philosophy, or non-standard philosophy, developed by Francois Laruelle. This will be a very elementary approach to a complex philosophical opus. Laruelle's work will be explored in relation to its relevance for art practices as this is discussed by Simon O'Sullivan (2017), also writing with David Burrows (2019) and also John O'Maoilearca (2015a, 2015b). Before considering the relevance of non-philosophy to art practice, I will provide a brief introduction to how Laruelle uses the notion of non-philosophy by drawing upon commentaries upon his work (Ray Brassier (2003, 2007); Robin Mackay and F. Laruelle (2012); Anthony Paul Smith (2012).

My discussion of Laruelle's complex writing on non-philosophy is far from exhaustive and only covers a very limited dimension of his work, in particular his notion of 'non', which relates to my concerns with educational and art practices. Laruelle's problem with philosophy is that it has acquired a particular autocratic functioning, aspiring to be the highest form of thought and where each new philosophical movement claims to outdo previous movements. John O'Maoilearca (2015a: 1) writes that Laruelle's approach to philosophy is to demonstrate its authority:

> Despite what appears to many as philosophy's benign, abstracted appearance, the stance adopted here takes it to be the supreme form of thought control, or to be perfectly clear, a device for controlling what counts as thought. … Its very form is transcendence.

What we might call standard philosophy for Laruelle invokes 'an aristocratism of thinking' by defining the act of thinking through its transcendent conceptualizations that are constructed within different philosophies: empiricism, rationalism, idealism, materialism, existentialism, scientism and even anti-philosophy. This aristocratism also applies to other disciplines that promote their transcendent positions as Laruelle states, 'Every discipline very soon arrives at its own sufficiency, in the sense that it tends to auto-finalise itself, raise itself to the level of a total, complete or all-powerful thought' (Mackay and Laruelle 2012: 20–1). We might consider other disciplines such as aesthetics or educational practices in order to expose their positions of sufficiency (authority) that dominate and regulate practice.

Non-philosophy challenges this autocratic or authoritative functioning, not by advocating anti-philosophy but by proposing a more horizontal or democratic approach in which all thoughts are equalized and where the 'non' does not infer a negative but signals a more expansive functioning equivalent to the 'non' demarcated by the term 'non-Euclidean geometry', which denotes an expansive field of geometry (see Brassier 2003). Non-philosophy therefore is, as Simon O'Sullivan (2017: 3) suggests:

> an attempt to practice philosophy (at least of a kind) without the aforementioned auto-positioning. Crucially, it does not involve a straightforward disavowal of the philosophical gesture (it is not non philosophy); nor does it involve a recourse to an 'outside' that might seem to be folded back in *by* philosophy. (italics in original)

Laruelle removes philosophical thinking from its elevated perch and advocates a flattened democratic topography of thought in which philosophy is just one way of thinking amongst many other modes. This seems to recognize the autonomy of different modes of practice which includes their modes of thinking whilst also recognizing the importance of their interaction or convergence that might lead to a collective expansion. Laruelle wants to acknowledge the different materialisms of thought produced in different domains of practice that may impact philosophy so as to expand and transform its domain. Non-philosophy does not reject philosophy; rather it refuses only the part of it that can be refuted, what Laruelle (2013a: 211–12) calls its *sufficient reason*. O'Maoilearca (2015b: 161) writes:

> As its name would imply, Laruelle's 'non-standard philosophy' (or just 'non-philosophy') poses as something other than standard philosophy. If it is connected to performance, then, it is not on account of its offering us a philosophy *of* performance. Indeed, to examine the means by which non-philosophy avoids becoming another 'philosophy of' x, y, or z, – *of* performance, for example – we must look at it in terms of its *activity*. What it attempts, Laruelle says, is '*not a new philosophical paradigm*' but the '*transformation of philosophy*' (Laruelle 2013b: 71). He is adamant that non-philosophy is a new 'practice of philosophy' rather than a 'philosophical taking of sides and thus inside philosophy'. (italics in original)

Maoilearca continues (162):

> While standard philosophical approaches take their conception of what proper philosophy is and then apply it to all and sundry objects – what Laruelle calls the '*Principle of Sufficient Philosophy*' – non-philosophy is a 'style of thought' that <u>mutates with its object</u> (Laruelle 2012: 259) (my emphasis). Hence, non-philosophy is neither 'theoretical nor practical nor aesthetic, etc., in the sense whereby philosophy defines separated regions of experience' (Laruelle 2013a: 285). It is all of these at once.

It is important to note that the 'non' in non-standard philosophy can also be applied to other autonomous domains of practice, as in non-pedagogy, or non-aesthetics, and so on, in order to question their 'sufficiency' and thereby open each to a more expansive field of practice.

In passing, the idea of 'mutating with the world', denoting an ongoing reciprocal process, seems close to Alfred North Whitehead's notions of *novelty* and *creativity* (1928: 21).

> 'Creativity' is the principle of novelty. An actual occasion is a novel entity diverse from any entity in the 'many' which it unifies. Thus 'creativity' introduces novelty into the content of the many, which are the universe disjunctively. The 'creative advance' is the application of this ultimate principle of creativity to each novel situation which it originates. … The novel entity is at once the togetherness of the 'many' which it finds, and also it is one among the disjunctive 'many' which

it leaves; it is a novel entity, disjunctively among the many entities which it synthesizes. The many become one, and are increased by one.

For Whitehead, creativity is not premised upon human experience but is fundamental to all existence (Halewood 2014). We cannot define creativity in itself but only point to its manifestations, what Whitehead calls its 'creatures' in novel instances or actual occasions (32). 'The function of creatures is that they constitute the shifting character of creativity' (32). A creative thought or other practice introduces novelty into the content of the many. Halewood puts it this way, 'Whitehead argues that change, novelty and process are integral both to existence and to our experience of existence. Therefore we need a philosophy to account for this. There is no meaning in "creativity" apart from its creatures.' This points to the difficulty relating to permanency and flux or being and becoming that, for Whitehead, permeate our lives and the world around us in that we feel a sense of endurance when in fact reality is constantly evolving and mutating. We might view one manifestation of this concern in the posture adopted by non-philosophy through its rejection of positions of authority within disciplines and a valuing of a democracy of thought and the constantly mutating reciprocities between thought and object. Whitehead puts this more lyrically by quoting from the hymn *Abide with Me* by Henry Francis Lyte (1847):

Abide with me;

Fast falls the eventide.

Here the first line expresses the permanences, 'abide', 'me' and the 'Being' addressed; and the second line sets these permanences amid the inescapable flux. (1978: 209)

This constancy of change through creative process that for Whitehead constitutes a 'buzzing world' (50), which requires us to acquire mutable and commensurate modes of understanding, the mutation of thought with its object, is close, I think, to Laruelle's call for the creative impulse of the 'non' in non-philosophy (or non-art or non-pedagogy) in that this 'non' should be viewed as an operator for an expansive and transformative approach to thought in each respective domain as it mutates along with its 'objects', thus avoiding hubristic or transcendent postures or 'auto-positions'. Of course, as Whitehead insists, we have to recognize that novel 'creatures' are not necessarily good, or they may appear in the wrong society (1978: 223).

The idea of non-philosophy mutating with its object suggests that if it is to try to grasp the modes of thinking inherent to art practice or pedagogical practice, that is to say, if philosophy is to be able to *engage* with art or pedagogical practice, it has to relinquish any auto-position of transcendence and try to mutate into art-philosophy or pedagogy-philosophy, that is to say, the mode immanent to each practice whereby thinking is materialized and folded into the being and becoming of each practice. This means that we cannot 'generalize' about practice but try to deal with each practice's particular concerns, but in doing so, this may provide transversal potential for thought that precipitates new coordinates for thought and practice.

Non-philosophy abandons positions of transcendence or authority and operates instead from a concern with *radical immanence* emerging in the haecceities of practice. Non-philosophy will function through concepts but only when these have been 'cleansed' of what Laruelle calls the 'Principle of Sufficient Philosophy'; this would suggest a kind of decolonization of the authority of 'philosophical' thinking. In passing, we might also think of art practice that escapes the 'principle of sufficient art', or of pedagogical practice that passes beyond the 'principle of sufficient pedagogy', that is to say, the authority of established discourses and practices in these domains. It's not a case of non-philosophy acting as a purging of philosophy because this would simply seem to produce a purer or less contaminated philosophy. It demands what Laruelle calls 'a change in vision'.

> Non-philosophy is a conception of philosophy (and all forms of thought) that allows us to see them as equivalent according to a broader explanatory paradigm. It enlarges the set of things that can count as thoughtful, a set that includes existing philosophy but also a whole host of what is presently deemed (by standard philosophy) to be non-philosophical (art, technology, natural science). (O'Maoilearca 2015a: 9)

This quote from O'Maoilearca hints at the autonomy, co-existence and interaction of heterogeneous modes of thought and practice, a 'radical horizontality between heterogenous practices', or transversality in Guattari's terminology (O'Sullivan 2017: 283). It seems to posit a democracy of thought (an ecology of practices) in which philosophy has no authority over other modes of thought and in which thought can take 'other' and evolving forms. It is important therefore to conceive thought as a practice that has numerous forms of life. Beyond philosophy the task would be to consider other practices, such as art, music, technology, science and other practices, in order to expose their colonizing authority in contrast to those practices that lie 'outside' and which may be marginalized or excluded. O'Sullivan is keen to explore such questions relating to the relevance of non-philosophy for art practice. How, for instance, does writing about art (philosophy, aesthetics, social criticism, etc.) capture or define art practice and its productions? How does non-philosophy help us to reconfigure the relationship between the authority of discourses about art practice and the real of art practice which escapes such discursive capture? What kind of 'thought' is art practice? O'Sullivan (284) writes:

> It seems to me that this is one of the most interesting areas of inquiry in relation to non-philosophy and art practice. The diagnosis of how philosophy or theory captures objects and practices (or, in fact, defines them as such in the first place)is important, but more compelling is how non-philosophy might reconfigure what counts as a theory of art and how it might contribute – however obliquely – to an understanding of how art itself works in practice, on the ground as it were (that is, when it is not explained, interpreted, or simply defined by philosophy). Two questions, then: what kind of framework does non-philosophy offer for thinking *about* art; and, what kind of thinking *is* art? (italic in original)

Laurelle's use of the 'non' in non-philosophy as an operator for an expansive field can be applied to the idea of the 'non-human'. We might say that an encounter with something new in art practice or in pedagogical practice (or other modes) produces a new thought, a new form of practice and thus a new mutation of the human. Along with those artists already discussed above, the performance art practices of Allan Kaprow, Maria Abramovich, Joseph Beuys, Carollee Schneemann, Lee Wen and many others, in their respective ways, have produced new, often scandalous mutations (materializings) of practice that challenge and question what art is and thereby what it is to be human. Indeed, such practices could be said to call forth what Deleuze and Guattari call a people yet to come. Such practices can invoke postures that puncture forces of assimilation to established orders of practice which try to incorporate them. This point can apply more generally to conservative forces that try to embrace 'that which disturbs', what we might call 'otherness', into their established frameworks of value. Such forces, by incorporating the new into established orders without themselves mutating, extend their imperialism of thought (O'Maoilearca 2015a: 46). We might then see how the idea of the 'non' in Laruelle's work has clear ethical and political ramifications for domains of human existence, including art and pedagogy, as it questions and problematizes how the human is conceived and constructed within particular practices and discourses.

Part Two

Towards an Ecosophic Pedagogy of Taking Care

The scandal of the truth of art, as described by Foucault at the beginning of this chapter, functions through various levels of affect to disturb established orders and in doing so can expose, on one level, social injustice, exploitation, victimization and marginalization and, on another level, disrupt established and inherited forms, practices and their aesthetic values, so questioning 'what art can be or become'. In Simondon's terminology this functioning can be described as a process of disparative transduction that produces individuations of affect and sensibilities. If these points regarding the centrality of affect are applied to art in education, then we might argue that rather than seeking for more effective assessment criteria, or delineating more appropriate competences, in other words trying to effect more efficient conceptual captures for quality assurance (consistent with the exponential increase in education of instruments for testing, inspection and audit), perhaps we might wish to place more emphasis upon how we can work with *ecologies of affect* that are generated through art encounters which can in turn effect new sensibilities and which may be more effective for developing educational programmes that value diversity and participation. However, a word of caution, market capitalism also works with the force of affect not only in promoting products but also in generating affective forces to 'influence' or provoke public sensibilities and desires. How might we understand, support and extend ecologies of affect? Guattari (2013: 203) states that 'affect is pre-personal'; it is something that arises before it is captured by identity. The difficulty is that flows of affect are not 'discursive'; they constitute intensities that emerge from existential coordinates of experiencing. Guattari (204) writes:

> As soon as one seeks to quantify an affect, one immediately loses its qualitative dimensions and its potential for singularisation, for heterogenesis, in other words the eventual compositions, the 'haecceities' that it promotes.

Following Assis above, we can refer to such affects as micro-haecceities that emerge in the ongoing process and contingency of practice. Guattari (204) continues by stating that 'affect is the process of existential appropriation by the continuous creation of heterogeneous durations of being'. This 'continuous creation' echoes Simondon's notion of transductive disparations, and the notion of 'existential appropriation' seems close to his idea of transductive structuration as discussed in the previous chapter. Affect can therefore be viewed as a 'structural germ' that generates an existential structuration (ritornello) as the intensities and relationalities of practice evolve. In pedagogic work in art education, rather than trying to frame such continuous creation and structuring by conceptual capture, we might be more effective by trying to respond through what Guattari (1995) calls an ethico-aesthetic paradigm that treats each practice by trying to 'feel' its value for each creator (trying to draw alongside its sensible affects and values, its rhythms of expression). Stengers (2005b: 184) writes about approaching a practice by feeling its borders. This paradigm draws upon Spinoza's notion of potential (what a body can do or a mind can think) as well as the immanence of becoming in order to contemplate the production of subjectivity. In *Chaosmosis* Guattari (1995: 133) directs his attention to education and asks, 'How do you make a class operate like a work of art? What are the possible paths to its singularisation, the source of a "purchase on existence" for the children who compose it?'

How might we construct possibilities for children and students that facilitate and encourage them to develop their individual 'purchase on existence' and the capacities and sensibilities that follow whilst equally valuing collective being and becoming-with? Such questions call for a revaluation of education that would shift the emphasis of the grounding of education upon economic imperatives towards what we might call, after Guattari, an *ecosophic education* that places emphasis upon the interdependent relations between subjectivity, social structures and the environment. These constitute what Guattari called the three ecologies.

> Without modifications to the social and material environment, there can be no change in mentalities. Here, we are in the presence of a circle that leads me to postulate the necessity of founding an 'ecosophy' that would link environmental ecology to social ecology and to mental ecology. (Guattari 1992)

The term 'ecosophy' is a combination of 'ecology' and 'philosophy'; the interdependence of the three ecologies that Guattari proposes does not imply the forming of a holistic process but emphasizes assemblages (*agencements*) of heterogeneity and difference, rhizomatic rather than holistic structures. Guattari's aim is to promote a re-invention or a renewal of social practices and relations that offer the possibility of a better, more convivial world than that which has evolved through market capitalism that entails the homogenization of passive subjectivities, the promotion of difference-within-limits, but also economic crises in global employment as well as environmental crises leading to global warming and the destruction of the environment (forests, oceans, species, cities). There has also been a retrenchment towards identity in the form of nationalisms and racism. In 'Remaking Social Practices' (1992: 1), Guattari writes:

> It is true that it is difficult to bring individuals out of themselves, to disengage them from their immediate preoccupations, in order to reflect on the present and the future of the world. They lack collective incitements to do so. Most older methods of communication, reflection and dialogue have dissolved in favour of an individualism and a solitude that are often synonymous with anxiety and neurosis. It is for this reason, that I advocate – under the aegis of a new conjunction of environmental ecology, social ecology and mental ecology – the invention of new collective assemblages of enunciation concerning the couple, the family, the school, the neighborhood, etc.

Ecosophy is therefore calling for modes of existence that recognize the interdependence of subjectivities, social and environmental systems. An educational ecosophy would place a similar emphasis upon such interdependence and would not, as in current education systems, place major emphasis upon the production of *homo economicus* and attendant values of competition, consumption, privatization, deregulation and human capital. Ecosophy demands an ethico-political as well as an ethico-aesthetic articulation between the three ecologies. How then might we move towards reinventing educational practices that place emphasis upon an ecosophic responsibility? Guattari (1995: 120) states, 'It is less a question of having access to novel cognitive spheres than of apprehending and creating, in pathic modes, mutant existential virtualities.' It is important to counter the pathic affective strategies of neoliberal or market capitalism with other, more collective pathic modes and sensibilities that lead to a new political praxis not governed by market economies but which try to articulate social collective values and practices with global problems. This would involve the production of new subjectivations as well as new universes of value and social assemblages. Implicit to this production is a sensitivity towards modes of existence and value that are marginalized or prevented from emerging but which may have potential for both individual and collective growth. Ecosophy calls for a generation of ethico-political alternatives that 'reappraise the ontological foundations of existing modes of valorisation in every domain' (1995: 127), and this will include education and its existing modes of valorization. By emphasizing the transversal relations between mutating existential territories, incorporeal universes of value of alternative social assemblages and evolving environmental systems, Guattari proposes a cartographic approach to different but interrelated 'ontological strata' (124) that recognizes that

> within each of these strata, each of these Becomings and Universes what is put into question is a certain metabolism of the infinite, a threat of transcendence, a politics of immanence. And, each one of them will require schizoanalytic and ecosophic cartographies which will demand that partial components of enunciation be brought to light where they exist but are unrecognised and where scientism, dogmatism and technocracy prevent their emergence. (125)

Such existential enunciations are not necessarily locatable within established discursive frameworks but 'come to being through an ontological heterogenesis' (1995: 125) that emerges in residual or marginal cultures, a heterogenesis that I have called the gift of otherness that ruptures established orders and frameworks of understanding. This ontological heterogenesis seems to me to chime with Laruelle's advocacy of the 'non' that seeks to explore and value different modes of thought and practice, a democracy of thought that takes no position as a transcendent authority.

The scandal of art, what we might also call 'non-art' in terms of the expansive potential of the 'non', can effect such an ontological heterogenesis that may precipitate deterritorializations, a creative processuality that leads to new subjectivations, new existential territories and universes of value. Guattari states, 'The primary purpose of ecosophic cartography is thus not to signify and communicate but to produce assemblages of enunciation capable of capturing the points of singularity of a situation' (128). Such singularities that emerge in diverse practices, such as art practice, and which hold ontological potential, may be unrecognized by established orders of discourse and practice. Here the gift of otherness is often ignored, for example, by the dogmatism of institutional discourse. The current allure of institutional abstractions such as standards or competences and their universe of values that function as transcendent enunciators could be replaced by a focus upon the immanence of practice and its value within local spaces of practice. Teachers in many countries today are regulated by inspection regimes that evaluate the effectiveness of their practice according to established authority of standards. Equally, teachers are expected to teach according to prescribed curriculum content and criteria for assessment. We might argue that they have become enslaved by the education machine. This situation suggests that what Guattari (129) refers to as 'an immanence of collective intellectuality' is repressed or marginalized. How might this 'immanence of collective intellectuality' in the world of teachers be tapped and released from the inhibitions placed around it by governmental forces that in turn are driven by the imperatives of economic ambition? This would be, I suggest, a priority of an ecosophic education that draws upon diverse ecological strata and their potential for all forms of life.

> The importance of art practice is that it is 'a practice of unframing, of rupturing sense, of baroque proliferation or extreme impoverishment, which leads to a recreation and a reinvention of the subject itself ... the event of its encounter can irreversibly date the course of an existence and generate fields of the possible 'far from the equilibria' of everyday life. (131)

To repeat Guattari's question then, 'How can we make a classroom of children, a pedagogic space, operate like a work of art?' a context of creative processuality in which each existential territory can evolve its universe of skills and collective values. Can we imagine a classroom, a studio, as an ecosophic assemblage that enables a creative evolution of individual and collective subjectivities? A space in which a difference can make a difference, where the gift of otherness extends capacities to act and think. A pedagogic space of 'aesthetic and ethico-political transversality' (132). Transversality here does not denote the neoliberal agenda for flexible skill sets, networking structures and adaptation to new and changing technologies and markets, all of which are controlled by and promoted for the interests of large corporations. Guattari used the term 'transversality' to refer to an immanent process inherent to learning prior to any institutional structuration. It is not concerned with the 'transmission' of knowledge from teacher to learner but with an idea of collective learning-with. Transversality in a pedagogic context concerns the here and now of learning-with and its different but interrelated ecologies – learning about the relationalities of existence, modes of practice, assemblages of knowledge and values that inform how we might act individually and collectively and which lead towards the production of what we might call (after Illich) more convivial subjectivities. Learning-with rather than learning-from involves a co-learning that requires a teacher to ask what might be happening in a learning encounter for a child or student; how do practices of thinking and action constitute the encounter? Does the learner's practice in combination with the teacher's response open up new possibilities and new sensibilities? Does the pedagogical relation increase the learner's capacity to act?

The importance of art in education embraces the three interrelated ecologies and develops an awareness of their interconnectedness as discussed above but with the added and crucial dimension of developing what Guattari called mutant coordinates, through art practice, for new sensibilities, capacities and possibilities for action. An ecosophic education is therefore grounded in a pedagogy of taking care that recognizes the interdependence of subject-social-environment relations and promotes creative possibilities for transversal enrichment.

Ecosophic Art Education

The implications for art in education of the scandalous nature of art, its poietic event that may refashion subjectivity through the emergence of new sensibilities and modes of practice, its potential for invention and transformation, deserve consideration in relation to an ecosophic education. The vital significance of art encounters in the intensity of actual practice lies in their transformative potential. Equally, encounters with art as an observer, experiencing the scandal of its truth, may invoke a rupturing of established modes of sensibility and thought and lead to new or modified modes. It may act as a catalyst to expose current sociopolitical conditions and their values so as to open up a possibility for new universes. In the latter case, the intensity of an art encounter acts as a 'war machine' as described by Deleuze and Guattari, and such encounters need to be considered carefully when organized in the domain of pedagogic work. In the former case, art encounters in actual practice allow individuals to take the risk of exploring and through this creative processuality have opportunities to develop new sensibilities and new ways of conceiving. It is through such encounters 'in' art practice or 'with' art practice that we can perhaps see, as jan jagodinski (2019: 73) puts it, 'that art and life are constantly making and unmaking one another'. We might say that the gift of art, its otherness, enables an ongoing metastable production of becoming, the continual experimentation and production of sensibilities, thought and action through new situations of practice: painting, drawing, ceramics, construction, performance, video, photography and more. The emergence of sensibilities, thought and action is not exclusive to art practice, but their production, affect and potential are particularly potent when generated through art practice. Guattari (1995: 106) puts it like this:

> Patently, art does not have a monopoly on creation, but it takes its capacity to invent mutant coordinates to extremes: it engenders unprecedented, unforeseen and unthinkable qualities of being.

The intensive affects and the generation of new sensibilities through art practice, whatever its subject matter, its concern, may impact other domains of subjectivation by problematizing how our lives are constituted within sociopolitical, economic and ecological environments, how we relate to others and their values, how we might expand our capacities to act individually and collectively and how we relate and respond to our surrounding environments.

This brings into play Guattari's three interrelated ecologies of subject, social relations and environment and how art practice and art education can generate transversal potencies and affects towards individual and collective flourishing. On an 'individual' level, this might involve the production of new sensibilities, values and modes of practice, on a collective level, as a scandal of the truth, when art practice exposes social, political or environmental 'wrongs' (when it functions as a war machine). The two levels are interrelated. What is at stake here in the words of Guattari (1995: 133) is 'an aspiration for individual and collective reappropriation of the production of subjectivity'. This point is made more substantially by Guattari (91) when he discusses the importance of inventing an 'ecology of the virtual' in contrast to 'ecologies of the visible world'. He views the arts, and I would argue art in education, as crucial to this virtual enterprise to invent new forms of sensibility in contrast and in opposition to current quotidian, economic and political forces. Forms that lead to a new gentleness, 'the creation and development of unprecedented formations of subjectivity that have never been seen and never felt' (91). The invention of new rhythms and intensities of living through experiencing otherness and its virtual potential. Art practice is not to be viewed as that conducted only by artists but in terms of the force of creativity, close to the notion of a fundamental creativity put forward by Whitehead, before it becomes captured by discursive or disciplinary positions. In a passage discussing performance art, Guattari (90) speaks of the 'vertigo' of such practice that ruptures what he calls 'the semiotic net of quotidianity' and projects us into a 'forward flight … capable of engendering mutant subjectivities'. He continues (90):

> In a more general way, every aesthetic decentring of points of view, every polyphonic reduction of the components of expression passes through a preliminary deconstruction of the structures and codes in use and a chaosmic plunge into the materials of sensation. Out of them a recomposition becomes possible: a recreation, an enrichment of the world, a proliferation not just of the forms but of the modalities of being.

An ecology of the virtual proposed by Guattari seems very important for art in education and is crucial for recomposing, enriching and proliferating forms of practice and modalities of being that can emerge from each student's rhizomatic and situated specificities of practice. We might conceive this ecology as close to the idea of speculation and speculative practice already mentioned above (Savransky, Wilkie and Rosengarten 2017: 4–5):

> It matters how we enter the future, what senses of futurity we bring into play, which modes of relating to the not-yet we enable knowing and thinking practices to nurture. Thus, rather than objects of knowledge or thought to be captured by a backward-walking present, possible futures are here engaged as vectors of risk and creative experimentation. It is futures themselves that, whenever one takes the risk of cultivating them, can escape the impasses of the present, and lure our own practices of thinking, knowing and feeling to unforeseen possibilities.

Ecologies of the virtual involve the invention of a future not simply in terms of cognition, of knowing, but also in terms of affect and feeling; they involve the complexities of 'existential apprehension' (Guattari 1995: 93) that await expressive form. We might relate these points to the different modes of apprehension that emerge in educational contexts when children and students are confronted with a learning encounter and how such modes find their respective forms of expression through art practice. Through such expressive ecologies, both actual and virtual, learners are lured into unforeseen possibilities, to new existential territories, within what I have called a pedagogy of taking care. Ecologies of the virtual are, we might say, concerned with an otherness that emerges in the assemblage of practice and whose gift may bring about new rhythms and cartographies of practice.

We might see a link here with Laruelle's notion of the 'non' as an otherness that extends possibilities of practice and, consequently, the idea of non-art education that puts aside any transcendent arbiters of practice in order to valorize the *creative art-life process and the uniqueness and potential of each existential creation* and what Guattari calls new 'ontological crystallisations'. A non-art education would try to travel beyond, but not reject, established definitions or the inherited practices of art education, perhaps drawing upon the heterogeneity of contemporary art practices and their new materialities and potentialities, to produce a proliferation of hypertexts through which learners are encouraged to follow their own pathways and create their own orders and meanings, their own artistic singularities and cartographies towards an ecosophic project.

7

The Gift of Otherness: Ontological Adventures in Pedagogic Work

What Might Pedagogical Practice Learn from the Ontological Turn in Anthropological Studies?

In this chapter I turn to some anthropological studies that seem, in some respects, to echo Laruelle's concern for a democracy of the practice of thought and a rejection of transcendent authority. I will refer closely to the exposition of the anthropological works of Roy Wagner, Marylin Strathern and Eduardo Viveiros de Castro, provided by Martin Holbraad and Morten Axel Pedersen (H&P) in their text, *The Ontological Turn: An Anthropological Exposition* (OT 2017). My aim is to consider what we might learn from such anthropological studies in order to advance an advocacy for an ecosophic pedagogy of taking care within the rhizomatic becomings in environments of learning. My purpose is to work with the idea of the gift of otherness in that it is through encounters with 'that which is other', that which might challenge established understandings and practices, that which prompts or worries us to rethink or think again, that learning in an expansive sense might occur. This is not to argue that established or inherited practices and knowledge are unimportant or to be left in abeyance, but it is to be concerned with how such inheritances may need to evolve and to what degree when faced with experiences that require new modes of thought and practice.

H&P provide an insightful and provocative discussion of the works of Wagner, Strathern and Viveiros de Castro, who, they argue, advanced in different ways a deep concern for ontology in anthropological studies. When I was reading *The Ontological Turn*, I found myself resonating with its unfolding of ontological issues in anthropological studies in that these seem highly relevant to pedagogic practices in which pedagogical encounters may at times generate 'vantages from which established forms of thinking are put under relentless pressure by alterity itself, and perhaps changed' (OT: 297). Such openness to change suggests that pedagogic work is ontologically political and ethical in its task of responding to alterity and its potentialities for what might be possible, what could be. This requires us to consider the idea of the political in pedagogic work, and I will return to this issue in the concluding chapters.

It is important to stress that my interest to think with H&P and their anthropological mentors is generated by the effects and affects that their exposition of the ontological turn has had upon my reflections on pedagogic practice; such effects and affects are both epistemological and ontological. Their work emphasizes for me the importance and potential of the gift of otherness and resonates with my advocacy for a pedagogy of taking are. Throughout my discussion therefore I draw parallels between their exposition of anthropological practices and my concern with pedagogical practices. H&P begin their study with reference to what they call 'a-ah!' moments (OT: 2) in anthropological experiences when confronted with 'strange' practices, customs or traditions that make the anthropologist question her basic assumptions about objects, relations or time. Over the years anthropology has formulated ways of conceiving such experiences through theories such as cultural relativism. H&P do not dismiss such theoretical frameworks and their application, but they wish to stay with what we might call the haecceities of such moments in order to deepen enquiry into their ontological grounds, an enquiry that may lead to a questioning of anthropological assumptions and the epistemologies that underpin these. Their task as they see it is that in staying with the ontological grounds of a-ah! moments, ontological questions may 'solve epistemological problems' (OT: 5). They propose a question that is fundamental to pedagogic enquiry of the kind I have tried to advocate throughout this book:

> How do I enable my ethnographic [pedagogic] material to reveal itself to me by allowing it to dictate its own terms of engagement, so to speak, guiding or compelling me to see things that I had not expected, or imagined to be there? (my insertion)

Put in other terms, how do we enable 'otherness' to reveal its gift in pedagogic practice without established frameworks of understanding constraining our capacity to receive such gifts? This suggests, in sympathy with H&P, that the 'epistemological problem of *how one sees things* is turned into the ontological question of *what there is to be seen* in the first place' (OT: 5; italics in original). The possibility for such a-ah! moments and their potential in pedagogical practice has been suggested in previous chapters, and in taking care, we might be able to witness 'what is there' in a learning encounter. For H&P (OT: 6), 'the ontological turn is not so much a matter of "seeing differently", it is above all a matter of seeing different things.' In pedagogic work, therefore, rather than trying to grasp the child's or student's point of view of what we *think* is *the same* object of practice or of enquiry, we might need to put our epistemological frameworks aside in order to allow that which is 'other' to grasp us. A turn to ontology would allow the contingencies of pedagogic experience to act as a platform for reconfiguring pedagogic practice in ongoing vectors of experimentation, reflexivity and conceptualization. Such vectors are possible in most if not all practices of pedagogic work.

The turn to ontology and its immanent reflexivity is not new in pedagogical enquiry. A concern for difference, otherness and potential was present in various guises in the past, in the works of John Dewey, Alfred North Whitehead, Maria Montessori, Jean Jacques Rousseau, Johann Heinrich Pestalozzi, Friedrich Frobel, Ivan Illich, bel hooks, Maxine Greene and many others. The distinct aspect of the ontological turn in pedagogic enquiry is that it re-engages with these previous studies that have been largely marginalized by current educational policies and directives that are driven by economic imperatives. Such re-engagement is achieved through what H&P (OT: 9) call an intensification of the processes of reflexivity, conceptualization and experimentation and which again are not uncommon in pedagogic enquiry. But with an emphasis upon ontological events, such processes become more radical by trying to realize the immanent potentials of such events rather than operating from established lenses of inquiry. This requires an openness to 'what is there' and how we might need to develop concepts to articulate this. It involves, by implication, an open reflexivity, an always incomplete process of not only developing new ways of understanding but also trying to expose those assumptions according to which practice has been understood and which may obscure 'what is there'. How might our established conceptualizations of 'learning', 'teaching', 'assessment' or 'practice' in their various modalities precipitate such obfuscation? Such questions may arise from the pedagogical events in which we are confronted with 'otherness' that disturbs the infrastructure of pedagogical thought. The task is to try to develop dispositions towards the haecceity of otherness that allow us to put aside established frameworks of practice and let this otherness show us that practice could be otherwise. I will now turn to the three anthropologists that H&P discuss and consider some key conceptualizations and their relevance for pedagogic practice and a pedagogy of taking care.

Roy Wagner: Jazz Pedagogies

Opening their chapter on the American anthropologist Roy Wagner and his work on the invention of culture, H&P (OT: 69) draw attention to the incredible skill and versatility of Jazz musicians, their consummate grasp of their instruments and their supreme ability to respond to the inventive playing of fellow musicians and to carve out their solo performances. A key point about these solo performances is that their content is not pre-planned but is full of improvisation, spontaneity and unpredictability, driven by the contingencies and inventions in playing together. The jazz solo is a performance of contingency and invention, a body-mind-sound assemblage (*agencement*). H&P's purpose in introducing the idea of the jazz solo is to conceive of human life as 'performing solos' in this improvised mode within collective assemblages rather than practising pre-established social norms, though these are also important for social life.

What if we set alongside the task of pedagogic work that is concerned with introducing learners to established practices, knowledge and values, whereby schools are viewed as practice rooms for the preordained tasks of future life, an approach to pedagogy that placed equal emphasis upon the contingencies and spontaneity of solo performance. This would be to acknowledge the value of inherited conventions but also of passing beyond these in order to promote invention and creative novelty. This may sound like heretical nonsense or scandalous mischief. But in a world that is changing so rapidly, physically, socially and technologically, where threats to life are increasing and insecurity is endemic, a requirement for enabling solo performance, improvisation and invention to expand and enhance collective and convivial relations seems to be important. We might see this scenario in pedagogic work as the constant iteration of inheritances through the spontaneity, contingency, improvisation and invention of solo performance.

Roy Wagner's work in anthropology, his studies of other cultures alongside Western cultures, and presented in his key text, *The Invention of Culture* (1981), is generally concerned with challenging convention and its constraining effects upon how we conceive the world, how we construe that with which we are confronted. This suggests that we tend to 'see' the world, in our case, pedagogic practice, through conventions, habits, disciplines, theories, guidelines and so forth that are frontloaded. Such frontloading allows us to learn and participate in social practices, and of course, such knowledge and modes of practice are important. However, problematizing the semiotics of convention is central to

Wagner's work in anthropology (OT: 85) in his project of viewing culture as a process of invention (OT: 70). Similarly, my concern regarding pedagogic work not only is to view this practice as one that operates from its inherited modes but also, in response to the haecceities of practice, is called upon at times to become a process of invention. We might actually go further and suggest that each pedagogical experience involves novelty. The task is to be vigilant towards the constraining effects of convention in order to be able to respond with openness towards the diversity of actual practices and to work with their possibilities and potentials. In relation to this point, particularly when confronted with 'otherness', Wagner (1981: 30–1) writes, 'We must be able to experience our subject matter directly, as alternative meaning, rather than indirectly, through literalization or reduction to the terms of our ideologies.'

The contrast between convention and invention that Wagner addresses is important for my advocacy for a pedagogy of taking care. It concerns the notions of meaning as convention or as invention and that at times the latter dimension of meaning can be obscured or constrained by the former. We might say that in a semiotics of convention, meaning is a precondition for expression; that meaning is already established and can be applied to something to express an aspect of it. Assessment practices in art education tend to follow such conventional meaning when, for example, they are applied to drawings (or other art practices) that are discussed through established terms such as composition, line, perspective, tone, texture and so on. The challenge arises when drawings that do not seem to accord with such conventional semiotics are considered and whether an opportunity is taken to explore and invent meanings that seem more commensurate to their modes of expression and in doing so extend and modify meaning in relation to drawings and to pedagogical practice. Equally, the task may be to expand the scope of these traditional terms akin to the expansive project of Laruelle's 'non' that opens them to wider iterations.

We might say that a conventional understanding of a drawing is that it is often viewed as a representation, which in turn assumes a series of dualisms: the distinction between a prior world (real or imagined) and the representation of it by the drawing, the distinction between drawer and drawing, the distinction, in school art educational practices, between assessment criteria that give meaning to a drawing and the actual drawing. But if we move from this conventional regime of representation to one in which such dualisms are abandoned in favour of viewing a drawing as a complex processual assemblage, a body-mind-material assemblage, then perhaps we might see that coordinates of meaning are shifted from ones in which the drawing is couched within a notion of comparison that is governed by criteria such as 'accuracy' or 'ability', to ones that emerge and are immanent and intensive to the actual process of practice within its situated specificity and which demand forms of understanding appropriate to its modes of expression. In the latter scenario, meaning is not simply 'applied' from conventional coordinates but 'mined' from the immanence of practice. Such 'mining' as an *inventive* process of meaning may propagate thinking afresh what we thought we already understood. As H&P (OT: 104) state, 'It is of the essence of meaning as a phenomenon ... that it contains within itself the horizons of its own renewal.' Such renewals, I have suggested, can arise in moments of encounter. And following H&P, an important pedagogic task, therefore, if we acknowledge their point, is that it contains within itself the horizons of its own conceptual renewal. And behind such renewal is the continuing question of how we understand pedagogic practice as a consequence of ontological encounters and transformations of practice that lead to reworking the meaning of practice through the interplays of convention and invention.

Marylin Strathern: Postplural Pedagogies

I turn briefly to the work of Marylin Strathern to consider her work on relation, comparison and postplurality and their implications for a pedagogy of 'taking care'. For Strathern, relation is not to be conceived as external to things, that is to say, as existing between things, individuals, objects and so on; rather she posits that there are no 'things' as such but only relations and different kinds of relations (OT: 115). Furthermore H&P (OT: 116) comment on what we might call the productive force or assumptions embedded in the term 'relation' as employed in ethnographic study. They state that for Strathern, 'social relations do not exist in an external world out there but are an intrinsic and inevitable effect of the manner in which anthropological analysis is conducted.' They continue (116), quoting Strathern, that 'far from being an indigenous term adopted by ethnographers in the hope of "grasping the native's point of view" ... then, "the relation" is a proxy by which "scholars trained in the Western tradition ... through deliberate choice ... glimpse what 'other' assumptions might look like ... through an internal dialogue within the confines of [their] own language"' (Strathern 1988: 4). The term 'relation' therefore is viewed as an anthropological invention that is employed in an experimental and heuristic approach to the practice of anthropological analysis. It involves a double articulation towards what we might call the 'object' of study and equally towards the study's conceptual framing (in this case, the term 'relation'); articulations that emerge from the contingencies of encounter and in the linguistic traditions and inventions in which these are framed. H&P state (OT: 120; see also Strathern 2018):

> Anthropologists do not study relations between the people they study, but the relations they need to 'invent' to study those people. For [Strathern] relations are not substantive in the sense of something that 'is', but contingent in the sense of something – an ethnographic moment – that happens in the encounter between anthropology and its subject matter.

The implications of this contingent notion of 'relation' that is not to be conceived as representing an external reality but as an experimental and heuristic 'technology of description' (OT: 120) emerging in pedagogic moments for pedagogic enquiry will be discussed shortly. Before that I move on to another related notion from Strathern, dealt with in detail in her text Partial Connections (2004), namely, the concept of *comparison*, which was mentioned briefly above.

Put very crudely, for Strathern, comparison is not a matter of comparing one thing with another according to some external arbiter, as when in a particular context of study, we require a means by which we can bring a sense of order and sense to a plurality of practices we witness. How, for example, do we make sense of the diversity of practices, the diversity of drawing or other art practices, for example, and give a sense of order to these when required to do so, as, for example, in assessment practices? Historically, within school art educational practices, this has taken the form of employing the use of particular criteria to assess the quality and efficacy of a drawing or other forms of art practice. To do this we might operate from established assessment criteria that in effect 'identify' or 'pedagogize' a drawing and, through such criteria, establish a child's or student's drawing *ability*. Strathern calls such criteria 'scales' in the sense that they constitute conceptual vectors and idioms used to convey information or knowledge. Such 'assessments' could involve quantitative modes of 'scaling' whereby we study in detail the properties of an individual drawing or study a large collection of drawings to gain an overview of what appear to be common graphic schema. In taking these options, we feel that we are gaining some understanding of the drawings and their graphic forms. In other words, we might say that we are using selected criteria or 'scalings' to scan the drawings in order to reduce complexity and invoke control over what we study. We must not lose sight of the point that the drawings are not understood 'in themselves' but through the pedagogical language and scalings, the descriptive technology of assessment in which the drawings are constructed.

To repeat, this kind of comparison of drawings is premised on a plural metaphysic of a world composed of an infinity of entities that are, as it were, brought under control through an external arbiter that demarcates differences between things, in our case, drawings. Strathern introduces the notion of a 'postplural conception of the world' (2004: xvi) which abandons the pluralist idea of comparison by external measures. In order to try to grasp the concept of the postplural, H&P (OT: 125–40) refer to the notion of *abstraction*. I will try to give a summary of how this term is developed by H&P in their exposition of Strathern's concept of the postplural and then discuss the implications of this term for pedagogical practice.

What would comparison mean in a world where there are no things understood as discrete beings or entities but a world of relations, transitions and connections, what we might refer to after Deleuze and Guattari, as a rhizomic world? In a pluralist world, abstraction refers to those arbiters or batteries of criteria that are more abstract than what is being compared (drawing practices) and which allow comparisons to be made. We might, as mentioned above, look at drawings from the abstract notions of 'texture', 'line', 'perspective' or other criteria that allow us to compare and assess the drawings. Such abstractions would appear to reduce the complexity and allow us to carry out the task of assessment when faced with a diverse range of graphic expressions. However, H&P (OT: 130) state:

> Whereas, on the plural imaginary, comparisons occur between different things, then, postplurally, they also take place within things, precisely because the postplural move is to treat everything – each and every thing in the world – *as* a comparison. (italic in original)

This idea of comparison is difficult to grasp, but it may have important implications for the way in which comparison is practised in some educational contexts. How can a drawing be a comparison? Could isolating particular features of drawings, a move that appears to reduce the complexity, actually precipitate new orders of complexity and comparison? Rather than viewing abstractions as external arbiters that are applied to phenomena in order to enact comparison and thereby reduce diversity, can we conceive abstractions as *internal differentiations* that open up immanent possibilities for practice and in doing so maintain or extend diversity? Could we apply this notion of internal differentiation to a drawing practice and the practice of conceptualization by a teacher? This idea of abstraction as differentiation reverses the more commonly held view of abstraction as the application of external criteria to facilitate comparison, referring instead to an internal or intensive operation functioning from within. So rather than reading a drawing from established authoritative criteria imposed from 'outside', we might focus upon the particular localized mark configurations immanent to a drawing (internal differentiations) and try to work with their immanent potential. This brings into play the inventive and creative work, the 'technology of description and invention', of pedagogical inquiry. The opportunity to explore and expand possibilities for practice, that of the child and that of the teacher. In such a move, a drawing becomes 'more than itself' both in terms of its internal differentiations and local potentials and in terms of how understanding drawing practices might be extended by a teacher.

Whilst in actual drawing practices, the intensive process of internal differentiation is crucial and constitutes what we might call immanent and intensive transformations across practice, in assessment practices, a drawing is constructed through assessment criteria abstracted from drawings which are then used to make comparisons between drawings. We might conceive these intensive transformations in terms of local rhythms of practice (or instaurations, a term I will discuss below) that provide the possibility for new directions to emerge. H&P (OT: 138) summarize these points succinctly:

> Comparison does no longer occur with reference to a higher level of abstraction and generalisation by reducing the individual complexities of and thus the differences *between* the objects of study, as in more conventional models of comparison. Rather, comparison occurs at the same order of reality and concretion as the object of study by unearthing differentiations *within* it. (italics in original)

This contrast between comparison that applies general criteria that reduce individual complexities and differences between objects of study to a set of 'external' criteria and comparison as an internal process of differentiation and mutation is echoed by Isabelle Stengers (2011a) as she comments on the imposition of comparative criteria applied across practice so as to define practice. For Stengers, practice:

> denotes any form of life that is bound to be destroyed by the imperative of comparison and the imposition of a standard ensuring equivalency, because what makes each practice exist is also what makes it diverge. It is crucial here

not to read 'diverge from others' as doing so would turn divergence into a fuel for comparison. (59)

This notion of internal lines of divergence or differentiation seems close to Strathern's notion of comparison as an immanent force. Stengers continues:

> Divergence is not between practices; it is not relational. It is constitutive. A practice does not define itself in terms of its divergence from others. Each does have its own positive and distinct way of paying due attention; that is, of having things and situations matter. Each produces its own line of divergence, as it likewise produces itself. (59)

The immanent coherence and divergence of a student's or child's art practice are paralleled in a pedagogy of taking care that needs to respond to this immanence through a capacity to invent a technology of description commensurate with this local coherence. The point of comparison developed by Strathern is not to 'generalise over', in our case children's drawing practices, but to 'recomplexify' such practices through paying due attention and careful conceptualization. We might say, following H&P (OT: 138), that engaging in pedagogical enquiry, the teacher becomes a 'bricoleur of concepts, not imposed on, but extracted from, the [pedagogical] moments studied'.

It is in such moments that what I call 'the gift of otherness' emerges. I am using the term 'otherness' in a number of associated ways. It can refer to those pedagogical moments already mentioned when we are confronted with the unfamiliar or the strange or those encounters with contemporary or other forms of art practice that we find challenging. But learning itself is dependent upon engaging with the other in the sense that learning is a process that passes beyond established ways of thinking to embrace that which lies beyond, that which is different or other. A learning encounter that expands capacities to think and act is therefore an encounter with otherness. This does not relate only to those aha! moments or moments of puzzlement that I have discussed, though these are moments in which otherness is perhaps more pronounced but is a process more common than we might think. The gift of otherness, therefore, includes encounters with that which we may find puzzling or different but also the process of becoming other as we expand our frameworks of practice in thought (conceptualization and reflection) and action. Its gift is to instigate a passing beyond what we might call the imperialism of established ways of thinking and acting or, in the terms of Wagner, to pass beyond the conformism of convention in order to generate the novelty of invention.

Eduardo Viveiros de Castro: Perspectivist Pedagogies, Pedagogies of Self-transformation and Careful Equivocation

Though Viveiros de Castro's work on perspectivism arises from his studies of Amerindian cultures, I will try to indicate its relevance for pedagogic enquiry and practice in relation to the ideas of ontology and difference. The political ambition of his work is to expose the ideological premises of Western anthropological enquiries in order to promote the interests of indigenous peoples. He employs the idea of perspectivism as a means to promote these political ends. We might say that the notion of multiculturalism promoted in the West is premised upon the notion of one nature, many cultures, in other words, cultural relativism, whereby different cultures interpret the world according to their respective viewpoints. Viveiros (2014: 14) counterposes the idea of multinaturalism through his idea of perspectivism. Put simply, perspectivism is not concerned with beings having different ways of viewing things in the world but with beings viewing different things so that, for example, for a European, a gift *is* an object given to someone, but for a Maori, it *is* a spirit. Anybody has an ontological perspective on the world and sees and feels other bodies from its specific perspective. There is divergence in what each perspective conceives the world to *be* (71–2). Put another way, it is not a case of seeing things differently but of seeing different things. For Viveiros, a body is not to be viewed as a single unified entity but, in some ways echoing Strathern's idea of the 'dividual', is constituted by an evolving assemblage of affects, intensities, dispositions, ways of moving and communicating, an ensemble of ways and modes of being that are singular to each body (72). This idea of a body is close to the notion of *agencements* or assemblage developed by Deleuze and Guattari. Such ontological perspectives are not to be considered as a form of cultural relativism but as emerging from what Viveiros calls 'corporeal mannerism' (73) that is particular to each body's capacities as a multiple assemblage. According to perspectivism, the difference between an anthropologist and someone from a culture being studied is primarily ontological in that they both see in the same way but what they see *is* different. In summing up the difference between cultural relativism and perspectivism, Marylin Strathern writes:

> It goes without saying the perspectivalism [cultural relativism] is the antonym of perspectivism. To be perspectivalist acts out Euro-American pluralism, ontologically grounded in one world and many viewpoints; whereas perspectivism implies an ontology of many worlds and one capacity to take a viewpoint. ... The relativity of perspectivism ... rests in the absoluteness of the body one inhabits; and it works by engaging the view of another upon oneself.

Here, as with Strathern and Wagner, the notion of comparison is important because perspectivism does not involve the production of a pure translation by the anthropologist of a culture being studied. Rather, for Viveiros, the notion of 'careful equivocation' characterizes the mode of perspectivist translation so that the latter is always to some extent incomplete. H&P (OT: 179) cite the example mentioned earlier of the gift in Maori culture, whereby a standard way of conceiving the way it is viewed by anthropologist and Maori is that the anthropologist 'sees' an *object*, whilst the Maori 'sees' a *spirit*. However, to repeat, in a perspectivist account, 'the divergence between the two perspectives consists, not in two ways of "seeing" the gift, but rather in two different ways of conceiving what the gift *is*' (italic in original). The emphasis shifts from an epistemological to an ontological focus; what a gift *is* is actually different. This ontological difference makes comparison a matter of *careful equivocation* rather than an absolute registration between two perspectives. Misunderstandings are always likely. It is not a case of the anthropologist developing an authoritative viewpoint upon Maori culture but rather a different ontological perspective to that of the Maori. But this experience of the 'other', its gift, we might say, is that through careful equivocation, new insights and transformations of thought and practice may emerge for the anthropologist. The gift of otherness may generate self-transformation through the inventions of careful equivocation (OT: 184–94). This gift can be viewed as precipitating a kind of transcendence, not in terms of an idealist position but in terms of a transcending of established perspectives and their conceptual frameworks through an encounter with otherness.

Following this example of the 'gift' from anthropology and the different ontological underpinnings to its respective meanings, we might shift across to pedagogical encounters in which a drawing (or other kinds of practices) is given meaning by a teacher and by a child or student, respectively. Is it a representation, or is it an invention? Are teacher and student talking about the same thing when discussing the drawing, or are they talking about different things? Something of this possible ontological mismatch is captured by Viveiros (2004: 10) discussing practices of translation and equivocation (error) in anthropology, which I think has some relevance for pedagogies of taking care:

> To translate is to emphasise or potentialize the equivocation, that is, to open and widen the space imagined not to exist between the conceptual languages in contact, a space that the equivocation [here *qua* error] precisely concealed. The equivocation is not that which impedes the relation, but that which founds it and impels it; a difference in perspective. To translate is to presume that an

equivocation always exists; it is to communicate with differences, instead of silencing the Other by presuming univocality – the essential similarity – between what the Other and We are saying.

A teacher may create a space of equivocation in which, when encountering aspects of a child's or student's work she does not register with, she asks, 'What is it about the way I conceive this practice that makes the child's or student's practice incongruous?' 'How might I change my conception?' On these points pedagogical enquiry begins to emerge as a more precarious, heuristic and experimental process that involves shifting alignments of pedagogic experiences and their conceptualizations that stand or fall by the degrees of insight they bring. Not to take otherness seriously, not to take care, is a way of silencing and controlling otherness.

Viveiros (2004: 11) tells us that in 'Amerindian cosmology there are no points of view *onto* things, things and beings are the points of view *themselves*' (italics in original). To see different things rather than seeing things differently implies an ontological difference between bodies viewed in terms of a 'dynamic assemblage of affects, dispositions or capacities which render the body of every different species unique' (Viveiros 1998: 478). Though he is referring to different species here, I think that we might adopt the ontological focus promoted by perspectivism for careful equivocation in pedagogic work, for example, when confronted, as discussed earlier, with the ontological grounds of children's drawings that we find puzzling. This problematizes the idea that we can directly access and understand such practices through objective observation and analysis. Taking a phrase from David Burrows and Simon O'Sullivan (2019: 189), we might propose that a perspectivist approach to pedagogic practice and enquiry proceeds through 'something like *alienation as method*' (italics in original). Such an approach seems to capture experiences with contemporary art practices, such as those discussed earlier, that challenge our comprehension of art practice and in doing so demand that we try to develop new articulations of practice as we are confronted with otherness.

The work of many contemporary artists may precipitate direct challenges for practices of art education in schools or elsewhere in that such work may disrupt the very grounds upon which art education functions. The ontological principle of 'becoming other' is an important and vital aspect of such experiences and of pedagogic practice. The gift of otherness is, therefore, not to be conceived objectively but in terms of a 'becoming-other-making' that is immanent to processes of learning and transformation. Becoming-other-making is possible because in a sense we possess the potential to become something else. This process is one of self-differentiation and self-transformation. The epistemological frameworks of pedagogic practice can be challenged by encounters with the ontology of otherness. Such challenges may reveal the limitations of pedagogic understanding, which place limits upon responding to alterity. A concern for the ontology of otherness brings with it, in the words of H&P (OT: 296), 'a certain kind of politics' that 'becomes immanent to the ontological turn'. If this in turn, in responding to otherness, functions by transmuting pedagogical encounters 'reflexively into forms of conceptual creativity and experimentation', which impact both teacher and learner, then it is continually and implicitly disposed to the production of otherness with all the epistemological and ethical obligations that emerge. We might therefore claim that pedagogy is *ontologically ethico-political* (OT: 296) in its obligations towards difference and its potentials that emerge in pedagogical encounters, whose affects and effects require that established frameworks of thinking may need to be modified or changed.

As H&P (OT: 175) state, whilst Wagner reworks the idea of culture as convention to culture as invention, Viveirios de Castro reconceptualizes the idea of a uniform nature to a multiplicity or a 'multinature'. My concerns are with developing pedagogies of taking care that call for a multiplicity of strategies that are able to respond effectively to the divergent ontological grounds of children's and students' modes of learning and which, in turn, expand pedagogical work. We might argue, looking awry, that perhaps the true purpose of pedagogy is the continuous education of teachers or educators.

Speculative Ontology, Creative Advance and Instauration

A pedagogy of taking care can be conceived in micropolitical terms as a war machine (Deleuze and Guattari), in the sense of a pedagogy that emerges in relation to otherness, that is to say, when it is confronted by and needs to respond to practices heterogeneous to established pedagogical frameworks and procedures. Such responses do not thereby assimilate the other to inherited pedagogical formats, but in receiving its gift, they challenge such formats and evolve new possibilities and parameters for transforming pedagogic work. Equally, such parameters are always subject to further disruption and change as such work encounters the contingencies and equivocations of practice. We might view this continual process of change in terms of what Alfred North Whitehead called the 'creative advance'. Otherness does not simply refer to that which is different or heterogeneous but also to the process of becoming other. We might say that otherness involves both relations of rupture and relations of transformation; it is inherent to processes of change.

The recent 'speculative turn' in philosophy involving a group of philosophers that includes Graham Harman, Quentin Meillassoux, Ray Brassier and Iain Hamilton Grant, often referred to as speculative realists or materialists, each adopting different philosophical approaches within this speculative adventure, has 'renewed' what Whitehead referred to as speculative philosophy. This turn has also been reflected in other fields such as social and cultural research (see Wilkie, Savransky and Rosengarten 2017) and also research in education (Rousell 2017). Stephen Shaviro (2011) contrasts the processual philosophy, or the philosophy of organism, of Whitehead to the substance philosophy of Graham Harman. He refers to Harman's remark that modern thought still remains largely enthralled by the idea of 'human access' or what Meillassoux names 'correlationism'. Essentially, these terms indicate that we cannot access the world or things in it directly; we cannot know things in-themselves; we can only access them through human forms of cognition. According to Meillassoux (2008: 5), correlationism is 'the idea according to which we only ever have access to the correlation between thinking and being, and never to either term considered apart from the other'. Variations of correlationism might include theories that interrogate the relation between mind and being, between language and being or between a transcendental ego and the world as set out in phenomenology. The fact that we only have access to the correlation takes us back to Kant and his ideas that we can never know reality as it is in itself but only as it appears to us. We cannot compare things as they appear to us with how things are in-themselves; because no direct access to things is possible, we can only 'think' of such access. One outcome of such correlationism is that epistemology seems to dominate ontology.

Whitehead is recognized by these speculative realists as someone whose philosophy did not privilege the human. In his philosophy of organism, he argues that all actual entities exist on the same ontological level; they are 'complex and interdependent' (Whitehead 1928: 18) in a continual process of becoming and perishing. Shaviro (281) comments, 'For Whitehead, human perception and cognition have no special or privileged status, because they simply take their place among the myriad ways in which all actual entities prehend other entities.' Actual entities emerge as a consequence of prehension, a key notion that does not relate only to humans but to all entities. Entities emerge and become what they are through prehending other entities. Prehension is a process (causal, perceptual, cognitive, affective) through which entities apprehend, respond or are affected by other entities as they in turn affect others. We might say that a human being is composed of multiple prehensions, psychic, affective, physical and so on (Whitehead 1928: 18; see also 1938: 150). Prehension then concerns awareness in the sense of an entity becoming aware of another entity, and such awareness is not immediately cognitive but affective, a kind of sensing or noticing, an ingression that registers a difference. This seems in some way to offset the correlationist argument by replacing the notions of human cognition and things 'in-themselves' by placing emphasis upon evolving relations.

Whitehead does not only name actual entities as fundamental beings but he also uses the term 'actual occasions' which gives his ontology a dual aspect involving things and events (1978: 119). This duality, following Shaviro (283), can be viewed in terms of 'contrasts', another term used by Whitehead (95) rather than incompatibility or opposition (1978: 348). We might say that Whitehead is proposing a contrast between being and becoming – a contrast that involves an actual real and a virtual real (Deleuze 1994: 208; Whitehead 1978: 214).

Whereas the term 'perception' may give the impression of a subject perceiving a world that exists 'out there', prehension is a creative process occurring within particular ontological coordinates. Prehending involves what Whitehead calls a 'subjective aim' or 'subjective form' which alludes to the particular manner in which something is grasped. Whitehead (1978: 23) writes:

> Every prehension consists of three factors: (a) the 'subject' which is prehending, namely the actual entity in which that prehension is a concrete element; (b) the 'datum' which is prehended; (c) the 'subjective form' which is *how* the subject prehends that datum.
>
> *How* an actual entity *becomes* constitutes *what* that actual entity is; ... Its being is constituted by its 'becoming'. (italics in original)

Each event of the coming together of these factors in a particular becoming is called a *concrescence*. Prehension can be viewed as a process of evaluation and transformation, as Shaviro (286) states, 'to prehend a datum is therefore already to "translate" it into a different form'. The subjective form which determines the manner in which prehension occurs and which distinguishes entities is equivalent to 'singular modes of decision and selection'. The decision is that from which novelty arises, 'whereby what is "given" is separated off from what *for that occasion* is "not given"' (Whitehead 1978: 42–3; my emphasis). The process of decision, a term that Whitehead uses in its root sense of a 'cutting off', 'constitutes the very meaning of actuality' (43). Whitehead states, '"Actuality" is the decision amid "potentiality"' (43). Something new, a new concrescence, is actualized in the act of decision: to take this action rather than that, to think this way rather than another, to view things this way and not that way. In *Modes of Thought*, he elaborates on this interrelation of actuality and potentiality (1968: 151–2):

> Thus in conceiving the function of life in an occasion of experience, we must discriminate the actualized data presented by the antecedent world, the non-actualized potentialities which lie ready to promote their fusion into a new unity of experience, and the immediacy of self-enjoyment which belongs to the creative fusion of those data with those potentialities. This is the doctrine of the creative advance whereby it belongs to the universe that it passes into a future.

In this final book, Whitehead (1968: 116) again emphasizes the importance of the subjective form of prehension he describes in *Process and Reality*, but he uses a different expression which reminds me of the constant obligation for a pedagogy of taking care.

> Our enjoyment of actuality is a realization of worth, good or bad. It is a value experience. Its basic expression is – Have a care, here is something that matters! Yes – that is the best phrase – the primary glimmering of consciousness reveals, something that matters.

The notion of how something matters to someone in 'this' situation and how it is subsequently expressed is what we might call the ontological fulcrum in relation to which a pedagogy of taking care is obligated to respond. This mattering brings together in a 'creative fusion', the 'actualised data presented by the antecedent world' and 'the non-actualized potentialities', thereby promoting a self-enjoyment of this particular fusion. If we bring together the notions of prehension, creative fusion and ontological pluralism and relate them to pedagogic work, we might see that such work is faced with innumerable creative fusions as learners prehend a learning encounter, with an obligation to respond to each fusion.

The ontology of 'the function of life in an occasion of experience' that involves the creative fusion of the actual and the potential leading to a creative advance might, to some extent, be captured by the gerund form *experiencing*, an occasion of experiencing. We often use the noun form *experience* in contrast to the gerund *experiencing*, and yet experience seems to lose the intensity and dynamism, the immediacy and situatedness of local affects and matterings that experiencing captures. In the next section, I will consider the notions of mattering, creative fusion and experiencing *vis a vis* learning encounters and pedagogic practice through the concept of *instauration* developed by Etienne Souriau in his text, *The*

Different Modes of Existence, published in 1943 during the German occupation of Paris, four years before the passing of Whitehead. According to Bruno Latour (2011: 308), Souriau's book raises a key question: 'In how many different ways can one say that a being exists?'

Etienne Souriau: Instaurations and the Ontology of Prepositions

Latour (308) points out that an 'ontology of prepositions immediately takes us away from the all-too-familiar inquiry into the philosophies of being'. It does not designate a domain or territory but a vector (on, in, at, near, between) that prepares a direction for becoming (a prepositioning), and so it concerns what we might call the key or the conditions in which becoming emerges (309), not what form becoming will take. Latour advises that enquiry into prepositions has to be differentiated from enquiry into substance or foundations but also that we require a term 'that allows us to link questions of language to the question of being, ... despite the demand that they should be distinguished' (309); this term is 'instauration'. A good way to begin to grasp this term is to consider the domain that was a major interest of Souriau, the creative processes of art practice. He considers a fairly traditional practice, sculpting in clay (1943: 42).

> A pile of clay on the sculptor's base. An undeniable, total, accomplished, thingy [*réique*] existence. But nothing of the aesthetic being exists. Each hand or thumb pressure, each stroke of the chisel accomplishes the work. Don't look at the chisel, look at the statue. With each act of the demiurge the statue little by little breaks out of its chains. It moves towards existence – towards the existence that will in the end blossom into an existence that is intense, accomplished, and actual. It is only insofar as the mass of earth is destined to be this work that it is a statue. At first only weakly existing via its distant relationship with the final object which gives it its soul, the statue slowly reveals itself, takes shape and comes into existence. First the sculptor is only pushing it into shape, then bit by bit he achieves it with each of the things he decides to do to the clay. When will it be finished? When the convergence is complete, when the physical reality of this material thing comes to correspond with the spiritual reality of the work to be made, and the two coincide perfectly. In its physical existence and its spiritual existence it then communes intimately with itself, each existence being the mirror of the other.

It would be a mistake to read this passage as if it was describing a hylomorphic process whereby form is imposed on matter, the artist's vision being imposed upon the clay. Rather we have to consider the whole process as a case of instauration (Latour 2011: 310). It is an ongoing process of invention-through-making which involves contingencies, surprises, mistakes, uncertainties, decisions, inspiration, deflation and so on. The making process can be viewed as a processual assemblage constituted by a range of actions, dispositions, affects, reflections and resolutions. It is not a one-way process in which the artist imposes their ideas or inspirations upon a passive material, whereby they are the origin of the work, but an ongoing relation in which the material affects, sometimes shocks, and opens new vistas and possibilities which the artist receives as a gift that informs the making process. The work is therefore the result not of a construction driven by the artist but of an instauration, an assemblage of becoming-making, invented and proceeding through the shifting movements and reciprocal relations of making. These shifting movements can involve in their becoming a feeling of potential, that which has not yet been achieved, that which the artistic assemblage is 'seeking' but which evades or which is illusive.

The Latin *instauratio* and *instaurare* suggest recommencement, restoration or resumption of that *which has not been able to be brought to fruition the first time*. This notion of incompletion is important. Instauration is concerned with the complex interrelating and evolving processes, already mentioned, of an assemblage; we might say an assemblage of prehensions, that which is impossible to capture, and that which is always incomplete. We might say that it is concerned with the ongoing evolution of an *ethos*, of the spirit of a making. It avoids any idea of origin, for example, the artist's intentions, and concerns the ongoing *collaborations* or *agencements* of practice. But I think it is reasonable to suggest that it does not just happen but is triggered by something or some event, or we might say an otherness or an ontological singularity that moves collaboration into a new or modified phase.

Latour (312) remarks that the Western philosophical tradition since the time of Parmenides has 'been obsessed with the identity of substance', that is to say, with a single mode of existence. Souriau's notion of multirealism is an attempt to explore different modes of existence. Latour (313) states:

In a strange passage, in which Souriau wonders at how rarely philosophy has attempted to multiply the modes of existence, he makes an astonishing statement: 'Absolute or relative, this [philosophical] poverty is in any case sufficient reason for conceiving and testing the Other as a mode of existence.' Here everything is defined: can we perhaps try alteration as a mode of subsistence, instead of always going to look for the substance lying beneath the alterations?

The term 'alteration' as a mode of subsistence has some affinity with notions of renewal, adaptation and mutation and is also connected to the idea of alterity or otherness, to process and difference. If we accept a metaphysics of process rather than substance, we might ask how many ways can a being alter, change or evolve, and this has direct relevance for pedagogical practice and the obligation to respond effectively to the ontological pattern of each child or student's mode of learning (mode of making) and the particular way in which such experiencings matter. In associating alteration with alterity, the ethos of each mode of learning will emerge in terms of its own ways of responding to, its own creative fusions with, that which is different or other in a learning encounter. More widely, does the way that knowledge is structured within educational domains presuppose and prioritize particular modes of existence and thus deny other modes? Does such structuring of being deny a wider range of existential potential? I will turn to these and related issues when discussing the mesopolitics of pedagogic practice in the concluding chapters.

From a teacher's point of view, we might consider different modes of learning that are encountered in pedagogical work through the experience of the *phenomenon* as explored by Souriau and which he approaches in its 'obviousness' (Latour: 317) or what Souriau calls *patuite* (patuity). We might refer here to the haecceity of the phenomenon and, thinking pedagogically, the obligation to respect the particular vectors that phenomena comprise. The need to respond to difference and multireality in pedagogic work may often degenerate to the use of educational platitudes, or established knowledge, without actually responding effectively to the singularity of the phenomenon and its particular vectors of difference and how such vectors become expressed. Commenting upon the all-embracing power of knowledge as *the* dominant mode of existence over other modes, Latour (320) states:

> The epistemic mode of existence has always been exaggerated, always made out to be the one mode that asks of all beings nothing other than how they can be *known*. This does not take away from its dignity, originality, or truth, but does deny its right to take originality, dignity, or truth away from the other modes of existence.

Obviously in the domain of pedagogic work, as in other domains, the development of knowledge is important, but it is also important to have an awareness of its imperial force particularly when we are confronted with alterity and the inherent patterns of different modes of existence. Latour (332) writes about the task of the philosopher which I think has relevance for a pedagogy of taking care and its task of responding to difference:

> If the philosopher is the 'shepherd of being', the job of a Souriau-type shepherd would require more care, more attention, and more vigilance, as well as more politeness. First, because each being must be instaured according to its own special procedure which can also go wrong; and then, because each flock is made up of animals of different sorts that take off in different directions.

There is some resonance with the pedagogic task of supporting others in their learning encounters and how these are instaured by each child or student in their respective patterns and the divergence of ecologies and ethologies of learning. Local processes of instauration relate closely to Whitehead's counsel 'have a care, here is something that matters', in that each mattering and creative fusion that constitute the creative advance can be viewed as ongoing instaurations, assemblages of practice in which body, mind, dispositions, tools, materials, inspirations, shocks and potentials emerge into an ethos and invention of becoming. Pedagogies of taking care do not abandon conventions of knowledge or practice but equally have to frontload a disposition towards varying degrees of alterity, a disposition that tries to be sensitive to each learner's assemblage of instauration and be able to invent commensurate modes of support and challenge.

The human world is currently trying to deal with a coronavirus pandemic that in many countries has revealed enormous degrees of inequality relating to housing, heating, food, clothing, education, physical and mental health and social welfare. In the light of such unacceptable inequalities in some quarters of government and the media, a call is beginning to emerge for a revaluation of education in schools and its purpose. Should there be such a major emphasis upon STEM subjects at the expense of the arts and humanities? Should more emphasis be given to individual and social well-being? Should we entertain a radical overhaul of the curriculum and devise new educational and pedagogical practices and structures that aim to enable individual and collective flourishing? Would such an overhaul challenge the conventional doxa, hierarchies and power relations of education? Should we build into educational processes an orientation towards what Deleuze and Guattari refer to as a people yet to come, a people not yet anticipated by current models of education? Should education be in the business of fabulating such a people? Current models and structures of education tend to presuppose modes of life for which their students are being prepared, and we might argue that learning encounters initiated within such a paradigm already anticipate particular modes of practice and solutions – a classroom of perpetual training for the increasingly pervasive world of capital production, competition and profit. In the final chapters, I will focus upon the molecular or micropolitics (and ethics) of pedagogic work and the micropolitics of art practice, which can be conceived as a micropolitics of the self, viewed in terms of ongoing ontological adventures of self-invention and transformation.

However, these notions of self-invention and transformation that have been discussed throughout this book are also key motifs of neoliberal modes of economic production in its perpetual search for new products, new desires, new sensibilities and new subjectivities for an ever-expanding market. The distinction has to be made between processes of transformation for the purpose of new convivial and civic collectives and those that serve the instrumental purpose of market capitalism and the perpetuation of *homo economicus*.

8

Thinking par le milieu: Pedagogic Work and Art Practice

Macropolitics and Micropolitics

On a couple of occasions in recent years, I have been accused of 'not having a political position' or that my work is 'politically neutral'. I found this challenging and a little puzzling in that I have always thought (perhaps wrongly) that my concern with how we might respond effectively to the problematics of 'otherness' in the domains of pedagogic practice is a deeply political and ethical challenge. For me, the idea of the political is an ever-present ontological, ecological and relational challenge and an always incomplete practice.

Perhaps the difficulty lies in how we approach the political, and I think this is where the problem, if it is a problem, might lie. There is a keen ontological difference between what we might call macropolitics and micropolitics, but they are inseparably linked as argued by Gilles Deleuze and Felix Guattari (1988: 213) in part 9 of *A Thousand Plateaus*, titled *Micropolitics and Segmentarity*. They make a distinction between the rigid segmentarity of molar systems and a more supple segmentarity of molecular flows; 'every society, and every individual, are thus plied by both segmentarities simultaneously: one molar, the other molecular.' State apparatuses, such as education, and their overcoding administrative structures constitute molar segmentarities, or striations, but they also depend upon a molecular diffusion and suffusion of their values and relations. Deleuze and Guattari argue that the 'stronger the molar organisation is, the more it induces a molecularization of its values, relations and elementary apparatuses' (215). On an individual molar level, we often adhere to modes and overcodings of practice and organization which we inherit, feel secure and which sustain us; these constitute 'the arborescences we cling to' (227) and which generate molecular resonances and desires. Translating the molar and the molecular into the political, Deleuze and Guattari (213) state, 'In short, everything is political but every politics is simultaneously a macropolitics and a micropolitics.' A macropolitics depends upon a micropolitical diffusion of its values and relations. But there is also a micropolitics of affects and experiencing that trigger an inventiveness that punctures or resists macropolitical forces and their micropolitical diffusion, generating what Deleuze and Guattari call 'lines of flight' that may bring about macropolitical change. Put in a different, metaphorical register, we might view this resistant or inventive notion of the micropolitical in terms of those growths that appear between solid blocks of paving slabs. Deleuze and Guattari (216) state, 'There is always something that flows or flees, that escapes the binary organisations, the resonance apparatus, and the overcoding machine.'

The macropolitics of neoliberal capitalism that has generated global practices of exploitation, corruption, extractivism and destruction of natural resources, coupled with its version of capitalist production, competition and marketization, simultaneously permeates a micropolitical diffusion and suffusion of its values. Here the macro and the micro (or the molar and molecular) are indissoluble. As Maurizio Lazzarato (2009) puts it, neoliberal capitalism continually constructs and reconstructs human capital within different assemblages; the subject is made to feel responsible for their training and to adopt a permanent state of self-surveillance.

The macro system of educational policies and practices that are today largely impelled by neoliberal economic forces and values depends upon a molecular diffusion that produces particular pedagogized subjectivities. And such subjectivities in turn are driven by molecular desires and affects channelled through the production and stratification of desire, semiotic atmospheres and codes of neoliberal economic forces that establish a particular micropolitics of becoming, a machinic enslavement to neoliberal commodification. According to Suely Rolnik (2017), the macropolitics of neoliberal capitalism has exerted a powerful capture of individuals and collectives through what she terms the micropolitics of a *colonial-capitalistic unconscious* (5) according to which life is reduced to what we might call a *viva economicus*. Other modes of existence that proffer different values and relations are marginalized. Rolnik argues that the subject as a macropolitical production is 'subject' to the power relations and overcoding of conduct that orders and polices what Ranciere (2004) calls the distribution of the sensible. This refers to established social modes or patterns of conduct, ways of speaking, hearing, seeing, feeling, sensibilities that operate inclusions and exclusions in relation to a policed social consensus. Resistance at a macropolitical level may seek to redistribute the sensible and its inherent power relations in the name of equality. One difficulty, however, is that resistant or opposing macropolitics tends to function in the name of 'empowerment' within the existing social milieu, the right to be recognized to have a voice (Rolnik 2017: 8). Such resistance is not to be dismissed or disapproved of and may be vitally important to support. In contrast, a micropolitical insurgency would be one that emerges not from established opposition but from 'the potentialization of life', of vital modes of existence that, in the words of Deleuze and Guattari, create new lines of flight to escape dominant macropolitical regimes, potentialities that open up possibilities for 'an effective transmutation of individual and collective reality' (8). Rolnik (5) writes:

> The problem of the colonial-capitalistic unconscious is the reduction of subjectivity to the subject, which excludes its immanent experience of our living condition: the outside-the-subject. This exclusion is extremely harmful to life.

This outside-the-subject, the subject as composed by the colonial-capitalistic unconscious, refers to those events and their vital affects and forces that may disturb established modes of subjectivation and, functioning at a molecular or micropolitical level, constitute what Rolnik calls an eco-ethological knowing (5). Such becoming extends before and beyond neoliberal capture, and it extends continuously beyond the subject, diffusing or 'dividualising' what we often think of as a unified independent individual into a complex of affects and relations, processes close to Whitehead's notion of prehension. Rolnik (5) captures this process:

> In our living condition we are constituted by the effects of forces, with their diverse and mutable relationships that stir the vital flows of a world. These forces traverse all the bodies that compose the world, making them one sole body in continuous variation, whether or not we are conscious of it. We can designate these effects as affects. It is an experience that is extra-personal (since there is no personal contour, since we are the variable effects of the forces of the world, which compose and recompose our bodies), extra-sensory (since it happens via affect, distinct from perception), and extra-sentimental (since it happens via vital emotion, distinct from psychological emotion).

We might say that this 'extra' experience is an experience of otherness and that we are constituted by its affects and effects, that it inhabits our being and becoming. Rolnik argues that in this sphere of outside-the-subject, we relate to the other through *empathy*, a process 'in which there is no distinction between the cognizant subject and external object' (5). She continues:

> In the subjective experience outside-the-subject, the other lives effectively in our body, it dwells in us through its effects, the affects. It is with its living presence that empathy takes place. By inhabiting our body, the forces of the world impregnate us, creating embryos of other worlds. These produce in us a sense of strangeness, distinct from the familiarity provided by our experience as subjects.

When we work with others as in a teaching-learning context, and we receive their gift which, in Rolnik's terms, may 'create embryos of other worlds', and we offer ours – when we function according to a pedagogy of taking care, an important medium of relation is empathy. It is not the imposition of established form, concepts or practice but an *empathic collaboration* that may give rise to new sensibilities and new possibilities. We might call this a micropolitics of empathy.

To be clear, Rolnik argues against the macropolitical sphere of the colonial-capitalistic world and what she refers to as 'the pimping of life' through its particular modes of exploitation, subjectivation and homogenization, because it invalidates and neutralizes alternative modes of existence or processes of singularization that could precipitate transmutations of social reality that prioritize convivial, civic and democratic values and relations as these are debated and transformed. This is not to reject the macropolitical sphere, only particular versions that perpetuate exploitation and greed, prejudice and bigotry. The task is therefore to work towards a macropolitical sphere in which processes of singular and collective invention promote conviviality and democracy, realizing that these will always be subject to new transmutations emerging from micropolitical or macropolitical forces. This would be a 'macrosphere' that acknowledges and values micropolitical invention, difference and even insurgency that may transmute the former sphere. This sense of the political in the micropolitical emerges therefore from the contingencies of singular creative events and their potentialization of life and a people to come.

In relation to the production of pedagogized subjectivities, we might view curriculum frameworks, guidelines, competences and standards, assessment criteria and teaching methodologies as constituting a macropolitical sphere that valorizes particular kinds of pedagogized subjects according to the parameters established by such apparatuses. Teachers encouraged or instructed to deploy such dispositifs are therefore working from pre-established templates according to which students and children as learners should conform in order to fulfil their current and future positions in the social complex, the distribution of the sensible, which in the current epoch is determined by the values of neoliberal economics. The effect and affect of these macro dispositifs are to generate a micropolitical unconscious that captures, controls, informs and perpetuates practice according to their values, relations, modes of organization and subjectification. Equally, within subject disciplines, such as art, there are what we might call inherited macropolitical structures according to which both teachers and learners tend to conform producing a pervasive micropolitical unconscious that captures and orients practice. The art curriculum consists of a taxonomy of practices, skills, techniques and knowledge; it also involves teaching methods, assessment and evaluation, project and lesson planning and evaluation. The difficulty, which has been raised throughout these chapters, is that such structures, functioning as macropolitical dispositifs coupled with their micropolitical diffusion, tend to omit, marginalize or invalidate some practices that emerge in the microsphere of existential practices. In doing so they suppress the potential of such practices as well as the potential for transmutation in the scope of pedagogical practice.

We might say that such prescribed pedagogical structures determine particular modes of teaching and learning and therefore function within a politics of representation that operates through particular identitarian schemas that define practices of teaching and learning and which produce particular forms of pedagogized subjects. Though we require pedagogical structures such as those just mentioned, their dogmatic insistence by government inspection regimes, for example, may restrict access to or acknowledgement of 'other' modes of practice and their micropolitical potential, thus impeding the advancement of more macroscopic pedagogical horizons.

The hegemony of macropolitical pedagogical structures coupled with their micropolitical affects may induce a kind of micro-fascism towards alterity and an inability to respond to the creative potentials of practices that do not accord with established dispositifs that govern and regulate practice. Can we avoid the capture of pedagogical dogmatism? This alludes to a continual tension between the desire for conservation and the desire of invention. The former would take the form of something to be attained, a prescribed object of desire, that the learner lacks. This can be contrasted with desire viewed as a creative force emerging in a particular evolving learner assemblage and its relationalities that constitute a becoming. The existential domain of convention that tends to dominate institutional practices such as those in education exerts forces of perpetuation and preservation and their respective values that may exclude or invalidate modes of practice and their desires that do not conform to and which may challenge their register.

We may need to consider desire on a 'personal' level and how, as teachers, it informs how we acknowledge the different ways in which children or students respond to practices we initiate. I am referring here on one level to what we might call our micro-sensitivities, our micro-dispositions, often unconscious, that include feelings, preferences and affects that 'in-form' our responses. These are complex assemblages shaping dispositions, attitudes and expectations, and whilst on a molar level, we may react in an anti-fascist way to established practices that we take to be culturally biased; we may not see the fascisms that we ourselves sustain and nourish and that consist of our predispositions and expectations. On a more macro level, pointing to more rigid curriculum and assessment structures according to which teachers are obliged to operate within a planned centralizing system that regulates practice, Deleuze and Guattari (1988: 227) comment:

> We are always afraid of losing. Our security, the great molar organisation that sustains us, the arborescences we cling to, the binary machines that give us a well-defined status, the resonances we enter into, the system of overcoding that dominates us – we desire all that.

Can we alter the scene of education and pedagogic work towards a pedagogy of taking care and all that this demands in relation to relaxing the grip of molar forces – a pedagogy that would be open to the micropolitical insurgence and potential of otherness without abandoning or devaluing those macro-practices and traditions that have at their root a concern for individual and collective flourishing? Can we develop a micropolitical and ethico-aesthetic approach to education and pedagogic practice that avoids the current pimping of education for economic ends and can build upon the potentialization of life in its diverse modes of existence? Ben Anderson (2017: 594) states, 'For me, the hope of micropolitics is that it invites us to learn how to act in the midst of ongoing, unforeclosed situations and experiment with ways of discerning and tending to the "otherwise". It opens up a potentializing space to effect new subjectivities, for changing the parameters of subjectivation.

Having made these points about the entanglements of macropolitics and micropolitics in the domains of pedagogic practices, it seems to me that this does not go far enough. Both macro and micro analyses help us to comprehend how molar forces, such as curriculum structures, assessment practices and inspection regimes, generate and perpetuate their values on a molecular level in the dispositions and expectations of teachers and the practices of learners. What such analyses do not seem to tackle are what Souriau called the instaurations, the becoming-making of practice, that is to say, the processual politics and ethics of emerging individuations and assemblages that may engender new or modified subjectivations.

Functioning at the Meso Level

Lazzarato (2014: 14) tells us that according to both Foucault and Guattari, 'the production of subjectivity and the constitution of the relation to the self were the sole contemporary political questions capable of pointing the way out of the impasse in which we still continue to flounder.' For Foucault, this production emerged through an aesthetics of existence and a politics sympathetic to this, whilst for Guattari, it was through existential affirmation and a new aesthetic paradigm moving beyond capitalist modes of subjection. The notion of becoming-making from Souriau taps into the relational flows of the actual existential assemblage process that exist prior to any micro or macro analyses. This relates to techniques, to having a feel for, what Isabelle Stengers calls 'meso-knowledge', to the procedures and processes of making within a particular milieu. She comments (2009a), 'The meso is a site of invention where the pragmatics of the question is much more alive,' than is the case in micro or macro analyses. With the meso we are dealing with that which rises up in practice, its contingencies, the malleability of materials, the affects they generate, their resistance and accommodations, in short, the contingencies of events of becoming-making. These concern a mesopolitics of becoming-making. Materials here refer not just to relations with things like paint, clay, wood, metal and so forth but also to concepts, bodies, plants, animals, computers, films, videos, instruments, sound and so on. Such becoming-makings and their material relations may produce new prehensions, new or modified assemblages or lines of experimentation that lead to new collectivities and their potentials. The meso dimension of becoming-making involves a mesopolitics that will involve pragmatic issues of failure as well as success. A mesopolitics is concerned with the relational materialities and affects of events of becoming-making that may lead to capacities to think and invent in situations of concern beyond established parameters of thought and practice and so bring about new or modified subjectivities.

Isabelle Stengers and Mesopolitics

Isabelle Stengers states that the terms 'macropolitics' and 'micropolitics' do not work for her and prefers the notion of mesopolitics. The term 'mesopolitics' is deeply concerned with the material, with material relations, properties, techniques, processes and procedures. As she puts it (2012a: 8):

> When you have a perfect crystal it can be understood in micro or macro terms. But as soon as you have something which can bend, or any other properties of materials stickiness, fatigue, plasticity, elasticity, limits of elasticity, you cannot understand it in macro or micro terms. Such properties need the introduction of the meso scale, a scale that is not fixed because it is the one which allows you to characterize interstices, defects, faults … and their consequences. The properties of matter may be derived from generalities. At the meso scale you have to follow and narrate.

The meso level is concerned with questions such as why does glue stick? Why do cracks appear? How is *this* encountered? How does *this* propagate (2009a)? We might view such questions as pointing to ontological events and their affective materialities. They point to events of relations-between or *intersticial events*. Meso refers to 'the middle' or the 'in-between'. In the actualities and contingencies of working with the relational capacities of materials, as an artist with her materials, such handling or comprehension does not emerge in micro or macro terms, but it functions at the meso level which is not fixed, but fluid, because of the very nature of working with materials, their resistance, acceptance, accommodation, receptivity, tolerance and so forth. Such forces and affects may change or modify a situation of practice presenting new possibilities. So the meso level involves a 'creative advance' (Whitehead), or it may not.

If we apply this notion of the meso to the actualities, events, affects, unpredictability, uncertainties and evolving materialities of human relations, we are concerned not with operating from general principles, codes or guidelines but working-with the contingencies of functioning that require not guidelines but ways of noticing and narrating. On a political plane, the meso level relates pragmatically to working-with the problematics of living and finding ways to cope and articulate such coping strategies.

We might say that a pedagogy of taking care operates at the meso level when a teacher is trying to respond to a child's or student's practice that she finds puzzling in relation to her expectations or anticipations. 'Taking care' of such events is a pragmatic concern which involves a teacher trying to find ways of understanding, maybe shifting her expectations, putting aside established habits of thought and thinking in a different mode, not rushing to conclusions but remaining open to 'other' possibilities. This process would constitute the mesopolitics of the pedagogical event as the teacher and the learner work with the evolving materialities of pedagogical relations in a particular situation and which may transform those who participate. We cannot generalize in such situations, though this tendency is often what happens, but try to treat each pedagogical occasion as a particular event, thus giving each 'situation the power to make us think' (Stengers 2005b: 185). Another way of putting this is to receive the gift of the situation, its 'otherness' to engage our thinking. A situation's power, its gift, is virtual and thus demands thought, as a practice to invent, to artefactualize ways forward. And such practices of thought are required to be careful not to occlude or dismiss those pathways to learning and their particular ways of mattering that do not meet our expectations. By paying attention to how something matters for each learner by implication means that there are often different ways in which a situation, such as a learning encounter, can matter.

Another way of putting this is given by Whitehead through his notion of 'common sense' which does not refer to common knowledge but, as Stengers (2014b: 200) suggests, to a common interest 'for the way others make their world matter, ... for tales about different ways of life, for experimenting with what may be possible. For wandering and wondering'. This idea of common sense when applied to pedagogic work and the task of initiating a learning encounter implies that a teacher is involved in making connections, developing a rapport, in which the aim is not simply to transmit knowledge but to generate a learning encounter that calls out for the child to make a leap, to induce a feeling of existential importance to the encounter that encourages a leap. The teacher's task is then to restrain from imposing their 'expert' knowledge and to work with the consequences and potentials of each leap, to support and extend each child's pathway of learning, which may also extend that of the teacher. Whitehead also provides a famous anecdote that characterizes each leap by referring to the flight and landing of an aeroplane. It leaves a ground that calls for the flight of experimentation and exploration, and it lands again with a renewed attention and more questions, which mean that the ground is then altered and renewed with the power to call for a new flight.

The collective resources produced through such meso-thinking and practice could open up alternative practices and an ethico-politics of education to the current dominant mode that is driven largely by economic concerns. Such educational alternatives are very difficult to materialize against the forces of economic capture. But the task of meso-thinking, or put in the words of Deleuze and Guattari, adopted by Stengers, thinking *par le milieu*, is to resist the almost unconscious move to register in advance how a particular pathway to learning matters for a learner. In other words, the task of meso-thinking as practice is to be open to the gift of otherness that such situations may present. This could generate a mesopolitics to subvert current macropolitical values of education and their micropolitical diffusion, through a pragmatic collective and its potentials for different matters of concern that could lead to a different world than that exploited and being destroyed by global capitalism. A mesopolitics and ethics of pedagogic work involves a pragmatic concern for the singularities emerging from composing-with, a materiality that involves experiment, success and failure, which can lead to new modes of practice and new conditions for both teaching and learning. In pedagogic work both teacher and student are in Deleuze's (1994) terminology 'apprentices in learning' where 'learning evolves entirely in the comprehension of problems' (192). Learning from the particular relationality of problems, the student responding to a learning encounter and the teacher responding to the student's response, is something we cannot 'know' in advance but, in each case, requires an art of fabrication towards the problem that is always local. How a learner fabricates their response has to be handled with care by a teacher in their fabrication so as not to stifle the student's pathways to learning and their possible potential for future practice. This taking care is both an ethical and a political concern on the meso level.

Can we dare to shift the driving force of education grounded in notions of competition, progress, self-improvement, careerism and work towards propositions in Whitehead's terms, as a lure for feeling, that would set the conditions for education to function in a different key, by invoking a politics and ethics of the meso level of functioning? This would involve a mesopolitics emerging from the level of existential problems that in turn might invoke micro and macro effects by acknowledging that education should not be 'conditioned' by a single transcendent purpose designated by particular interests that excludes others but should be open to a multitude of as yet unknown and diverging futures – conditions that lure us into an acknowledgement that there are different ways in which a learning encounter matters and whose subsequent learning pathway cannot necessarily be subsumed under a common measure. Such daring may seem irrational, and such conditions are difficult to bring about in the current era of education. But can we invent or *reclaim* (Stengers 2012b) propositions, in Whitehead's sense, for a world that might be possible that may lure us into confronting the notion that our current systems of education are failing many children and students whose pathways to learning are so often occluded, marginalized or stymied. This could be a reclaiming from thinkers and educators, such as Whitehead, Dewey, Illich, Greene, Hall, hooks and others, that attempts to recover educational/conceptual practices not in terms of going back but in terms, as Stengers (2012b: 4–6) advises, of 'recovering', which in the context of education today would involve a reclaiming of *ethos* and *oikos* through an ecosophic education as discussed in Chapter 6, of learning from experiencing that which animates, of developing capacities for taking responsibility for our modes of relating to others and our environments. Stengers comments:

> Reclaiming means recovering what we have been separated from, but not in the sense that we can just get it back. (2012b: 4)
> Reclaiming means recovering, and, in this case, recovering the capacity to honour experience, as not ours but rather as animating us, making us witness to what is not us. (7)

Here the notion of otherness returns in this case as that which animates coupled with the task of recovering the capacity to honour experience.

In a conversation with Henk Oosterling moderated by Sjoerd van Tuinen (Stengers 2012a), van Tuinen remarks (2) that what Isabelle Stengers teaches us is

> that when it comes to difference, what counts is not so much a passive openness to the other, but rather the ability to actively introduce oneself to the others and this ability to make oneself relevant to the other is precisely the precondition for any civilized encounter.

Van Tuinen (2) then combines the notion of introducing oneself to others by quoting Gilles Deleuze from his text *Negotiations*:

> Mediators are fundamental. Creation is all about mediators. Without them nothing happens. They can be people but things too, even plants or animals. If you're not in some series, even a completely imaginary one, you are lost. You are always working in a group, even when you seem to be on your own.

The actual working practice of mediation, as is involved in pedagogical encounters, functions at the meso level; it operates *par le milieu*, from, as Stengers (2) puts it, 'the feeling something may grow here without imposing an aim on it ... the aim is present but not in a commanding way, not as defining its means.' This pedagogical orientation, which I have termed a pedagogy of taking care, operates through meso processes of experimentation and learning through which people engage individually and collectively. It emphasizes the singularities and divergence of practice and its local pathways of concern and potential that require care. A meso level of taking care, as mentioned repeatedly, involves vigilance towards and constantly working on one's own dispositions, expectations and sensibilities as well as a constant openness to the concerns, matterings and potentials of those we work with and try to encourage and support. To enable the production of new or modified assemblages (Deleuze and Guattari), practices that produce agency in terms of individual and collective modes of existence will involve working with micropolitical differences and events (otherness) towards resolution – sometimes with success, sometimes with failure. But Stengers (2012a: 10) warns us that mesopolitics in such situations is about 'treating this divide not in terms of micropolitics but as a learning process of the collective'. Can we consider such situations not from individual perspectives but from how a situation raises questions for a virtual 'we', thus creating an active dynamic between individual and collective subjectivities, a dynamic *par le milieu*? In terms of pedagogical (and other) practices, what Stengers calls 'the art of the meso' is about creating possibilities for something to happen, and learning from the meso is all about learning from the contingencies, fluctuations, unpredictabilities, uncertainties, possibilities and dynamics of those practices with which we are engaged or are party to and share, coupled with the statements we can make about them. We might say that the art of the meso is an invention emerging from the event which involves a coming together of materials and affects, as in art practice, of body, affects, materials such as brush, paint, canvas, clay, fabrics and computers, where the event is not reducible to any of its components, because they are all participants in the assemblage and ecology of practice. The art of the meso is therefore always an art of the in-between, *par le milieu*. The assemblages of actual working practices of pedagogical relations always demand a working 'in the middle', and the sense of such assemblages is not attributed only to a knower (artist, teacher, student) but involves multiple components in both actual and virtual realities. We might take from this that assemblages of learning are processes which are both actual and virtual, constituting a meso level of becoming-making, which involves multiple, unpredictable participants not reducible to knowledge.

'Evaluation assemblages', a ubiquitous term in educational contexts along with its partner assessment, tend to function on a macro level and are normally concerned with the products and processes of practice considered through pre-established criteria. From a mesopolitical level, evaluation concerns how a practice situation is inhabited. This could involve coping with surprises, disappointments, frustrations, excitements, failures and successes. Evaluation at the meso level concerns a craft of learning from a situation towards the becoming-making of the assemblage of a particular learning pathway, its particular arrangement and connections in process (a connection between situations and enunciations arising from them and which they form parts), whereas at the more macro level, it succumbs to established hylomorphic forces. Evaluation at the meso level is concerned with a learning from the situation, from the forming of assemblages of concern (arrangements and connections) and their potential that may allow further experimentation for individual and collective flourishing.

Being sensitive to the practice of others and their evolving assemblages of practice, feeling that something may grow here without imposing an aim or your views, sensing that the student is making connections no matter how tentative, giving confidence to explore and experiment, allowing the student to feel the engagement in practice, all of these are important to a pedagogy of taking care. It is a pedagogy in which both teacher and student are equals and where evaluation involves a mutual collaboration, a pragmatic negotiation, which is part of the ongoing practice and not something external to the practice.

This idea of equals is given a historical illustration by Stengers (2012a: 14) who mentions the establishment of the *école mutuelle* in France from 1747 and in the UK around 1795, spreading more widely at the beginning of the nineteenth century. It functioned on the basis of equals through 'mutual teaching' whereby children teach each other. Variants of this practice have been developed much more recently in Germany by Jean-Pol Martin and others, under the name 'Lernen durch Leheren', and in Paris by Vincent Faillet through the concept of 'mutual class'. A related variant was set up by Sugata Mitra (2006) in 1999 in India who established an educational project titled 'The Hole in the Wall' that developed the concept of 'Minimally Invasive Education' whereby children of various ages organized their own learning. Implicit to this idea of mutual education is an acceptance that students learn in different ways, at different speeds and rhythms; it respects and values heterogeneity. Stengers (2012a: 15) makes a crucial point here about working with and through difference:

> I think that a process which not only takes its heterogeneity for granted, but understands this heterogeneity as an active and important aspect of the situation, is politically very robust. Because if you start from an ideal of homogeneity and identity, it will be vulnerable to any difference. Difference will always be perceived as a defect.

A working condition of difference and divergence is implicit to a pedagogy of taking care, and such 'working with' functions on the meso level of practice where a teacher has to work with how a learning encounter matters for a student and how such mattering can be enhanced at the local level of skill development.

Micropolitics in the form of 'minor gestures' discussed by Erin Manning (2016: 75) runs close to the notion of mesopolitics formulated by Stengers. Writing about the artistic process as a minor gesture, Manning states:

> Minor gestures trouble institutional frameworks (macro) in the same way they trouble existing forms of value. This is their potential: they open the artistic process beyond the matter-form of its object, beyond the prestige value that comes with all the artistic conclusions that surround us. The minor gesture is the felt experience of potential (micro), the force that makes felt how a process is never about an externally situated individual, but about the ecology it calls forth. (my brackets)

Yet in some ways, this does not fully embrace that sense of the meso Stengers identifies, which relates to the contingencies of practice and how these might be experienced and managed. For her, the meso level lies 'in the middle', in what we might call the material and affective relationalities of practice and its milieu, together with emerging potentials. Mesopolitics is concerned therefore with the politics and intensities of the as yet unknown, with the becoming-making of an ecology of practice. This would be a politics-in-the-middle, a politics of the rhizome, working and reworking assemblages of practice.

I turn now to consider the notion of mesopolitics in art practices and consider some implications for a mesopolitics of art in education in relation to an ethics and aesthetics of subjectification in Foucault's terms – the creative practice of the becoming-making of a life.

The Mesopolitics of Art Practice and Art in Education: Subjectivation *par le milieu*

Before I consider mesopolitical functioning in contexts of art in education, perhaps an illustration of such functioning within a very different context may be helpful, a context that involves everyday practices of educating for social survival, consideration and respect. The illustration comes for a recent BBC film titled *Lets Talk about Race* (2021), presented by Naga Munchetty who interviewed black people to talk about their experiences of racial discrimination and victimization. She spoke to two teenage boys sitting with their father. They mentioned a particular instance in school when their mates were fooling around, and a passing teacher commented, 'It's always the black ones isn't it.' The conversation continued along these lines, and one of the boys said that his father, a retired athlete who represented England in the Olympics, told him, 'You have to play the game, the rules are not the same for you.' Munchetty then turned to the father and engaged in the following conversation:

> **NM:** 'Did you give this advice to your son?'
> **Father:** 'Absolutely. Because what was becoming clear is that he was becoming labelled and that label was sticking ... so he was getting in trouble ... that was my advice as a father, as a black man who was born and raised here ... don't attract too much attention to yourself.'
> **NM:** 'Do you think a white father has to say that to a white son?'
> **Father:** 'Certainly not!'
> **NM:** 'Then how does that make you feel?'
> **Father:** 'It makes me feel sad, in one sense, but there is something about living life pragmatically.'

A second interview takes place with another black father talking about the prejudice and injustice of police 'stop and search' policy in the UK, a policy in which far more black people are subject to its prosecution. He was talking about his teenage son, insisting that he wear clothes that would not draw attention, such as black hoodies. 'I can't allow him to wear the clothes he wants to wear to be himself ... even though he is not harming anyone ... because I know it's the way he will be perceived ... I will wait for a call from the station.'

These conversations concern the politics of living with injustice, discrimination, abuse and violence. On one important level, we can develop, support, demand and instigate a politics of resistance or opposition to social inequalities and injustices, and this is absolutely necessary, as the uprisings in London and other cities, following the New Cross fire in London in 1981, clearly confirm. Such uprisings were the consequence of institutional racism in the police and the continual condoning of such attitudes by government. The uprisings demanded another kind of politics and ethics to the apartheid politics of discrimination, abuse, persecution and prejudice condoned by macro social forces, manifestations of which, sadly, still exist.

But the day-to-day living-with such situations as described by the fathers in the interviews above seems to demand a more nuanced or meso notion of politics that emerges through a pragmatics of life-in-the-making, as stated by one father and implied by the other. Such pragmatics do not imply simply accepting the situation with resignation and 'getting on with it', far from this, but strategies of concern and care that facilitate an assemblage of coping whilst also opposing and resisting the status quo, advocating and demanding change. The notion of mesopolitics as proposed by Isabelle Stengers captures the spirit of a becoming-politics, of a politics emerging in the middle of a pragmatics of living.

Perhaps we can think of the mesopolitics of art practice as that which is concerned with assemblages of becoming-making, with the exploration and experimentation with materials (of all kinds, including concepts) that lead to new consequences and possibilities for expression and the emergence of new sensibilities, new modes of existing and new collective relations –an existing not as a subject but, as Foucault argued, as a work of art, which would entail a continuous process of becoming-making *par le milieu*.

Art practices, such as drawing, painting, sculpting, performance, film and other modes, involve materials as media for expression and conceptualization within particular situations and surroundings. An artist feels and thinks in and with paint or other materials, an ongoing experimenting and composing in and with materials. It is not a case of the artist driving and orchestrating this composing but rather a reciprocal adventure in which artists and materials ask questions of each other and from which particular decisions, propositions, consequences and potentials may emerge. In other words, such practice is a composing of a particular artistic assemblage. Stengers (2005b: 185) comments on this reciprocity referencing Whitehead, 'I would speak of a decision, more precisely a decision without a decision-maker which is making the maker.' Decisions, consequences and potentials emerge from what Stengers calls a 'relationship of relevance', arising in the event or adventure, which constitutes a particular assemblage of composing. The milieu of such adventures of composing involves singularities, nuances and affects that precipitate pathways of practice involving contingencies and shifts in direction, stumblings, breakthroughs, surprises, disappointments and impasses that have the capacity to change both practice and its milieu. Acting in the middle is therefore concerned with the contingent, affective and conceptual forces of adventures of composing in and with a milieu, with their consequences and potentials that may lead to iterations of new sensibilities and modes of practice. The consequences and potentials, and their actualizations, can lead to the seeding and flowering of new questions and new challenges. The connection between body and paint, or other materials, and the reciprocal composing, whereby we allow a situation the power to make us think, alerts us to each existential import and potential of such composing and the need to avert pigeonholing according to established practices or discourses. Such events of experience, an epiphany in painting, sculpting and filming, for example, expose us to their unpredictability, and their decisions and consequences can trigger an expanded milieu of becoming-making. We are always exposed to materials and forces that surround and those that are within us, being and becoming in the middle.

The composing of practice in the middle constitutes all art practices. Its decisions and consequences can be particularly 'felt' as Guattari (1995: 106) claims as 'it engenders unprecedented, unforeseen and unthinkable qualities of being' that open up new sensibilities, new modes of existence, new subjectifications and as such an ongoing mesopolitical dimension – a politics of ongoing becoming-making within an ecology of coexistence and co-becoming.

Historically, we might think of the individuations of 'Claude Monet's' painting assemblages, or those of 'Jackson Pollock', or in more contemporary times, the assemblages of 'Albert Irvine', 'Oscar Murillo', 'Anselm Kiefer', 'Yayoi Kusama', 'Cindy Sherman', 'Sonia Boyce', 'Lavette Ballard', 'Yinka Shonibare', 'John Mawurndjul' or 'Cold War Steve'. We might think of the assemblages of 'Barbara Hepworth's' sculpting or carving, 'Bridget Riley's' painting, or those performances of 'Marina Abramovic'; such assemblages suggest an ecology of practices in their particular milieus and the new possibilities and connections for practice that emerged from them. Considering these practices as ongoing assemblages of practice means that we think of practice as an ongoing divergence, not as exhibiting 'progress'. This suggests a multiplicity of possibilities that in Guattari's terms may render unforeseeable qualities of being.

I think we are obliged to think in a similar way about children's and students' art practices, not in terms of progress according to some ultimate arbiter but in terms of divergence within a social technology of common sense that aims to acknowledge the way in which such divergent practices make their world matter and what might be possible.

The issue of divergence, the divergence of assemblages and their local ecologies, and the notion of advancement in terms of common sense as this term is used in its Whiteheadian form bring us to the issue of 'responsibility'. If an assemblage includes an ongoing reciprocal composing involving an artist and their materials as discussed above, responsibility does not flow from the artist but from a kind of reciprocal 'concern' for the 'thisness' or haecceity of a situation and the contingent and unknown unfolding of practice, what we might call its otherness. It is a responsibility forming an etho-ecology, one that may open up new possibilities for practice, each in their own particular way – a responsibility of co-composing with the otherness of a situation and its power to matter in its particular way (Stengers 2005a: 192), a co-composing whose outcomes we await. In a recent interview on BBC 4, Bridget Riley said something close to these ideas; she said, 'If I know what I am going to get I lose interest, I need just a small connecting point from the present known to an unknown that lies just beyond what I have already seen.'

The challenge of art practice then is not to be viewed in terms of the creative artist working independently with their materials whatever these may be. It is a process of risk *par le milieu* – a meso practice. Will the materials accept the way they are manipulated; will they resist? Will such interaction precipitate new propositions as lures in Whitehead's sense that lead to new possibilities, new leaps, that on returning to the ground of practice change its ground, which will also involve precipitating new risks?

The challenge and responsibilities of art education (and other subject domains) in schools and elsewhere, involving all participants, are characterized by Stengers (2005a: 196), speaking more widely on an ecology of practices:

> The problem for each practice is how to foster its own force, make present what causes practitioners to think and feel and act. But it is a problem which may also produce an experimental togetherness among practices, a dynamics of pragmatic learning of what works and how. This is the kind of active, fostering 'milieu' that practices need in order to be able to answer challenges and experiment changes, that is, to unfold their own force.

It is the obligation of the social technology of a pedagogy of taking care, as advocated throughout these chapters, that the diverse learning pathways of children and students, and those of educators, may be allowed and encouraged to unfold their own force and their potential.

Mesopolitics and Divergence

Whereas we might say that macropolitics and a micropolitics resistant to the former's values can be said to articulate established positions, mesopolitics is concerned with the pragmatic becoming-making of practices through the working of relations and materials of whatever kind.

This might involve, as discussed above, a member of an ethnic minority trying to offer guidance to their children faced with their particular situations of discrimination, to formulate pragmatic modes of continuing survival. In relation to art education and a pedagogy of taking care, paying due attention to the local ecologies of students' learning pathways, their ways of mattering, connecting and organizing (assemblages) and holding back the tendency to impose the authority of established and valued modes of practice, would constitute a continually negotiating mesopolitics and ethics of pedagogic practice – a politics and ethics that is concerned with the becoming-making of students and also their teachers. It is guided by contingency, heterogeneity and divergence rather than identity and homogeneity. This would suggest a pedagogical space of symbiosis or one close to Ivan Illich's notion of conviviality. Stengers (2011a: 60) writes:

> Symbiotically related beings go on diverging, go on defining in their own manner what matters for them. Symbiosis means that these beings are related by common interests, but *common* does not mean having the same interest in common, only that diverging interests now need each other. Symbiotic events are a matter of opportunity, of partial connection, not of harmony. (italic in original)

A symbiotic becoming-making of practice is a practice *par le milieu*, involving local assemblages (connections and organization) of materials, affects and cognitions. As discussed in Chapter 3, Isabelle Stengers (2011a: 59) argues that 'what makes each practice exist is also what makes it diverge', for each practice has its distinct way of paying due attention, of forming how something matters. Each assemblage of practice has its own existential lines of divergence. Comparison, according to a standard of equivalence, would destroy this divergence. Divergence, according to Stengers, is not to be viewed as 'divergence from' others because this would turn it into 'fuel for comparison'.

> Divergence is not between practices; it is not relational. It is constitutive. A practice does not define itself in terms of its divergence from others. Each does have its own positive and distinct way of paying due attention; that is, of having things and situations matter. Each produces its own line of divergence, as it likewise produces itself.

In *Introductory Notes on an Ecology of Practices* (2005b), Stengers writes:

> Approaching a practice means approaching it as it diverges, that is, feeling its borders, experimenting with questions which practitioners may accept as relevant, even if they are not their own questions ... rather than posing questions that precipitate them mobilising and transforming the border into a defence against the outside. (184)

If the notion of symbiosis is related to a classroom or other such collective educational contexts, then it concerns what William James proposed as the becoming-making of a *pluriverse* in which each new event of learning or teaching (itself a learning process), each divergence of practice, adds new variety, new dimensions. Such additions do not imply an automatic harmony and a general goodwill but will probably involve conflicting interests. As Stengers (62) puts it, 'Ecological, symbiotic events, the creation of rapport between divergent interests as they diverge, mean novelty, not harmony.' This suggests that the very notion of symbiosis implies a mesopolitics of becoming but a becoming in which each may continue to 'define and develop in their own manner what matters to them'; this will involve disagreements, silences and awkwardness but existing within a rapport of common sense as proposed by Whitehead, an interest for the way others make their world matter and for experimenting with what might be possible. Such rapport by implication then involves a concern for otherness and its gift.

A mesopolitics concerns the pragmatics and opportunities for a becoming-making of local assemblages within a context of equals where such making will involve agreements, resistances, deliberations and disputes. And such a mesopolitics of becoming is never finished in that becoming endures by continually renewing itself. Mesopolitics and ethics therefore are not concerned with what we might call the persistence of existence in its own being but rather with 'becoming other' through what Whitehead called a creative advance into novelty. In contrast to the molar force of macropolitics and the minor forces of micropolitical resistance, the mesopolitics of becoming-making presents itself through its pragmatic lines of divergence that add new dimensions and new creative advances, strategies and potentials to the world which may, in turn, facilitate new modes of micropolitical forces that precipitate changes to macropolitical values and structures. We might therefore see the mesopolitical as an operator for an expanded domain of local practices and their potentials, which, in relation to established practices of art education, expand the possibilities and potentials of this domain.

What we might call *meso-pedagogies* are pragmatically ethico-political in that they are concerned with the immanence of becoming-making that may challenge, disrupt or modify established frameworks of practice through the intensities, disruptions, potentials and divergence of local problematizations of practice that lead to new sensibilities and ways of thinking, thus continuing what we might call the adventures of subjectivation in pedagogical or other modes of practice.

In the concluding chapter, I continue with explorations of the meso or the in-between through the notion of a pedagogy of the interstices and a pluriverse of pedagogies.

9

Pedagogy of the Interstices: Trust and Uncertainty

Introduction

In this concluding chapter, my aim is to consider the notion of a pedagogy of the interstices and the implications this notion has for pedagogic practice. Attendant to this notion is the practice and feeling of trust as well as a kind of coalition of practice with uncertainty. This incorporates a shift from the idea of knowledge as eliminating uncertainty towards accepting uncertainty and contingency as part of the process of learning that leads to an expansion of knowledge. A pedagogy of the interstices allays cultures of identity and in doing so operates a generative and inventive disposition in relation to working-with and valuing the divergence of practice, the outcomes of which, in pedagogical terms, may only be dimly envisaged and not fully understood but constitute a possible opening for new modes of practice to emerge. The insistence of otherness or otherwise as manifested by the terms, 'and', 'or', 'maybe' or 'perhaps', constitutes the risk and the challenge of pedagogic practice as it is confronted with the divergence of practice and the togetherness of divergence. Such difference and its possibilities are both generative of practice and also highlight the limits and constraints of established modes of practice.

The notion of otherness, the gift of otherness, on which I have ruminated in these chapters, constitutes the 'outside', the 'or' or the 'perhaps' in the sense given by William James (1912) that wanders on the edge of our modes of practice and which initially, in some inchoate sense, signals how practice might be otherwise, or that we might conceive it otherwise. Equally, this raises the problematic of how to respond effectively and empathetically to the divergence of different practices and their potentials. This links the importance of trust with the interstices of 'perhaps' in a double sense in pedagogic practice – the trusting of the teacher in the becoming-making of a learner's practice and its potential and the trusting of the teacher's guidance by the learner. The adverbs 'perhaps' and 'maybe' and the conjunctions 'and' and 'or' therefore refer to the evolving contingencies and connectivities of living practices, to possibilities around the corner. They denote, as James (2004: 90) puts it, that experiencing of activity is 'synonymous with the sense of life'. His 1909 Hibbert Lectures that constitute the text, *A Pluralist Universe*, do not refer to an existing totality but to a pluriverse (James uses the term 'multiverse') always in-the-making where 'things are "with" one another in many ways, but nothing includes everything, or dominates over everything' (2004: 71). According to his notion of pluralism, the pluriverse is always being constructed so that it cannot be totalized; 'the word "and" trails along after every sentence. Something always escapes. "Ever not quite"' (71). The open-ended nature of a pluriverse-in-the-making must therefore include those possibilities that are not yet realized. For James (72), 'the word "or" names a genuine reality'.

William James was a philosopher who influenced Alfred North Whitehead, and something of James's emphasis on the contingencies, uncertainties, otherness and possibilities implied by the adverbs 'perhaps' or 'maybe' is captured by Whitehead in his book *Process and Reality* (105–6), where he writes, 'Life lurks in the interstices of each living cell and in the interstices of the brain.' How might we comprehend this puzzling statement? How might it be of importance for the life of pedagogic practice with which I am concerned? What might be the relevance of the term 'interstices' for pedagogic practice or indeed for the ideas of trust, knowledge and uncertainty in the context of such practice? Before I respond to these questions, I will provide a brief account of Whitehead's work on process and becoming with reference to his ideas of societies, prehension and concrescence. I refer to Isabelle Stengers's notion of a culture of interstices and combine this with Whitehead's idea of abstractions to facilitate an engagement with the pluralism of 'perhaps'. These ideas are then applied to the domain of artist–teacher assemblages and conversations to advocate pluralist pedagogies that are always incomplete and that require both invention and decolonization implicit to a pedagogy of taking care. Such taking care requires a notion of trust that embraces speculation and uncertainty as it encounters divergence and otherness, and the chapter closes with a discussion of these issues.

Societies, Prehension, Concrescence and Interstices

Whitehead uses the term 'society' not just to refer to human societies but to all *enduring* entities. In general terms a society consists of a nexus that 'enjoys social order' (1978: 34), that is to say, particular immanent aspects or characteristics that constitute and sustain its make up. Michael Halewood (2014: 365) writes, 'Societies are those elements of existence that exhibit and express orderliness of existence and therefore comprise those enduring things of the world encountered by other enduring things of the world.' The idea of endurance of a society means that it involves what Whitehead calls 'antecedents and its subsequents', a society 'enjoys a history expressing its changing reactions to changing circumstances' (1967: 204). A society is always, apart from death, 'adding to itself, with the creative advance into the future' (204). A society could be a molecule, a tree, a human being, a pond or even the evolutions of a manifesto or a theory. Thus, all the enduring things that we experience are, for Whitehead, societies, and societies have their own reasons, that is to say, their own immanent modes of composition, sensing, feeling and becoming, a point that is important to bear in mind when we think, in common parlance, of individual learners or teachers, because we can view each learner or teacher as a 'society' consisting of its immanent sense of order and feeling. Here the term 'society' seems close to the notion of assemblage; it does not invoke a separation of 'individual' and 'environment' but a dynamic ecology of practices.

The idea of an enduring society, or an assemblage, is indissoluble from the processuality of events of its becoming. But becoming is not a continuous process because continuity has itself to become; it is never given beforehand simply because each actual occasion or event adds something new, something novel. Whitehead (1978: 35) states, 'There is a becoming of continuity but no continuity of becoming.' In human terms every encounter is a new event which does not happen to the 'same' subject but which, in the process of encounter, produces a new or modified subject. We might say that each encounter involves what Whitehead calls a new *prehension*, a term that refers to the particular manner in which a society (a molecule, a tree, a person, etc.) takes account of something and how this matters thereby leading to a new *concrescence* or a new form of concreteness or unity. The concrescence subsequent to the prehending of an encounter, though seemingly immediate and happening all at once, involves an informing past as well as current situations and future possibilities. In human terms it refers to the emergence and constitution of new subjectivations. At any given moment, we are positioned in relation to what we might call a determined past and a not-yet-determined future – events experienced and those yet to come. We are always coming into being, always prehending and concrescing different kinds of experiencings, physical, conceptual, visual, tactile, acoustic and so on, and giving these what Whitehead calls 'subjective form' which constitutes the particular manner in which we structure or compose our experiences. These forms are accompanied by 'subjective aims' that relate to current decisions and future possibilities, which lead in turn to new subjectivations.

The production of novelty is a crucial ontological principle for Whitehead, whereby something new emerges, not from nowhere, but from the coincidence of lines of inheritance and their levels or patterns of conformity, with new encounters and their capacity to challenge thought/practice, which bring about change. Stengers (2014a: 58) writes, 'The possibility of a breaking of social continuity by some new, non-conformal occasional mode of becoming one is why actual occasions matter.' But such novelty has to be *relevant* and generate the power to force new subjective forms/practices of expression that lead to new subjective aims and their forms of coherence.

Whitehead distinguishes between life and established social orders. 'Life is a bid for freedom; an enduring entity binds any one of its occasions to the line of its ancestry' (1978: 104). He continues, 'The root fact is that "endurance" is a device whereby an occasion is peculiarly bound by a single line of physical ancestry, while "life" means novelty. … What has to be explained is originality of response to stimulus' (104). Developing his idea of life, he states further that 'the characteristic of life is reaction adapted to the capture of intensity, under a large variety of circumstances. But the reaction is dictated by the present and not by the past. It is the clutch at vivid immediacy' (1978: 105). Life is evocative of 'intense experience without the shackle of reiteration from the past' (105). Life exists therefore not in the established territory of social spaces, but it 'lurks in the interstices' of such spaces and the intensity of new encounters. It is the interstices that are the places where new possibilities for practice may emerge. We might view this notion of life as that force or capacity that enables a living organism to adapt to changing circumstances, to produce novelty and, in order to adapt to changing circumstances, established orders of being require life-as-novelty-in-becoming. 'The very inconspicuous kind of novelty,' writes Stengers (2014a: 60), 'that is the capacity of any living being to adapt to a changing environment.' What matters in such situations is the ability to be able to respond to those aspects or features of a particular situation that challenge established modes of practice and thought and which may come to matter, a response that calls for innovation, for *relevant* novel and coherent modes of expression. And such modes of expression may involve developing relevant stories, appropriate abstractions or concepts or visual and other forms that are called for by the interstices opened by the challenge.

Another way of putting this contrasts the seeming continuity of inheritance and traditional values with the necessity for experimentation in changing circumstances when such inheritance is inadequate – an experimentation that may betray existing practices and recuperate them into new forms of coherence. 'Every social inheritance is a betrayal, in the sense of "recuperation", but that which, as it makes society, inherits what was original, is transformed by what was betrayed, and creates the possibility of new interstices' (Stengers 2011c: 329). This is not too far removed from the experiencing of an encounter, a learning encounter that challenges existing or assimilated modes of practice and demands novel responses. Responses that in turn stabilize until future encounters disturb them and demand further transformation.

The gaps or interstices created, for example, in encounters where assimilated modes of practice and thought no longer 'work' constitute the locations, nonsensical intervals, for new lures to emerge that generate potential for new modes of practice. Such lures may consist of new concepts or, as in art practice, new modes of expression, or in Whitehead's terminology, new propositions as lures for feeling that lead to novel modes of practice. The pedagogical task is to not only help children or students to engage with encounters in such a way that established patterns of practice are secured but also, crucially, provoking or stimulating interstices, through encounters, for the possibility for new modes of practice and understanding to emerge. This would constitute the challenge of novelty for the life of becoming – relevant novelty that will make a positive difference. It could be the challenge of new and relevant concepts not met with before or modes of practice not previously encountered that disrupt assimilated practices.

Culture of Interstices

In an important sense therefore, we might think of pedagogic work as trying to develop and maintain what Stengers (2011c: 328) calls a 'culture of interstices'.

> The culture of interstices is not the privilege of personal experience. It may also be a way of understanding ritual trances, divinatory utterances, and the objects manipulated by therapists, (or artistic and other assemblages) which open a human collectivity to an outside whose intrusion suspends habitual social functioning. (my bracket)

This would be a culture medium in which the purpose of encounters would be to provoke interstices that lead to relevant novelty and new forms of coherence.

Stengers (328) refers to the slow process of percolation and the becoming of continuity: 'propagating from interstice to interstice until the flow itself becomes recognisable, describable, socialised, no longer intersticial but the thread of a living person'. She reminds us that for Whitehead education was *the* crucial human and social science and that its chief concern should be to 'provide habits of sensitiveness against dead abstractions, to provide habits that may be compared with a *culture medium for interstices*', a culture that generates stimulation, excitement and passion. Stengers (2006: 15) states:

> When a teacher feels that what she is doing is important, that it is not only a transmission of useful knowledge, … she indeed participates to what may be called a cosmic adventure, because the manner the children will experience new possibilities, feelings and ideas, or stubbornly keep to their abstractions, to their judgement about what matters and what does not, is indeed a cosmic stake.

The cosmic adventure of pedagogic work therefore calls forth existential transformations of self and world, and we might want to argue, in the spirit of Whitehead and his work in education, that today education requires new abstractions to resist the totalizing force of current cultures of economization, to counter inert professionalization and cultures of audit and promote a 'taking care' that facilitates the valuing of difference and divergence. In *The Aims of Education* (1962: 2), he wrote, 'Education with inert ideas is not only useless: it is, above all things, harmful … Except at rare intervals of intellectual ferment, education in the past has been radically infected with inert ideas.' As James Williams (2014: 250) infers, it is a pedagogical obligation to initiate experiences for children or students that stimulate imagination and induce new possibilities and sensibilities.

We need to invent abstractions that allow us to avoid the capture by established categories or generalizations that prevent us from acknowledging that which does not fit, abstractions that try to embrace the problematics of an increasingly complex and challenging world. This would constitute the adventure of pedagogic work, and when we accept that such work has a deep concern for the creative potentials of all children and students, a concern for a people and a world yet to come, it is indeed an adventure with a cosmic stake.

Such an abstraction coined by the musician Brian Eno is 'scenius' in contrast to 'genius' coupled, respectively, with the notions of ecosystem and egosystem. The term has direct relevance for the classroom as a space of collective practice and invention. Eno's book, *A Year with Swollen Appendices* (1996: 354–5), contains a letter to the musician Dave Stewart in which Eno introduces his novel term:

> A few years ago I came up with a new word. I was fed up with the old art-history idea of genius – the notion that gifted individuals turn up out of nowhere and light the way for all the rest of us dummies to follow. I became (and still am) more and more convinced that the important changes in cultural history were actually the product of very large numbers of people and circumstances conspiring to make something new. I call this 'scenius' – it means 'the intelligence and intuition of a whole cultural scene'. It is the communal form of the concept of genius. This word is now starting to gain some currency – the philosopher James Ogilvy uses it in his most recent book.
>
> Now I would love to be involved in making something to explore this idea – to support my thesis that new ideas come into being through a whole host of complicated circumstances, accidents, small incremental contributions made in isolation (as well as gifted individuals, of course) that in total add up to something qualitatively different: something nobody has ever seen before and which could not have been predicted from the elements that went to make it up.
>
> One of the reasons I am attached to this idea is that it is capable of dignifying many more forms of human innovation under its umbrella than the old idea of 'genius', which exemplifies what I call the 'Big Man' theory of history – where events are changed by the occasional brilliant or terrible man, working in heroic isolation. I would prefer to believe that the world is constantly being remade by all its inhabitants: that it is a cooperative enterprise.

Alex Gentry (2017), commenting upon Eno's new abstraction, identifies important factors concerning the geography of scenius: mutual appreciation which is like motivational peer pressure, exchange of tools and techniques so that new inventions are shared amongst everyone, celebration of success and tendency for novelties and a flourishing nonconformity. Gentry summarizes Eno's concept in the following statement:

> Scenius is like genius, only embedded in a scene rather than in genes. Brian Eno suggested the word to convey the extreme creativity that groups, places or 'scenes' can occasionally generate. His actual definition is 'Scenius' stands for the intelligence and the intuition of a whole cultural scene. It is the communal form of the concept of the genius.

Eno points to older and recent sceniuses in art including the Dada movement, the experimental music scene in America through the late fifties and early sixties, the art scene at Goldsmiths College in the mid to late eighties, all of which 'were fed by a vigorous and diffuse cultural scene'. The important point stressed by Gentry is to acknowledge that sceniuses can emerge anywhere in any scale and form, which leads me back to a consideration of the classroom or art studio as a scenius for an ecology of practices and a culture of interstices. Equally, this takes us back to Guattari's (1995: 133) question, 'How do you make a classroom operate like a work of art?' How can we forge articulations between creative singularity and potential and collective values and practices?

These questions and Brian Eno's abstraction bring me back to Whitehead's rather enigmatic phrase, 'life lurks in the interstices', and to the notion of mesopolitics discussed in the last chapter. In other words, an answer might be that we need to pay attention to that which exists or emerges in the interstices of practice, to the small incremental contributions that can make a positive difference. Perhaps we might view Whitehead's phrase as indicating what Didier Debaise (2008: 1), following Isabelle Stengers, calls 'the point of departure of a new coherence, yet to be constructed'. It would designate Whitehead's 'speculative approach towards the living' and its potentials, and for my purpose, it designates what we might refer to as a becoming-making of pedagogic practice which involves trying to notice what emerges in the interstices, those flows of life that emerge between established assemblages of practice. Whitehead argues that life is the name for originality and not for tradition (1978: 104); it occurs in the interstices, in the empty spaces (1978: 105) between bodies. Debaise (2008: 2) writes, 'Life produces innovation.'

The spatial connotation of interstice can be contrasted with a temporal one such as an interval between sounds or between actions. Such intervals may be considered as an emptiness separating sounds or actions, but as Debaise (2008: 3) points out referring to William James's example of silence after thunder (James 1950: 240), the event of thunder followed by another is an event 'in contrast' whose existence incorporates a phase of silence. As James puts it, 'What we hear when the thunder crashes is not thunder pure, but thunder-breaking-upon-silence-and-contrasting-with-it.' Another way of thinking about this is that the existence of thunder is inextricably linked with the otherness of silence. When we apply this contrast to human existence, we might say that this process consists of contrasts between that which has been established and inherited and that which emerges within current conditions and encounters, not necessarily thunderclaps but tremblings, which may open up interstices in that which is inherited and which generate new possibilities. When we are faced with a difficult or puzzling situation that disrupts our established orders and relations of practice, the disturbance functions as an interstice, a gap, that 'calls' for new or modified relations and practice, new abstractions that ask us to think anew about practice. Debaise (2008: 12) writes, 'Everything happens in zones in between bodies and their environment,' in what we have described as 'interstices', and further, 'Everything happens in the encounter.'

Life is always lurking in the interstices of relations; we are always affecting and being affected, or as Isabelle Stengers (2011c: 184) puts it, functioning within a dynamics of 'infection'. We are continually altering, modifying, redesigning, revising and transforming within such dynamics.

Artist–Teacher Assemblages: Taking Care of the Interstices

We can apply Whitehead's aphorism of 'life lurking in the interstices' and Stengers's notion of a culture of interstices to the practices of the artist-teacher. The notion of the artist-teacher has been developed in recent decades in different manifestations including regional working groups and master's programmes, in different parts of the world (Addison and Burgess 2020; Daichendt 2010; Vella 2016). In their final publication, *What Is Philosophy?* (1994) Deleuze and Guattari write about the 'umbrellas' we construct that protect us from chaos. They focus upon the disciplines of art, science and philosophy that 'cast planes over chaos' (1994: 202) and whose quest, generated by encounters that throw up questions that established modes of practice and thought cannot 'answer', is to push beyond the boundaries of practice and plunge into chaos to construct more relevant and novel modes of practice. Deleuze and Guattari (203) refer to a text by D. H. Lawrence (1955) titled 'Chaos in Poetry' and point to a particular passage relating to the notion of interstice:

> People are constantly putting up an umbrella that shelters them and on the underside of which they draw a firmament and write their conventions and opinions. But poets, artists, make a slit in the umbrella, they tear open the firmament itself, to let in a bit of free and windy chaos and to frame in a sudden light a vision that appears through the rent.

Lawrence's text is worth further attention because he continues to comment upon the aftermath of such artistic rents when they are painted over by what he calls 'common place man' (1955: 235, online) and what Deleuze and Guattari (204) refer to as the 'crowd of imitators who repair the umbrella with something vaguely resembling the vision, and the crowd of commentators who patch over the rent with opinions: communication'. Lawrence (235, online) continues:

> So long as the umbrella serves, and poets make slits in it, and the mass of people can be gradually educated up to the vision in the slit: which means they patch it over with a patch that looks just like the vision in the slit: so long as this process can continue, and mankind can be educated up, and thus built in, so long will a civilization continue more or less happily, completing its own painted prison. It is called completing the consciousness.

Repairing the slits in the 'painted firmaments' by imitators and commentators who produce resemblances inevitably diminishes the novelty and interruptive force of art and brings life back to its painted prison. Such reparations may, unconsciously or uncritically, inform the practices of art education so that its practices may, inadvertently, perpetuate these imitations through its curriculum content, modes of assessment and examination whilst failing to grasp the vital force of art practice. As for artists it is probably the case, as argued by Deleuze, Guattari and Lawrence, that their struggles with the otherness of chaos are less of a problem than their confrontations with the established orders of opinion, imitation and tradition.

This idea of a painted firmament is germane to the wider notion of culture, to the values and conventions that become invisibly embedded and which can frequently and unconsciously invoke different forms of prejudice, bias, discrimination, inequalities, exclusion or marginalization. The umbrella of cultural norms generates invisibilities such as that of white privilege, which excludes or marginalizes other cultures from its firmament. The importance of Stengers's notion of a culture of interstices as a pedagogical tool is that encounters with otherness call for counter-narratives to expose such unconscious exclusion or marginalization – narratives that in her words 'open a human collectivity to an outside whose intrusion suspends habitual social functioning' to reveal prejudices and discriminations, in order to challenge them and construct new visions, new narratives, for a more convivial world. A crucial function of art is to create the interstices, the rents in established orders, through which such visions can emerge.

The idea of life emerging in the interstices applied to the notion of the artist-teacher brings with it the conflict mentioned above, that between the established firmaments of practice in both education and art, and the interstices created by interruptions, interventions and questions that puncture such firmaments and which await new forms of relevance and coherence. It is the interstices created by artists that need to be taken care of, those propositions and their modes of expression that may emerge, disrupt and bring about change in the form of new practices, modes of expression and thought.

In pedagogic practice it is the interstices that emerge in the process of a learning encounter either for the teacher or for the student – those interruptions, gaps, challenges and disruptions to assimilated modes of practice that offer possibilities for new or modified practice that require taking care. Such challenges may result in reverting back to the settled ground of practice as the interstice is closed down, or to new divergences and new possibilities in the adventures of practice. A constant challenge for pedagogic practice is that its informed ground of practice, composed of abstractions such as competences, guidelines, standards and inherited methodologies and conventions, may fail to grasp the immediate experiencing of a learning encounter for a child or student; 'this reaction to that situation in this environment' (Whitehead 1968: 38). This challenge, in Whitehead's terms, is one where we need to take care of our abstractions, to civilize our abstractions so that they do not lead us too far away from the immediacies of experience. This returns us to Lawrence's umbrella. We might view pedagogic practice as putting up an umbrella on the underside of which is constructed its own firmament of practice, conventions and values that become invisible in the sense that they generate an invisible authority of practice, a sufficiency that regulates practice. In today's digital world, we might view this firmament as composed and mediated by series of algorithms that regulate practice and go unquestioned or unchallenged. Such authority may then occlude those modes of practice that occur beyond its firmament. George Perec (1973) comments upon a similar unquestioning that affects our daily existence which has some relevance to the points above about pedagogic practice.

> To question the habitual. But that's just it, we're habituated to it. We don't question it, it doesn't question us, it doesn't seem to pose a problem, we live it without thinking, as if it carried within it neither question nor answers, as if it weren't the bearer of any information. This is no longer even conditioning, it's anaesthesia. We sleep through our lives in a dreamless sleep. But where is our life? Where is our body? Where is our space?

In summary, the firmament of pedagogic work in art education may be interrupted by children's or students' practices that do not subscribe to its conventions or values. Equally, new art practices may make slits in this firmament and allow new visions and modes of practice to emerge. The artist-teacher is therefore operating with and between (*par le milieu*) established pedagogical firmaments and the divergences of student practices as well as between the firmament of established art practices and those new art practices that create tears in this firmament. The artist-teacher may thus be affected by two interstertial tremors.

The practice of the artist-teacher engages with the here and now of each child's or student's practices, with the immediacy of such practice and with its potentials; it attempts to engage with the interstices created by existential learning encounters. Such engagement calls for a language that does not allow established abstractions to occlude the immediacies and divergence of practice. A recent development of artist-teacher enquiry was initiated in 2019 by Andy Ash at University College London in collaboration with Henry Ward at the Freelands Foundation in London and Kate Thackara, Head of Art at Lady Margaret School in London. It involves a network of artist-teachers who meet monthly to generate enquiry and share practice with a view to extending the possibilities for artist–teacher assemblages. Members usually meet once a month at the Freelands venue, but during the lockdown imposed by government during the coronavirus pandemic, the network met online. I will draw upon conversations that emerged from the online sessions organized by Andy Ash and Kate Thackara, from April 21 and May 18, 2021, which focused upon the questions 'What does it mean to be an artist-teacher?' and 'How do the "artist" and the "teacher" influence each other?' We might view these conversations as constructing an evolving collective language, developing a series of working abstractions, questions, provocations, visions and discussions that tackle issues of practice, that formulate the concerns, visions and values of practice for those in the artist-teacher network. Such conversations may create slits or intervals in the established firmament of practice as constructed, for example, by curriculum orders or examination syllabuses, in order to open new possibilities for more effective, equitable, speculative and perspicacious modes of practice. The conversations constitute a practice of becoming-making whose purpose is to inform, expand and evaluate the pedagogic work of an artist-teacher. They function to proposition, question, facilitate, innovate and invent coherences yet to be constructed in relation to the different and diverging dimensions of learning-with in what I would call a pedagogy of taking care. This would echo Foucault's and Guattari's notions of life as an ethico-aesthetic and political adventure of becoming.

Coupled with these conversations, as already mentioned, we can also view the productions of art practice as constituting propositions that may facilitate new modes of practice and thought as they create openings that challenge established orders in relation, for example, to issues of race, gender, class, sexuality, issues relating to the social and natural environment and other sociocultural and political issues. The novelty and challenge of some of these art practices may impact upon artist-teacher pedagogies; they may infect thought and effect interruptions to their current firmament and lead to developing new modes of pedagogical practice that may, for example, conflict with examination structures and assessment criteria.

Artist–Teacher Conversations: Artefactualizing Practice

We can view these conversations in terms of Brian Eno's notion of the cooperative enterprise of *scenius* already discussed above which was in fact mentioned by a member of the artist-teacher network (Thomas Eke) during the April webcast, that is to say, a cooperative and creative enterprise developed by the network, 'the intelligence and intuition generated by a cultural scene' and its interstices. During the session on 21 April, members broke up into discussion groups in which several issues were raised in relation to the initial question 'What does it mean to be an artist-teacher?' Some groups were critical of what they perceived as a closed-mindedness embedded within the art examination system in that its standardized conceptions of art bore little appreciation of contemporary art practices, such as performance. They felt that the diversity of current art practices was not reflected in the examination system. One suggestion was for the examination boards to consult more widely with teachers to discuss these issues and to bring the examination system in line with the possibilities for practice that emerge continuously from contemporary art practice which transform what constitutes art practice and how it is performed. Of course, this would suggest a constantly evolving flexible system in order to accommodate art practices that undermine or challenge the premises of the system.

An issue that was raised in some groups was that of 'learning from and with the child or student'. This was proposed as a counter-narrative to a more didactic approach to teaching and learning that tends to proliferate in schools due to current curriculum and assessment orders. The notion of the child or student acting as a 'teacher' (which brings into question just what this term can mean) was viewed as a valuable source coupled with the idea of the teacher as facilitator and not a font of knowledge or an unquestioned leader – a facilitator of potentials in a pedagogical context where every member is valued, where children, students and teachers learn from one another within a convivial collective space.

Labelling and boundaries, putting students as well as teachers into categories, was a concern that was also expressed with a sense of equivocation. Labels were viewed as useful, but they can limit both teaching and learning. We might witness this in examination and assessment discourses applied to children or students and in inspection discourses that determine a teacher's capabilities. Such categorizations of learners and teachers were viewed as a handicap and needed to be relaxed in that holding to particular definitions or beliefs about what constitutes an artist, student or a teacher can be dangerous. There is therefore a need to challenge preconceptions and to view these practices in the spirit of a continuous becoming-making. This relates closely to the notion of subjectivity as an assemblage, a process-in-making which will be discussed shortly. Challenging preconceptions imply what we might call a decolonisation of thought that attempts to expose established and perhaps unconscious attitudes and values in order to view other possibilities for practice and ways of conceiving practice.

The session on 18 May led by Kate Thackara considered how modes of being of 'artist' and 'teacher' influence each other. How are these terms 'artist' and 'teacher' conceived? Whitehead's notion of abstractions (concepts) is important to bear in mind. In *Science and the Modern World* (1967: 59), he writes, 'You cannot think without abstractions; accordingly it is of the utmost importance to be vigilant in critically revising your modes of abstraction. … A civilisation that cannot burst through its current abstractions is doomed to sterility after a very limited period of progress.' We might apply these thoughts to the terms 'artist' and 'teacher' in order to view them as abstractions that are continually being renewed or reclaimed through active, critical, creative and speculative practices of pedagogy and art, crucial for the generation of new ideas and a flourishing of new practices. An important task therefore is, wherever possible, not to allow imposed or dominant notions of 'teacher', 'learner' or 'artist' to dominate or be perpetuated without question.

Stengers (2008: 50) informs us that Whitehead sought to unpack, 'What our modes of abstraction are doing to us, what are they blinding us against?' How are the notions of teacher and learner conceived within educational policy? How do individual teachers conceive what it is to be a teacher? How are the notions of art practice and artist conceived by artists, teachers or examination boards? We require abstractions in that they generate thought and 'lure our feelings and affects'. But it is crucial that we are able to take care of our abstractions, 'never to bow down in front of what they are doing to us'. Put in other terms already mentioned, such abstractions compose the often invisible authority of the firmament of practice that has been fabricated and which fabricates us as practitioners, often complicitly and without question. Such abstractions therefore are part of the very milieu of practice and, as Stengers points out, 'may empower or poison it'.

The Freelands artist-teacher network functions partly as a critical space that involves producing counter-narratives emerging from the functioning realities of teaching art to those produced and perpetuated by government curriculum orders, competences and standards as well as by examination discourses and assessment criteria – in other words discourses of authority that appear to know how to define and legitimise art practice. In passing, we might want to question who benefits from such knowledge. The artist-teacher network creates a space in which teachers artefactualize ideas, visions, propositions and concepts from their local and collective ecologies of practice, in order to lure thought and practice to wider experiences and modes of practice, acknowledging the divergences and potentials. This means affording the pedagogical and artistic situations that artist-teachers experience an authoritative force to *collectively* feel, imagine, think and speculate future modes of practice. Such feeling and speculation do not have to emerge from major events or epiphanies but may occur gently from little incidents or surprises within contexts of mutual sharing and listening.

In order to respond to the question, 'How do the "artist" and the "teacher" influence each other?' the focus for the session on 18 May, several members of the network gave a brief presentation describing how they interconnected these two identities. The first presentation was given by Kate Thackara who reflected upon the artist-teacher identity as a spectrum which she depicted through a series of diagrams that depicted several relations between that mode of being we call 'artist' and that mode of being we call 'teacher'. These included a relation of opposition, a relation of attraction, a cyclical relation, a parallel relation and a fluctuating relation. The mode of functioning we call the artist-teacher may be composed of all these recurring relations plus many others we might conceive. We might say that there are as many modes of the artist–teacher relation as there are artist-teachers. Kate stressed the point that in functioning as an artist-teacher, she found what she termed 'magic moments', moments and situations that arise when working with students and which may seem unimportant to a teacher but *can* be important and significant for the student. This echoes the advice given by Whitehead (1968: 116), to 'have a care, here is something that matters', for this something may be generative of expanded fields of practice. Taking care involves a practice of careful noticing that trusts and works with the flows and outcomes of a learner's practice, and it can facilitate moving beyond the teacher's established frameworks of practice and understanding to expand pedagogic work.

Louise Evans, a teacher from Glasgow, spoke about materials and the fluidity of making through which meaning emerges. For Louise, the notions (abstractions) of 'boundary' and 'curiosity' are crucial to both her work as an artist and her practice as a teacher. In a personal statement before this session, Louise states:

> Two words I keep circling around are 'curiosity' and 'boundary'. In the studio, I make paintings fuelled by my ongoing curiosity with colour, surface and boundaries between painting and sculpture. In the classroom, I aim to adopt similar ways of working and thinking. I want to allow students to be curious and to ask questions of 'what if …?' when making. To observe rules and boundaries and investigate what happens if rules are broken and lines are blurred.

The 'what if' is resonant of William James's emphasis upon the realities of 'perhaps' or 'or'. An important aspect of her teaching is the dialogue that she tries to promote after a making session in which she talks to her students about how she conceives their work and encourages students to express their intentions, questions and concerns.

Joseph Critchley, a London teacher, spoke about the importance of taking risks, of propositioning or challenging students to experiment and so expand their modes of practice. In a project concerned with the theme of identity, working with digital programmes such as photoshop, he used the portrait work of Cindy Sherman to challenge students to experiment on themselves. As a provocation he transformed his own facial identity on photoshop and asked his students to experiment with theirs. The project thus precipitated a host of issues relating to how identities are created within social media platforms, advertising, television and streaming networks, magazines and so on, issues relating to appearance, the body, desire, moral codes and more. It asked them to take some personal risks, to experiment and, most important, to interrogate the idea of identity and how it is constructed.

Sorcha Tucker spoke about the challenges she has experienced on moving schools, from an art department that placed value upon exploration to one in which outcomes are paramount. This clash of pedagogic ideologies and the challenge she faces in her new school are reminiscent of the conflicts discussed in Chapter 1 when university teacher educators were faced with having to fit into a new school-based model of 'teacher training'.

These discussions are by no means exceptional or unique and are mirrored in other artist-teacher groups or formats in the UK and other countries. Their importance relates to what we might call a pluralist approach to pedagogic practice, which will be discussed shortly, and the collective effort to evaluate practice that produces new or modified ways of thinking, however slight or innovative, coupled, when viewed necessary, with a decolonizing of thought and practice. The becoming-making of each artist-teacher practice illustrates the divergence and diversity of such practices as they emerge within their local ecologies and environments in contrast to the notion of a controlled and regulated curriculum that tends to suggest a mythical common denominator. This raises the value of the notion of a mesopolitics of practice, or meso-pedagogies, considered in the previous chapter. It concerns the *concerns and creative advance* of local ecologies of practice, their becoming-making and their potentials with all their attendant successes, floundering, uncertainties, frustrations and screw-ups.

A Pluriverse of Pedagogies, Trust and a Decolonization of Practice

In this closing passage, I want to reflect upon the always unfinished practice of a pedagogy of taking care obligated to respond to the ongoing divergence and multifarious ways in which children and students learn. This may also involve, for the educator, what we might call a decolonization of thought and practice, or at the least its constant revision, when confronted with the gift of otherness. What matters in this approach to pedagogic work is not the constant search and development of general principles and frameworks but the progressive emergence of new and relevant forms of enquiry to respond to the divergence of practice that materialize from a culture of patient noticing. I have conceived otherness in all its differences and divergences as a gift and taking care as a multiple obligation. Taking care entails a pluralism, an attentive and careful noticing, a pragmatics of the suddenly possible (Buck-Morss), experimenting with and constructing new narratives that may run counter to those already established, rejecting forms of intolerance, prejudice and discrimination that produce marginalization and exclusion.

Rather than developing and refining educational programmes, systems or frameworks that aim to promote universal or general principles, standards, competences, or benchmarks that tend towards a monification of education, this book seeks to advocate the notions of divergence and plurality and a pedagogy of trust in which the words such as 'and', 'or', 'maybe' and 'perhaps' function as pedagogical leitmotifs for noticing and feeling-with otherness, other worlds in this world – leitmotifs that pluralize what might be possible and which characterize the adventure of a pedagogy of taking care that I have attempted to articulate with the help of those whose work I have drawn upon to guide and inform my task.

In my practice as a teacher, there are some moments that stand out as personal epiphanies or, to use a term from Martin Savransky's recent text, *Around the Day in Eighty Worlds*, personal *worldquakes*, that I now view as gifts of otherness that challenged what we might call the existing metaphysical framework of my learning and teaching. And there will have been other, perhaps gentler or subtler moments or quakes, that paused me to think, to partly notice and then absorb back into the flows of practice without the disturbance of stammering.

In a mathematics lesson I worked with an eleven-year-old girl who I thought was struggling to grasp the notion of 'three', as in questions such as, 'How many lots of three can you see?' I held up three fingers and asked, 'How many lots of three are there?' She replied, 'Three.' After trying again, I received the same answer. I asked her to show me as I held up three fingers that for me constituted one lot of three, and to my surprise, she counted the three sections of each finger giving me three lots of three!

A class of six-year-old children were looking at trees in the playground and talking about their structure with their teacher. After talking the teacher asked them to choose a tree and draw a picture of it thinking about its structure. The drawing one little boy produced, see Figure 6 below, was, for me, a seminal moment as I tried to grasp its 'logic', and as this experience percolated, I wondered more about how we assess and evaluate drawings, how assessment criteria 'frame' or even constitute drawings.

Another little boy (three to four years) is making what some have called a scribble drawing, consisting of lots of rotational actions and their corresponding marks and configurations. Then he shouts, 'They're going round and round,' and I notice he is watching his playmates riding their sit-on toys. I wondered, is it really a scribble drawing inferring something random and fortuitous?

I remember watching a video titled *Windows of the Mind* (BBC 1993) of a young girl in Australia from the Walpiri people at Yuendumu, working with Rosemary Hill. The girl is asked to draw a picture of herself sitting on a chair. Figure 7 is my representation of her drawing taken from the video. It shook my foundations.

Pedagogy of the Interstices 231

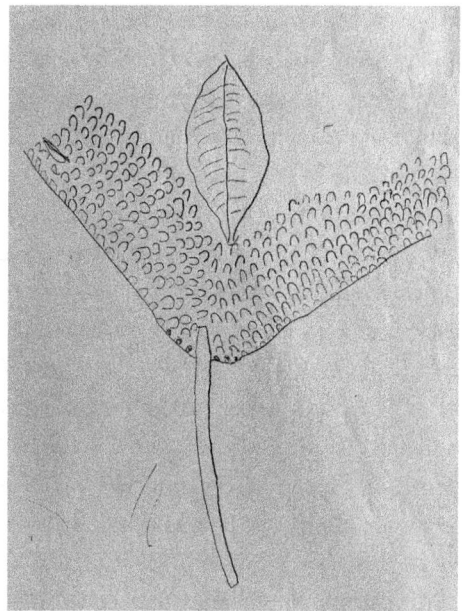

Figure 6

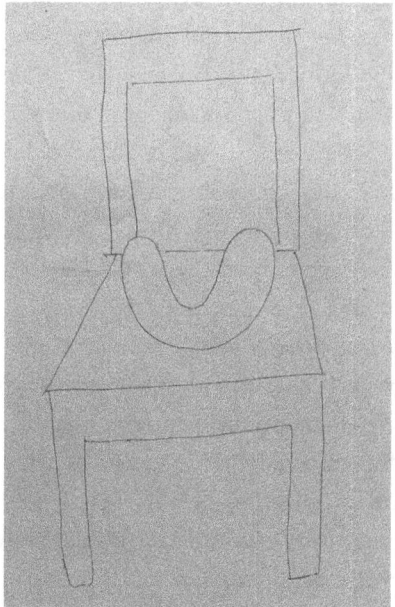

Figure 7

I recall these personal moments to indicate that a classroom, studio or other educational sites are composed of a diversity of worlds and their manners of practice and that the pedagogical adventure of taking care is not therefore concerned with facile notions of inclusion and equality but with a constant opening towards the 'and', the 'or', the 'perhaps' and with the creating of habits that allow human and non-human flourishing. These worlds diverge, some perhaps radically, from each other and from established orders and values of practice. But divergence does not imply separation but rather a togetherness that the idea of conviviality, as employed by Ivan Illich, implies. Divergence indicates what William James called a multiverse in his book, *A Pluralistic Universe*, and the notions of 'and', 'or', 'perhaps' indicate the interstices created by the gift of otherness which intimates the possibility and potential of other worlds in this world and their potential to expand how we conceive practice.

In pedagogical terms we might take James's notion of a multiverse as a sharp contrast to what we might call a monism of pedagogical practice inferred by notions of standardization and uniformity that effect a kind of educational imperialism. More recent texts in fields of philosophy and anthropology, such as *A World of Many Worlds*, by Mario Blaser and Marisol de la Cadena; *Designs for the Pluriverse: Radical Interdependence, Autonomy and the Making of Worlds*, by Arturo Escobar; and *The Ontological Turn: An Anthropological Exposition*, by Martin Holbraad and Morten Axel Pedersen, have emphasized the notion of pluralism and the notion of a cosmos composed of divergence and the task of building a world otherwise, not knowing in advance the pathways that which confronts us will follow. Though such texts have emerged in the domains of anthropology and philosophy, their key message relating to a togetherness of divergence is directly relevant for pedagogic practice.

Thus, the notions of 'and', 'or' and 'perhaps' demand an ever new or developing pedagogy, one which may require the invention of new concepts that enable a concern with difference, otherness and its gift. Pedagogical work therefore becomes an adventure amongst the matterings, noticings, transformations, stutterings, hesitancies, uncertainties, surprises, achievements, failures and potentials of the many worlds of learners in this world. Adventures which, in meeting with such divergence, may induce educators to evaluate and perhaps transform our modes of thought and practice. This point relates to the stories from practice shared by the artist-teachers above, how they construct and initiate their practices, how they respond, notice, evaluate and modify their practice. It is a matter of feeling the many 'ands' and 'perhaps' that we experience along with their possibilities and uncertainties. This is not a straightforward or unproblematic enterprise because it nudges the desire for standardization of its authoritarian perch and creates the pragmatic issue of how to create educational programmes that give serious attention to divergence and conviviality. However, such an enterprise does not seem unreasonable in our epoch, our histories of colonialism, ecological devastation, capitalist exploitation and educational programmes that have fed or still feed these political and economic forces.

Plurality is therefore implicit to a pedagogy of taking care, plural pedagogies not concerned with an imperialism of practice which establishes and polices pedagogical borders according to specific pre-planned agendas such as economic ambition but perhaps a guarding of divergence and its potentials. It animates a politics and ethics that refuses the monism of standards, and it remains open to a speculative pragmatics, to worlds of becoming and their ecologies of practice, to modes of existence yet to arrive. Essential to such a pedagogy is the notion of trust – trust in the adventure that may result in success or disappointment but whose aim is to induce new feelings, ideas and sensibilities that lead to new habits and convivial modes of practice. It does not require a globalization whose aim is homogenization or a monism that smooths out differences but a globalization grounded in a togetherness of divergence, a pluriverse that evolves and mutates through its interstices, which generate possibilities for practice and beg the continual question what a teacher or a learner is capable of.

A pedagogy of taking care that anticipates the construction of plural pedagogies as a teacher encounters the plurality and divergence of her children's or students' learning pathways means, inevitably, that the teacher's metaphysical frameworks may be constantly shifting and reforming according to the force of the encounter. Here the idea of general principles or competences seems redundant, and such situations require modes of dramatization commensurate with divergence and different ecologies of practice. Such forms of dramatization are emerging in the artist–teacher conversations discussed briefly above. Conversations and discussions about the different worlds of practice from which, in the interstices of their partial connectivity, may emerge new ideas, concepts, ways of working and modes of practice that effect pedagogical transformations. Such processes again bring to the fore the persistence of our words 'and', 'or', 'perhaps'. Here again also comes to light the importance of what Stengers calls a culture of interstices, implicit to a pedagogy of taking care as this involves the coming together of different worlds and what emerges between them.

As mentioned briefly above, the artist–teacher conversations I have presented are not exceptional in that similar engagements happen in many regions of the UK and other countries – collective engagements in which evaluations of practice can lead to an expansion of how we understand pedagogic work in this domain. For me they demonstrate a pedagogy of taking care that involves a concern for difference and how to develop effective pedagogical strategies as well as a critical vigilance towards established dispositifs of practice no matter how difficult these may be to overcome. Such taking care demands a trust in the 'perhaps' and in taking leaps towards it (the child's or student's mode of practice), which may embrace the possibility that such leaps may disrupt the teacher's framework of understanding. The feeling of engaging with another reality as the child's or student's reality enters the teacher's experiencing. Taking such leaps involves a trust and uncertainty but driven by a pragmatics of a 'perhaps', of what might be possible. Martin Savransky (2021: 66) argues that such trust is not reciprocal in the sense of a contract of exchange because this would reduce the irreducible difference that persists between a teacher's held out hand and the hand of the child or student stretched out to meet it. Trust, rather, is a recursive relation between the teacher's offer of engagement, of stimulation, challenge and support, and the student's response – a recursive assemblage of relays that involves what we might call a 'tremorous form of togetherness' (Savransky: 68), a togetherness of divergence. Such togetherness of divergence involves what we might call a recursive worlding and unworlding of worlds.

A pluriverse of pedagogies is constituted, but never completed, by the togetherness of divergence and the interstices of 'perhaps' that precipitate the recursive relation of trust. A classroom or studio and other sites of learning are composed of a multiplicity of worlds in this world along with their gifts that may pose equivocations, uncertainties or revelations, as the feelings of other worlds impinge upon a teacher's framework of understanding. Pluralist pedagogies, as illustrated in the artist-teacher narratives, emerge from encounters with others and the feeling of difference, thus asking for an openness to a 'perhaps' and its gift that may generate new opportunities for practice. Such pedagogies, embracing a pedagogy of taking care, also require a vigilance towards pedagogical abstractions that may limit a response to difference and divergence and thereby generate an epistemology of control. The importance of the artist-teacher narratives lies in their ability to invent, artefactualize or modify abstractions (conceptual, visual) that allow practice to be depicted anew and thereby inhabit pedagogic work otherwise. Such a pluralism offers no permanent ecumene but the constant interruption or noticing of a 'perhaps' that may generate a power to make us think and act in more expansive directions. For example, do the artist–teacher conversations create possibilities for advancing practice or not? Pedagogic practice is always in-the-making, and its test and trust lies in the crafting of stories, generating conceptualizations and modes of practice that constitute pedagogical tools for learners and teachers to make creative advances in the adventures of practice.

Trusting the 'perhaps' is thus a pedagogical challenge and adventure that accommodates the insistence of 'perhaps' that may be only a vague or uncertain presence, a perhaps, as Whitehead puts it, that 'lurks in the interstices'. In other words, 'perhaps' denotes the insistence of life. The artist–teacher conversations *matter* because their difference and divergence make other worlds appear along with their possibilities and potentials; they whisper a pragmatics of the suddenly possible. And such whispering will be needed more and more in the coming years as we try to develop modes of living together, humans and non-humans, in the face of global challenges.

Ontology and Epistemology

And finally, the relationship between epistemes of practice and the being or becoming of practice can be equated to the relation between epistemology and ontology. The discussion of the ontological turn in Chapter 7 briefly considered the issue of avoiding epistemological relativism when articulating the practices of the other, that is to say, capturing the other's practice in terms of the anthropologist's conceptual framework in contrast to trying to articulate the ontological encounter in terms that are immanent to the other's practice. A key concern therefore in such encounters is to put aside presumptions about the other embedded within the anthropologist's episteme and to try to decolonize thought. This has some relevance to pedagogic practice in which a teacher's pedagogical episteme is confronted with the divergent ontologies of students' or children's practices. The 'perhaps' of such encounters, if not pushed aside, may constitute an existential tremor for a teacher that may provoke a similar decolonization, or at least a disturbance, a process of thought and practice that precipitates a process of existential transformation. This seems to suggest that a pedagogy of taking care constitutes an epistemological and an ontological challenge in responding to divergence and difference if it can put aside the power of pedagogical control operationalized through enforced curriculum orders and their modes of subjectivation.

This is not to suggest that the children and students who are taught have radically different ontological experiences, though some may. It is a call for a noticing of difference and divergence, however nuanced or abrupt, without immediately reading such difference through established theories or frameworks that assimilate difference. It is also a call, by implication, to extend our abstractions, to develop the art of artefactualizing terms to try to embrace ontological differences however slight.

What would a metaphysic of 'perhaps' look like? It seems to involve a recursivity between ontology and epistemology in which neither realm is complete, a recursivity which is subject to a pragmatics of the suddenly possible or 'perhaps'. The relation between the ontology of practice and stories *from* practice, and not *about* practice, constitutes an open-ended recursive relation involving trust and uncertainty as well as already assimilated practices. This pragmatic reading of the relation between ontology and epistemology illustrates that ontology is always a becoming-making and that any epistemological novelty or invention is thus also an ontological novelty. This pragmatic recursivity is captured by Simondon (see Chapter 4) who prefers the notion of *ontogenesis* to ontology. The creative force of this recursivity, if allowed to function, is vitally relevant today; it is powered by our *creative initiative* maintaining an ongoing tension between our established knowledge and practice and our infinite potentiality, what Cecile Malaspina (2019: 221) calls 'a reservoir of potentials and virtualities that we may activate collectively in order to invent a solution to the problems we face'. The artist-teacher narratives, in relation to their particular domains of practice, illustrate for me the force and power of such initiatives to collectively create or invent solutions to the tensions, differences, divergence and challenges of practice, initiatives that stem from a pedagogy of taking care.

References

Addison, N., and Burgess, L. (2020), *Debates in Art and Design Education* (2nd edn), London: Routledge.

Agamben, G. (1988), *Homo Sacer: Sovereign Power and Bare Life*, Stanford: Stanford University Press.

Agamben, G. (2009), 'What Is an Apparatus?' in *What Is an Apparatus? And Other Essays*, trans. David Kishik and Stefan Pedatella, 1–25, Stanford: Stanford University Press.

Anderson, B. (2017), 'Hope and Micropolitics', *Environment and Planning D: Society and Space*, 35 (4): 593–95.

Arendt, H. (1977), *Between Past and Future*, London: Penguin.

Arnason, J. (2007), 'The Idea of Negative Platonism: Jan Patocka's Critique and Recovery of Metaphysics', *Thesis Eleven*, 90: 6–26.

Assis, P. (2017), 'Gilbert Simondon's "Transduction" as Radical Immanence', *Performance Philosophy*, 3 (3): 695–716.

Atkinson, D. (2011), *Art, Equality and Learning: Pedagogies against the State*, Rotterdam: Sense Publishers.

Atkinson, D. (2018a), *Art, Disobedience and Ethics: The Adventure of Pedagogy*, London: Palgrave Macmillan.

Atkinson, D. (2018b), 'Art, Pedagogies and Becoming: The Force of Art and the Individuation of New Worlds', in L. Knight and A. L. Cutcher (eds), *Arts-Research-Education: Connections and Directions*, 3–16, Cham, Switzerland: Springer.

Balch, O. (2013), 'Happy Parents = Happy Workforce', *Guardian*, 4 February.

Baldacchino, J. (2020), *Educing Ivan Illich: Reform, Contingency and Disestablishment*, New York: Peter Lang.

Bakhtin, M. M. (1986), *Speech Genres and Other Late Essays*, Austin: University of Texas.

Bell, V. (2017), 'On Isabelle Stengers' Cosmopolitics: A Speculative Adventure', in A. Wilkie, M. Savransky and M. Rosengarten (eds), *Speculative Research: The Lure of Possible Futures*, 185–97, London: Routledge.

Berlant, L. (2016), 'The Commons: Infrastructures for Troubling Times', *Society and Space*, 34 (3): 393–419.

Blanchot, M. (1989), *The Space of Literature*, trans. A. Smock, Lincoln: University of Nebraska Press.

Blaser, M. (2016), 'Is Another Cosmopolitics Possible?' *Cultural Anthropology*, 31 (4): 545–70.

Blaser, M., and de la Cadena, M., eds (2018), *A World of Many Worlds*, Durham, NC: Duke University Press.

Brassier, R. (2003), 'Axiomatic Heresy: The Non-Philosophy of Francois Laruelle', *Radical Philosophy*, 121: 24–35.

Brassier, R. (2007), *Nihil Unbound: Enlightenment and Extinction*, Basingstoke: Palgrave Macmillan.

Brown, W. (2015), *Undoing the Demos: Neoliberalism and Stealth Revolution*, New York: Zone Books.

Brown, W. (2017), 'Apocalyptic Populism', *Eurozine*.

Brown, W. (2019), *In the Ruins of Neoliberalism: The `Rise of Antidemocratic Politics in the West*, New York: Columbia University Press.

Brown, T., Rowley, H. and Smith, K. (2015), *The Beginnings of School Led Teacher Training: New Challenges for University Teacher Education*, School Direct Research Project.

Buck-Morss, S. (2013), 'A Commonist Ethics', in S. Zizek (ed.), *The Idea of Communism 2*, 57–75, London: Verso.

Burrows, D., and O'Sullivan, S. D. (2019), *Fictioning*, Edinburgh: Edinburgh University Press.

Clarke, J. (2015), 'Stuart Hall and the Theory and Practice of Articulation', *Discourse: Studies in the Cultural Politics of Education*, 36 (2): 275–86.

Cole, J. (2008), 'Raymond Williams and Education: A Slow Reach Again for Control', in *The Encyclopaedia of Pedagogy and Informal Education*, https://infed.org/mobi/raymond-williams-and-education-a-slow-reach-again-for-control/.

Combes, M. (2012), *Gilbert Simondon and the Philosophy of the Transindividual*, Cambridge, MA: MIT Press.

Daichendt, J. (2010), *Artist Teacher: A Philosophy for Creating and Teaching*, Bristol: Intellect Books.

Debaise, D. (2008), 'The Living and its Environments', *Process Studies*, 37 (2): 1–15.

Debaise, D. (2012), 'What Is Relational Thinking?' *Inflexions*, 5: 1–11.

Debaise, D. (2017), 'The Lure of the Possible: On the Function of Speculative Propositions', in A. Wilkie, M. Savransky and M. Rosengarten (eds), *Speculative Research: The Lure of Possible Futures*, 210–17, London: Routledge.

Debaise, D. (2018), 'The Minoritarian Powers of Thought: Thinking beyond Stupidity with Isabelle Stengers', *Substance*, 47 (1): 17–28.

Deleuze, G. (1994), *Difference and Repetition*, London: Continuum.

Deleuze, G. (1995), *Negotiations*, New York: Columbia University Press.

Deleuze, G. (2004), *Logic of Sense*, London: Continuum.

Deleuze, G. (2006), *Two Regimes of Madness, Texts and Interviews 1975–199*, ed. D. Lapoujade, trans. A. Hodges and M. Taormina, New York: Semiotext(e).

Deleuze, G., and Guattari, F. (1988), *A Thousand Plateaus*, London: Athlone Press.

Deleuze, G., and Guattari, F. (1994), *What Is Philosophy?* London: Verso.

Dewey, J. (1929), *Experience and Nature*, Chicago, IL: Open Court.

Dewey, J. (2000), *Liberalism and Social Action*, Amherst: Prometheus Books.
Dewey, J. ([1931] 2008a), *Philosophy and Civilization*, New York: G. P. Putnam's Sons.
Dewey, J. ([1929] 2008b), *The Quest for Certainty: The Later Works 1925–1953, Vol 4*, Carbondale, IL: Southern Illinois University Press.
Diprose, R. (2017), 'Speculative Research, Temporality and Politics', in A. Wilkie, M. Savransky and M. Rosengarten (eds), *Speculative Research: The Lure of Possible Futures*, 39–51, London: Routledge.
Duchamp, M. (1973), *The Writings of Marcel Duchamp*, ed. M. Sanouillet and E. Peterson, New York: Da Capo Press.
Eno, B. (1996), *A Year with Swollen Appendices*, London: Faber & Faber.
Foucault, M. (2001), *Fearless Speech*, Los Angeles: Semiotext(e).
Foucault, M. (2010), *The Government of Self and Others, Lectures at the College de France 1982–1983*, New York: Palgrave Macmillan.
Foucault, M. (2011), 'The Courage of the Truth: The Government of Self and Others', in F. Gros (ed.), *Lectures at the College de France 1983–1984*, New York: Palgrave Macmillan.
Furlong, R. (2001), 'Reforming Teacher Education, Re-forming Teachers: Accountability, Professionalism and Competence', in R. Phillips and J. Furlong (eds), *Education, Reform and the State: 25 years of Policy, Politics and Practice*, 118–35, London: Routledge.
Gasche, R. (2018), 'Patocka on Europe in the Aftermath of Europe', *European Journal of Social Theory*, 21 (3): 391–406.
Gentry, A. (2017), *What Is the Scenius*, Circuit Youth Salvo, https://medium.com.
Gerlach, J. (2014), 'Lines, Contours and Legends: Coordinates for Vernacular Mapping', *Progress in Human Geography*, 38 (1): 22–39.
Gerlach, J., and Jellis, T. (2015), 'Guattari: Impractical philosophy', *Dialogues in Human Geography*, 5 (2): 131–48.
Goffey, A. (2019), 'Automation Anxieties and Infrastructural Technologies', *New Formations*, 98: 29–47.
Gros, F. (2011), 'Course Context', in M. Foucault, *The Courage of the Truth (The Government of Self and Others II)*, 343–58, Basingstoke: Palgrave Macmillan.
Grosz, E. (2008), *Chaos, Territory, Art: Deleuze and the Framing of the Earth*, New York: Columbia University Press.
Grosz, E. (2017), *The Incorporeal: Ontology, Ethics and the Limits of Materialism*, New York: Columbia University Press.
Guattari, F. (1992), 'Remaking Social Practices'. This article appeared under the title 'Pour une Refondation des Pratiques Sociales', *Le Monde Diplomatique*, October 1992: 26–7. Translated by Sophie Thomas.
Guattari, F. (1995), *Chaosmosis: An Ethico-Aesthetic Paradigm*, trans. P. Bains and J. Pefanis, Sydney: Power Publications.
Guattari, F. (1996a), 'Subjectivities: For Better or Worse', in G. Genosko (ed.), *The Guattari Reader*, 193–203, Oxford: Basil Blackwell.

Guattari, Félix (1996b), 'Ritornellos and Existential Affects', trans. J. Schiesari and G. Van Den Abbeele, in G. Genosko (ed.), *The Guattari Reader*, 158–71, Oxford: Basil Blackwell.

Guattari, F. (2011), *The Machinic Unconscious*, Los Angeles: Semiotext(e).

Guattari, F. (2013), *Schizoanalytic Cartographies*, trans. A. Goffey, London: Bloomsbury.

Halewood, M. (2014), 'The Order of Nature and the Creation of Societies', in N. Gaskill and A. J. Nocek (eds), *The Lure of Whitehead*, 360–78, Minneapolis: University of Minnesota Press.

Hall, S. (1985), 'Signification, Representation, Ideology: Althusser and the Post-structuralist Debates', *Critical Studies in Mass Communication*, 2 (2): 91–114.

Hall, S. (1997), 'Culture and Power', interview with Peter Osborne and Lynne Segal, June, *Radical Philosophy*, 86: 24–41.

Hall, S. (2007a), 'Epilogue: Through the Prism of an Intellectual Life', in B. Meeks (ed.), *Culture, Politics, Race and Diaspora: The Thought of Stuart Hall*, 269–91, London: Lawrence & Wishart.

Hall, S. (2007b), 'Richard Hoggart, The Uses of Literacy and the Cultural Turn', *International Journal of Cultural Studies*, 10 (1): 39–49.

Hampe, M. (2018), *What Philosophy Is For*, Chicago: University of Chicago Press.

Hill, Rosemary, Sachs, Andrew, British Broadcasting Corporation, Educational Media Australia and Open University (1993), *Windows on the Mind*, London: BBC, Open University.

Holbraad, M., and Pedersen, M. A. (2017), *The Ontological Turn: An Anthropological Exposition*, Cambridge: Cambridge University Press.

Illich, I. (1969–70), *Celebration of Awareness*, Garden City: Doubleday.

Illich, I. (1973), *Deschooling Society*, Harmondsworth: Penguin.

Illich, I. (1992), *In the Mirror of the Past: Lectures and Addresses, 1978–1990*, New York: M. Boyars.

Illich, I. (2009), *Tools For Conviviality*, London: Marion Boyars.

Ingold, T. (2015), *The Life of Lines*, London: Routledge.

jagodinski, j. (2019), 'The Excessive Aesthetics of Tehching Hsieh: Art as Life', in K. Tavin, M. Kallio-Tavin and M. Ryynanen (eds), *Art, Excess, and Education*, 55–75, Cham, Switzerland: Palgrave Studies in Educational Futures.

jagodinski, j. (2020), 'The Non-Art of Tehching Hsieh: Art as Life, Life as Art', in P. de Assisi and P. Giudici (eds), *Machinic Assemblages of Desire: Deleuze and Artistic Research 3*, Leuven, Belgium: Leuven University Press.

James, W. (1907), *Pragmatism and the Meaning of Truth*, Milton Keynes: Watchmakers Publishers.

James, W. (1912), *Essays in Radical Empiricism*, London: Longmans Green and Co.

James, W. (1950), *The Principles of Psychology*, vol. 2, New York: Dover.

James, W. (1956), *The Will to Believe and Other Essays in Popular Philosophy*, Mineola, NY: Dover.

James, W. (1996), *Some Problems of Philosophy*, Lincoln: University of Nebraska Press.

James, W. (2004), *A Pluralistic Universe*, Blackmask Online, http://www.blackmask.com. (1996) Lincoln: University of Nebraska Press.

Kant, I. (1900), *Kant on Education (Ueber pädagogik)*, trans. A. Churton, Boston: Heath.

Kleinherenbrink, A. (2015), 'Territory and Ritornello: Deleuze and Guattari on Thinking Living Beings', *Deleuze Studies*, 9 (2): 208–30.

Lapworth, A. (2013), 'Habit, Art, and the Plasticity of the Subject: The Ontogenetice Shock of the Bioart Encounter', *Cultural Geographies*, 0 (0): 1–18.

Lapworth, A. (2016), 'Theorizing Bioart Encounters after Gilbert Simondon', *Theory, Culture & Society*, 33 (3): 123–50.

Laruelle, F. (2012). *From Decision to Heresy: Experiments in Non-Standard Thought*, ed. Robin Mackay, 257–84, Falmouth UK: Urbanomic/Sequence Press.

Laruelle, F. (2013a), *Anti-Badiou*, trans. Robin Mackay, London: Bloomsbury.

Laruelle, F. (2013b), *Philosophy and Non-Philosophy*, trans. Taylor Adkins, Minneapolis: Univocal.

Latour, B. (2011), 'Reflections on Etienne Souiau's Les Different Modes d'Existence', in L. Bryant, N. Siccek and G. Harman (eds), *The Speculative Turn: Continental Materialism and Realism*, 304–33, Open Access, Prahan, Victoria: re.press.

Lawrence, D. H. (1955), 'Chaos in Poetry', in A. Beal (ed.), *D.H. Lawrence, Selected Literary Criticism*, London: Heinemann. Online text: http//theorytuesdays.com.

Lazzarato, M. (2009), 'Grasping the Political in the Event', interview with Maurizio Lazzarato by Erin Manning and Brian Massumi, *Inflexions*, 3: 141–63.

Lazzarato, M. (2014), *Signs and Machines: Capitalism and the Production of Subjectivity*, Los Angeles: Semiotext.

Lazzarato, M. (2015), *Governing by Debt*, Cambridge, MA: MIT Press.

Lippard, L., and Piper, A. (1972), 'An Interview with Adrian Piper', *The Drama Review: TDR*, March, 16 (1): 76–8.

Mackay, R., and Laruelle, F. (2012), 'Introduction: Laruelle Undivided', in R. Mackay (ed.), *François Laruelle, From Decision to Heresy: Experiments in Non-Standard Thought*, 1–32, Falmouth: Urbanomic/Sequence Press.

Malaspina, C. (2019), 'Pure Information: In Infinity and Human Nature in the Technical Object', *Culture, Theory and Critique*, 60 (3–4): 205–22.

Manning, E. (2016), *The Minor Gesture*, Durham, NC: Duke University Press.

Massumi, B. (2002), *Parables for the Virtual*, Durham, NC: Duke University Press.

Massumi, B. (2011), *Semblance and Event: Activist Philosophy and the Occurrent Arts*, Cambridge, MA: MIT Press.

Massumi, B. (2018), *99 Theses on the Revaluation of Value*, Minneapolis: University of Minnesota Press.

Mbembe, A. (2003), *Necropolitics*, trans. Libby Meintjes, *Public Culture*, 15 (1): 11–40.

McNamara, O., and Murray (2013), 'The School Direct Programme and its Implications for Research-Informed Teacher Education and Teacher Educators', in L. Florian and N. Pantic (eds), *Learning to Teach: Exploring the History and Role of Higher Education in Teacher Education*, York: The Higher Education Academy.

McRobbie, A. (2000), 'Stuart Hall: The Universities and the "Hurly Burly"', in P. Gilroy, L. Grossberg and A. McRobbie (eds), *Without Guarantees: In Honour of Stuart Hall*, 212–24, London: Verso.

Medvedev, P. N., and Bakhtin, M. M. (1978), *The Formal Method of Literary Scholarship: A Critical Introduction to Sociological Poetics*, Baltimore: John Hopkins University Press.

Meillassoux, Q. (2008), *After Finitude: An Essay on the Necessity of Contingency*, New York: Continuum.

Mitra, S. (2006), *The Hole in the Wall: Self-organising Systems in Education*, Research Gate, January. New York.

Munchetty, N. (2021), *Lets Talk about Race*, BBC 1 Panorama, 8 March.

Negri, T. (1998), *Exil*, Paris: Editions Mille et Une Nuits.

Neshat, S. (1997), *Women of Allah*, University of California: Marco Noire Editore.

Okeke-Agulu, C. (2010), 'Conversation with Zarina Bhimji', *Art Journal*, 69 (4): 66–75.

O'Maoilearca, J. (2015a), *All Thoughts Are Equal: Laruelle and Nonhuman Philosophy*, Minneapolis: University of Minnesota Press.

O'Maoilearca, J. (2015b), 'Laruelle's "Criminally Performative" Thought: On Doing and Saying in Non-Philosophy', *Performance Philosophy*, 1: 161–7.

O'Sullivan, S. D. (2006), *Art Encounters Deleuze and Guattari: Thought beyond Representation*, London: Palgrave Macmillan.

O'Sullivan, S. D. (2010), 'Guattari's Aesthetic Paradigm: From the Folding of the Finite/Infinite Relation to Schizoanalytic Metamodelisation', *Deleuze Studies*, 4 (2): 256–86.

O'Sullivan, S. D. (2017), 'Non-Philosophy and Art Practice (or, Fiction as Method)', in J. K. Shaw and T. Reeves-Evisson (eds), *Fiction as Method*, Berlin: Sternberg.

Patočka, J. (1988), 'Fünf Bruchstücke zum Geschichtsschema', in Ivan Chvatík and Pavel Kouba (eds), *Jan Patočka, Péče o duši, Vol 3, Soubor statí, přednášek a poznámek k problematice postavení člověka ve světě a v dějinách*, 343–53, Prague: Archivní soubor (samizdat).

Patočka, J. (1996), *Heretical Essays in the Philosophy of History*, ed. J. Dodd, trans. Erazim Kohák, Chicago, IL: Open Court.

Patočka, J. (2002), *Plato and Europe*, trans. Petr Lom, Stanford: Stanford University Press.

Patočka, J. (2007), *L'Europe apre`s l'Europe*, trans. E. Abrams, Paris: Verdier.

Paul Smith, A. (2012), *François Laruelle's Principles of Non-Philosophy*, Edinburgh: Edinburgh University Press.

Perec, G. (1973), *The Infra-Ordinary*, UbuWeb Papers.

Piper, A. (1996a), *Out of Order, Out of Sight Volume 1: Selected Writings in Meta-Art 1968–1992*, Cambridge, MA: MIT Press.

Piper, A. (1996b), *Out of Order, Out of Sight Volume 2: Selected Writings in Art Criticism 1967–1992*, Cambridge, MA: MIT Press.

Pollard, I. (1987), 'Pastoral Interlude' or 'Wordsworth Heritage', in *Postcards Home* (2004), London: Autograph.

Ranciere, J. (1999), *Disagreement, Politics and Philosophy*, Minneapolis: University of Minnesota Press.
Ranciere, J. (2004), *The Politics of Aesthetics: The Distribution of the Sensible*, London: Continuum.
Ranciere, J. (2010), *Dissensus on Politics and Aesthetics*, London: Continuum.
Raunig, G. (2016), *Dividuum: Machinic Capitalism and Machinic Revolution*, Los Angeles: Semiotext.
Roberts, T. (2019), 'Guattari's Incorporeal Materialism: From Individuation to Aesthetics (and Back Again)', in T. Jellis, J. Gerlach and J. D. Dewsbury (eds), *Why Guattari? A Liberation of Cartographies, Ecologies and Politics*, 45–57, London: Routledge.
Rolnik, S. (2017), 'The Spheres of Insurrection: Suggestions for Combating the Pimping of Life', *e-flux journal*, 86: 1–11.
Rousell, D. (2017), 'Mapping the Data Event: A Posthumanist Approach to Art|Education|Research in a Regional University', in L. Knight and A. Cutcher (eds), *Arts, Research, Education: Connections and Directions*, 203–20, Cham, Switzerland: Springer.
Sauvagnargues, A. (2012), 'Simondon, Deleuze, and the Construction of Transcendental Empiricism', *Pli, The Warwick Journal of Philosophy*, Special Volume on Simondon: 1–21.
Sauvagnargues, A. (2016), *Artmachines: Deleuze, Guattari, Simondon*, Edinburgh: Edinburgh University Press.
Savransky, M. (2017), 'The Wager of an Unfinished Present', in A. Wilkie, M. Savransky and M. Rosengarten (eds), *Speculative Research: The Lure of Possible Futures*, London: Routledge.
Savransky, M. (2021), *Around the Day in Eighty Worlds: A Politics of the Pluriverse*, Durham, NC: Duke University Press.
Savransky, M., Wilkie, A. and Rosengarten, M. (2017), 'The Lure of Possible Futures', in A. Wilkie, M. Savransky and M. Rosengarten (eds), *Speculative Research: The Lure of Possible Futures*, 1–24, London: Routledge.
Sehgal, M. (2014), 'Diffractive Propositions: Reading Alfred North Whitehead with Donna Haraway and Karen Barad', *Parallax*, 20 (3): 188–201.
Shaviro, S. (2008), 'Performing Life: The Work of Tehching Hsieh', *Performancelogia*, January.
Shaviro, S. (2011), 'The Actual Volcano: Whitehead, Harman, and the Problem of Relations', in L. Bryant, N. Siccek and G. Harman (eds), *The Speculative Turn: Continental Materialism and Realism*, 279–90, Open Access, Prahan, Victoria: re.press.
Simondon, G. (1964), *L'individu et sa Genèse Physico-Biologique; L'individuation à la Lumièr des Notions de Forme et d'Information*, Paris: Presses Universitaires de France.
Simondon, G. (1989), *L'Individuation Psychique et Collective*, Paris: Aubier.
Simondon, G. (1995), *L'Individu et sa Genèse Physico-Biologique*, Grenoble: Jérôme Millon.

Simondon, G. (2007), *L'Individuation Psychique et Collective: à la Lumière des Notions de Forme, Information, Potential et Métastabilité*, Paris: Aubier.

Simondon, G. (2009), 'The Position of the Problem of Ontogenesis', *Parrhesia*, 7: 4–16.

Simondon, G. (2013), *L'Individuation à la Lumière des Notions de Forme et d'Information*, Grenoble: Jérôme Millon.

Simondon, G. (2014), *Sur la technique*, Paris: Presses Universitaires de France.

Souriau, E. (1943, 2015), *The Different Modes of Existence*, Minneapolis: Universal.

Stengers, I. (2004), 'The Cosmopolitical Proposal', *Wordpress*, online.

Stengers, I. (2005a), 'The Cosmopolitical Proposal', in B. Latour and P. Weibel (eds), *Making Things Public: Atmospheres of Democracy* 994–1003, Cambridge, MA: MIT Press.

Stengers, I. (2005b), 'Introductory Notes of an Ecology of Practices', *Cultural Studies Review*, 11 (1): 183–96.

Stengers, I. (2006), 'Whitehead and Science: From Philosophy of Nature to Speculative Cosmology', Lecture at McGill University, Montreal, https://www.mcgill.

Stengers, I. (2008), 'Experimenting with Refrains: Subjectivity and the Challenge of Escaping Modern Dualism', *Subjectivity*, 22: 28–59.

Stengers, I. (2009a), 'History through the Middle: Between Macro and Mesopolitics', interview with Brian Massumi and Erin Manning, *Inflexions*, 3: 183–275.

Stengers, I. (2009b), 'William James: An Ethics of Thought', *Radical Philosophy*, 157 (September/October): 9–19.

Stengers, I. (2010), 'The Care of the Possible', interview with E. Bordeleau, in *SCAPEGOAT: Architecture/Landscape/Political Economy*, 01 'Service': 12–17.

Stengers, I. (2011a), 'Comparison as a Matter of Concern', *Common Knowledge*, 17 (1): 48–63.

Stengers, I. (2011b), *Comopolitics II*, Minneapolis: University of Minnesota Press.

Stengers, I. (2011c), *Thinking with Whitehead: A Free and Wild Creation of Concepts*, Cambridge, MA: Harvard University Press.

Stengers, I. (2012a), 'Ecosophical Activism – Between Micropolitics and Mesopolitics', conversation between Isabelle Stengers and Henk Oosterling, moderated by Sjoerd van Tuinen at De Unie in Rotterdam on 31 May 2012, following a tour to the primary school Bloemhof – the home base of the Rotterdam Skillcity program *Physical Integrity* – and a Masterclass by Stengers at the Erasmus University Rotterdam earlier that day, 1–20.

Stengers, I. (2012b), 'Reclaiming Animism', *e-flux journal*, 36: 1–10.

Stengers, I. (2014a), 'A Constructivist Reading of Process and Reality', N. Gaskill and A. J. Nocek (eds), *The Lure of Whitehead*, 43–64, Minneapolis: University of Minnesota Press.

Stengers, I. (2014b), 'Speculative Philosophy and the Art of Dramatization', in R. Faber and A. Goffey (eds), *The Allure of Things: Process and Object in Contemporary Philosophy*, 188–217, London: Bloomsbury Academic.

Stengers, I. (2015), *In Catastrophic Times: Resisting the Coming Barbarism*, Luneburg: Open Humanities Press in collaboration with Meson Press.

Stengers, I., and Savransky, M. (2018), 'Relearning the Art of Paying Attention', *Substance*, 47 (1): 130–45.
Strathern, M. (1988), *The Gender of the Gift: Problems with Women and Problems with Society in Melanesia*, Berkeley: University of California Press.
Strathern, M. (2004), *Partial Connections* (updated edn), Oxford: Altamira Press.
Strathern, M. (2018), 'Relations', in F. Stein, S. Lazar, M. Candea, H. Diemberger, J. Robbins, A. Sanchez and R. Stasch (eds), *The Cambridge Encyclopedia of Anthropology*, http://doi.org/10.29164/18relations.
Suvak, V. (2019), 'Patočka and Foucault: Taking Care of the Soul and Taking Care of the Self', *Journal of the British Society for Phenomenology*, 50 (1): 19–36.
Tava, F. (2016), 'The Brave Struggle: Jan Patocka on Europe's Past and Future', *Journal of the British Society for Phenomenology*, 47 (3): 242–59.
Teacher Development Agency (TDA) (2008), *Standards in Teacher Training*.
Toscano, A. (2006), *The Theatre of Production: Philosophy and Individuation between Kant and Deleuze*. London: Palgrave Macmillan.
Vella, R. (2016), *Artist-Teachers in Context: International Dialogues*, Rotterdam: Sense Publishers.
Verhaeghe, P., and Declercq, F. (2002), 'Lacan's Analytical Goal: "Le Sinthome" or the Feminine Way', in L. Thurston (ed.), *Essays on the Final Lacan: Re-inventing the Symptom*, 59–83, New York: The Other Press, Online: 1–17.
Viveiros de Castro, E. (1998), 'Cosmological Deixis and Amerindian Perspectivism', *Journal of Royal Anthropological Institute*, 4 (3): 469–88.
Viveiros de Castro, E. (2004), 'Perspectival Anthropology and the Method of Controlled Equivocation', *Tipiti*, 2 (1): 3–22.
Viveiros de Castro, E. (2014), *Cannibal Metaphysics: For a Post-Structural Anthropology*, ed and trans. Peter Skafish, Minneapolis: Univocal Publishing.
Wagner, R. (1981), *The Invention of Culture*, Chicago: University of Chicago Press.
Watson, J. (2008), 'Schizoanalysis as Metamodeling', *The Fibreculture Journal* (12), https://twelve.fibreculturejournal.org/fcj-077-schizoanalysis-as-metamodeling/.
Whitehead, A. N. ([1932] 1962), *The Aims of Education and Other Essays*, London: Ernest Benn Limited.
Whitehead, A. N. ([1925] 1967), *Science and the Modern World*, New York: Free Press.
Whitehead, A. N. ([1928] 1978), *Process and Reality*, New York: Free Press.
Whitehead, A. N. ([1938] 1968), *Modes of Thought*, New York: Free Press.
Wilkie, A., Savransky, M. and Rosengarten, M. (2017), 'The Wager of an Unfinished Present', in *Speculative Research: The Lure of Possible Futures*, 25–38, London: Routledge.
Willerslev, R., and Suhr, C. (2018), 'Is There a Place for Faith in Anthropology?' *HAU: Journal of Ethnographic Theory*, 8 (1/2): 65–78.
Williams, J. (2014), 'Whitehead's Curse', in N. Gaskill and A. J. Nocek (eds), *The Lure of Whitehead*, 249–66, Minneapolis: University of Minnesota Press.
Williams, R. (1958), *Culture and Society*, London: Chatto and Windus.

Williams, R. (1993), *Border Country: Raymond Williams in Adult Education*, ed. J. McIlroy and S. Westwood, Leicester: National Institute of Adult Continuing Education.

Zepke, S. (2011), 'The Readymade: Art as the Refrain of Life', in S. D. O'Sullivan and S. Zepke (eds), *Deleuze, Guattari and the Production of the New*, 33–44, London: Continuum.

Zepke, S. (2017), 'A Work of Art Does Not Contain the Least Bit of Information, Deleuze and Guattari and Contemporary Art', *Performance Philosophy*, 3 (3): 751–65.

Index

actual reality 117
actual and virtual 117
Agamben Giorgio 82, 87
alethurgy 67
apeiron 103
Arendt, Hannah 126
artfulness 140, 141
articulation 22
artist-teacher assemblages 221
artist-teacher conversations 225
assemblage 31, 32
Assis, Paolo de 118, 120
Atkinson, Dennis 121, 126

Bakhtin 35–7
Baldacchino, John 16, 71, 79–86
Balibar Etienne 82, 83
Bell, Vicky 127, 134, 135, 138, 140
Berlant, Lauren 87, 88
Bhimji, Zarina 155
bios 56, 59
Blanchot, Maurice 136
Brown, Wendy 16–18
Buck-Morss, Susan 90

careful equivocation 182
Castro, Eduardo Viveiros de 181, 182, 183
Combes, Muriel 102, 104, 112
common sense 201
concrescence 214
contingency 79
conviviality 75–8
cosmopolitics 86, 135, 136
cosmopolitical proposal 94, 95, 134, 139
cosmos 137
creative instance 43
culture 20, 21, 174
culture of interstices 217, 218
Cynic 53, 57, 59

Debaise, Didier 103, 133, 136, 142, 220
decolonisation 229

dehiscence 126
Deleuze, Gilles 108, 150, 156, 203
Deleuze, Gilles & Guattari, Felix 103, 108, 114, 120, 122, 136, 150, 156, 193, 194, 198, 221
deschooling society 80
Dewey, John 13, 18, 94, 129–32
Diprose, Rosalyn 126
disestablishment 79, 85
disparation 106, 108
dispositif 82
distribution of the sensible 123
divergence 88, 210, 211
Dostoyevsky 93
Duchamp, Marcel 123, 148

early drawing practices 114
ecole mutuelle 205
ecologies of practice 86, 91, 210
ecologies of the virtual 169
ecosophic art education 168
ecosophic education 164
ecosophy 164, 165
education and care 66
Eno, Brian 219
epimeleia 51–3, 56
epistemology 235
equaliberty 82
ethico-aesthetic 34, 39
ethos 54, 56, 138
eudamonia 24
Euripides 54
events of individuating 99
existential territories 35

Foucault, Michelle 52–60, 146, 147, 208
Freelands Foundation 224, 227
Fromm, Erich 80

Galindo, Regina Jose 155
Gasche, Rodolfe 60
Gentry, Alex 219

Goffey, Andrew 31
grasping 45
Green, Maxine 24
Gros, Frederic 53
Grosz, Elizabeth 114
Guattari, Felix 2, 14, 16, 35, 39–49, 148, 163–9, 220, 221

haecceities 120
Halewood, Michael 215
Hall, Stuart 13, 16, 21–3, 51, 68
Hampe, Michael 90, 94
Haraway, Donna 93
heteroglossia 63
heterotopia 63
Hoggart, Richard 13, 16, 19, 29, 51
Holbraad, Martin 171
Holt, John 24
hooks, bell 24
Hseih, Tehching 152, 153, 154
hylomorphism 101

idiotic events 93, 94, 137
Illich, Ivan 74–9, 84, 85
individuation 97, 104, 106, 109, 209
instauration 184, 187, 189
interstices 213, 214, 221

Jagodinski, jan 152, 168
James, William 2, 93, 213, 214
jazz pedagogies 174

Kant, Immanuel 83

Lapworth, Andrew 98
Laruelle, Francois 157, 158, 161, 162
Latour, Bruno 188–91
Lawrence, D. H. 221, 222
Lazzarato, Maurizio 30, 35, 194, 199
learning with 119
learning from 119
Le Sinthome 147
lines of flight 194
Lippard, Lucy 151
lure for feeling 131, 202

machinic enslavement
macropolitics 38, 193

Manning, Erin 140, 141, 206
Maritain, Jacques 84
Massumi, Brian 46, 70, 73, 74, 85
McRobbie, Angela 23
Merleau-Ponty, Maurice 126
meso-knowledge 199
meso level 199, 203
meso-pedagogies 212
mesopolitics 199, 202, 204, 210, 212
mesopolitics of art education 206
metamodelization 39
metastability 104
micro-haecceities 120
micropolitics 38, 193
minor gestures 206
Mitra, Sugata 205
modulation 101, 102
Munchetty, Naga 206
mythopoesis 145

Negri, Tony 112
neoliberalism 16
neoliberal rationality 17
Neshat, Shirin 124
non-philosophy 161, 162

oikos 138
O'Maoilearca, John 158, 159, 161
ontogenesis 97, 109
ontology 235
ontological turn 171
Open University 19, 24
O'Sullivan, Simon 162

par le milieu 201, 204, 208, 210
parrhesia 51–60
Patocka, Jan 52, 60
pedagogy 71
Pedersen, morten Axel 171
Perec, George 223
perspectivism 181
phronesis 56
Piper, Adrian 151, 152
pluralism 214
pluriverse 211, 229
Pollard, Ingrid 154, 155
post-plural pedagogies 176
prehension 186, 214, 215
pre-individual 102, 103

preposition 188
proposition 134, 135

Ranciere, Jacques 123, 194
readymade 148, 149
reform 79
Riley, Bridget 209
ritornello 108, 114
Rolink, Suley 194–6

Sauvagnargues, Anne 101, 102, 105, 106, 108, 122
Savransky, Martin 129, 130
scandal of art 122, 166
scandal of the truth 145
scenius 219
schizoanalysis 45
schizoanalytic metamodelling 39
school curricula 24
Shaviro, Steven 154
signs 108
Simondon, Gilbert 97, 98, 99, 105, 107, 109, 110, 112, 119
Smith, Adam 18
social subjection 30
society 215
Socrates 54, 56
Souriau, Etienne 188–90
speculation 127, 129, 135
speculative ontology 184
speculative pedagogies 89, 125
speculative practice 92, 132
speculative sensibility 90
speculative turn 185
speech genres 35

Spinoza, Baruch 90
Stengers, Isabelle 69, 88, 91, 93, 95, 105, 131, 136–9, 142, 179, 180, 199–205, 210–13, 216–18, 221
Strathern, Marylin 176–8, 181
subjectivation 14, 15

teacher education 26
Thatcherism 4
Tocqueville, Alexis de 18
Toscano, Alberto 108–10, 120
transduction 106, 107, 118–21
transductive disparation 105
transindividual 111
trust 213
truth 66

uncertainty 213

vernacular potential
virtual reality 103

Wagner, Roy 174
war machine 156
Whitehead, Alfred North 42, 68, 69, 70, 89, 131, 134, 141, 159, 160, 185–7, 201, 202, 208, 215–18
Williams, Bernard 13, 16, 20, 21, 51
Wilson, Fred 124
without criteria 88, 89

Yevtushenko 86

Zepke, Stephen 123, 148, 150, 151

www.ingramcontent.com/pod-product-compliance
Lightning Source LLC
Chambersburg PA
CBHW062135300426
44115CB00012BA/1934